Diddlebury

The History of a Corvedale Parish

Diddlebury

The History of a Corvedale Parish

by

Martin Speight

Logaston Press

LOGASTON PRESS
Little Logaston Woonton Almeley
Herefordshire HR3 6QH
logastonpress.co.uk

First published by Logaston Press 2007

ISBN 978 1904396 66 6

Typeset by Logaston Press
and printed in Great Britain by
Bell & Bain Ltd., Glasgow

This book is dedicated to the memory of
Bill Woodhouse,
Upper House Farm, Middlehope
(1937-2006)

Contents

Foreword

I was first privileged to set foot in Diddlebury in June 1965, when, newly-appointed to the adult education staff of Salop County Council, I spent a day exploring the area with Trevor Rowley, then completing his thesis on the historic landscape of the Corvedale, who was going to teach a local history class in the village the following autumn. We were warmly received by the late Frank Mitchell, head of the school, who features in this book both as historian and schoolmaster. Since that time Diddlebury has always seemed an especially interesting parish, with an Anglo-Saxon church, magnificent timber-framed farmhouses, the most impressive rural malthouse in Shropshire, the evocative mounds that mark the site of Corfam Castle and the glimpses from the road of the Victorianised castle at Broncroft. In the decades that followed I led many walks studying the landscape of Diddlebury and surrounding parishes, and became acquainted with some of the documentary sources for its history through a research class that I organised in the Clee Hills region. I listened to imaginative tales about the largest cowshed in the world, and discovered, by invitation of the then residents, the amazing medieval landscape of the hamlet of Lawton, with its well-preserved house platforms and ridge-and-furrow.

It would be pleasurable to welcome the publication of any book that adds to our knowledge of Diddlebury, but Martin Speight's history of the parish is a work of scholarship of unusual quality, an excellent example of traditional English Local History. Many approaches to the history of a village can be enlightening, but Martin Speight's choice of a thematic analysis of the history of Diddlebury proves to be rewarding. Our understanding of English history grows as we learn how land has been farmed or how provision has been made for the poor over many centuries. The pattern of landownership in Diddlebury in some periods is similar to that in many other parishes, but in the 20th century the influence of P.G. Holder was highly unusual. This book has many high spots. The measured account of church life over many centuries will be of interest to historians far beyond the boundaries of Shropshire. We see that Methodism in this deeply rural area was a relatively short interval in the history of religion, that lasted for about a century and a half. In the context of many centuries of church history, we come to appreciate the long-term significance of the general decline in religious observance in the late 20th century. The concluding chapter provides an account of Diddlebury's historic buildings more detailed than is possible in any county-wide survey, and shows how, through the contributions of many scholars, our understanding of vernacular architecture in Shropshire has greatly increased since the 1960s.

Martin Speight does not merely relate the contents of sources. He uses them imaginatively to interpret the past for his readers. His analysis of Nicholas Proude's record of tithes and Easter offerings of 1657-62 provides illuminating insights into society in 17th-century Diddlebury. His employment of the many records of the village school gives us a picture of life in the late 19th and early 20th centuries that extends far beyond the gates of the playground. Much published local history at the present time concentrates on living memory, on those stories that every individual has to tell. In this book we see the benefits of a longer view, of looking at topics over many centuries. At the same time we learn much about the 20th century. Diddlebury was a relatively remote rural parish but its inhabitants saw many changes during the Second World War. The huge cowshed built by P.G. Holder at Peaton was used for the manufacture of aircraft parts. Local homes and the village school accommodated evacuee children from the school by the entrance to Goodison Park football ground. The well-known Charlie Edwards gained publicity as an opponent of the county 'War Ag' committee. The army established a depot in the park of Delbury Hall, while Corfton Hall was used as a hostel for the Women's Land Army. It is good to have these aspects of the history of a parish so thoroughly recorded.

This book illuminates many aspects of the history of Shropshire and of England, and will be of interest to readers well beyond the bounds of Corvedale. Diddlebury is fortunate that its past had been recorded by an accomplished practitioner of the art of history.

Barrie Trinder

Acknowledgements

In the course of 20 years of research, I have received help from a great number of people, to whom I offer my sincere thanks. I am most grateful to Barrie Trinder for kindly agreeing to write a foreword. Barrie probably did more than any other individual to stimulate an interest in local history in Shropshire in the 1960s, and his Corvedale classes are still remembered with pleasure in the area. I am particularly indebted to the archivists of Shropshire, Herefordshire and Staffordshire and their ever-helpful staffs, without whose co-operation and assistance the work would never have been possible. Particular thanks must also go to Michael Faraday and Christopher Potter, who have freely made available to me the fruits of their own researches where they relate to Diddlebury. To Michael I owe an extra debt, for painstakingly reading the drafts of the book. Peter and Rosalind Bolton also performed this onerous task, for which I am most grateful. The scholarly comments of these readers have removed many potential ambiguities and stylistic infelicities, and I hope made this a better book.

Local historians are a naturally helpful group of people, and I should like to thank all those who have assisted me by drawing my attention to sources of which I was unaware, sharing their findings with me and assisting in many other ways. In particular I should like to record my thanks to Madge Moran, Derek Williams, George Baugh, David Cox, Marion Roberts, Jim Tonkin, Brian Smith, Sylvia Watts, the Revd. Ian Gibbs, and Maldwyn Thomas. I would also like to draw attention to the work of my predecessor as parish historian, the late Frank Mitchell, whose papers relating to the parish I have found most useful. Kathleen Woodhouse has been an enormous help in locating photographs and other items, and I offer my grateful thanks to her and also to all the many other residents of Diddlebury and the Corvedale, too numerous to name, who have allowed me into their homes, lent me material, or helped me with information and introductions. All loans of photographs etc. have, I hope, been duly acknowledged. If I have omitted anyone's name from these acknowledgements, it was by oversight, for which I apologise.

Andy Johnson of Logaston Press has been a tower of strength, and has put up with the delays which inevitably tend to occur when a book is gestating. My wife Megan has had to bear the full brunt of the disruption to domestic life caused by authorship, and I should like to thank her most sincerely for her unwavering support and tolerance, particularly over the months when the final draft was being written.

I should like to express my gratitude to the following for allowing me to use their material as illustrations: Mrs. N. Aingell, Shifnal (42); Mr. and Mrs. D. Beaumont-Nesbitt (52); Clwyd Powys Archaeological Trust (6, 45); National Portrait Gallery (32); Peter Reavell and the Portable Antiquities Scheme (18); Shropshire Archives (7, 12, 27a and b, 28, 34, 35, 38, 48, 51, 65); Maldwyn Thomas, Haverfordwest (26, 32, 41); Dr. Peter Toghill (3); J.W. Tonkin, F.S.A. (57); Vicar and Churchwardens of Diddlebury (25a); Mrs. A. Walters, Wall under Heywood (19); Mrs. K. Woodhouse (13, 33). All other illustrations are from the author's own collection.

Introduction

There are a number of reasons why I have undertaken this history of the parish of Diddlebury, where my family and I have lived happily for the last two decades. I have always believed that, wherever possible, the results of historical research should be published and made available to all, as I have seen numerous instances where the work of competent and enthusiastic local historians has gone with them to their graves. Furthermore, the recent regrettable decision to close down the Victoria County History of Shropshire means that there is now little likelihood that the parishes of Lower Corvedale will ever feature in a companion publication to the superb study of the Upper Corvedale parishes in Volume X of that series. Perhaps more significantly, as I have researched the history of Diddlebury over the past 20 years, I have been struck by its intrinsic interest as an extensive rural parish comprised of a comparatively large number of townships and manors.

This situation poses both drawbacks and advantages compared with studying a single manor parish. On the debit side, it may be difficult to make a meaningful synthesis of a parish composed of so many diverse areas, and it may be added that the parish is such an artificial entity that the value of such a unit of study is very limited. Certainly Sparchford, for example, has traditionally looked towards Culmington, and Broncroft has, for equally valid geographical reasons, tended to have an affinity with Tugford. Nevertheless, it is to Diddlebury that these townships have ultimately belonged and continue to do so for ecclesiastical, and perhaps more significantly today, local government purposes.

On the credit side, the existence of a number of manors and estates means that a dearth of documentary sources in one township may be compensated by an abundance in another. There is, for example, comparatively rich documentation of medieval property holding in Little Sutton, but relatively little for the period immediately after 1600. By contrast, the situation in neighbouring Peaton is almost exactly reversed,

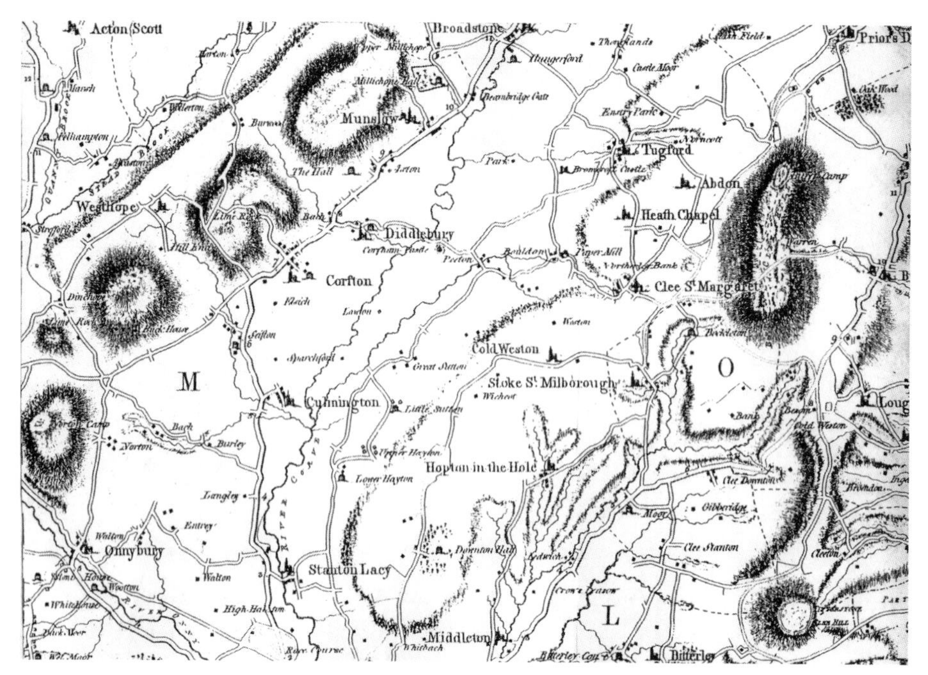

Fig. 1 From Robert Baugh's Map of Shropshire, 1808

with a series of 17th- and 18th-century surveys providing a wealth of detail about landholding and agricultural practices. On the whole the townships of Diddlebury and Corfton have the most comprehensive records, including the only really large collection of medieval deeds in the parish. This is the happy result of the Baldwyn family's apparent reluctance to discard any records relating to the process by which they acquired the lands which made them the dominant family in the parish. It is sometimes possible by examining records for one part of the parish to draw inferences about another which is less well documented, particularly if they occupy a similar location, like Middlehope and Westhope, or Sutton and Peaton.

In arranging the contents of this book, I have attempted to follow a thematic approach based loosely upon that employed by the Victoria County History, rather than the more traditional chronological organisation. Having come to medieval history comparatively late in life, I have been struck by the way that the period is often glossed over in local histories. Despite the obvious problems posed for the researcher by medieval handwriting and the use of Latin, a wealth of material may be obtained from a systematic study of printed sources such as the Inquisitions *post mortem*, the Calendars of Close and Patent Rolls, and other similar published works. As will be

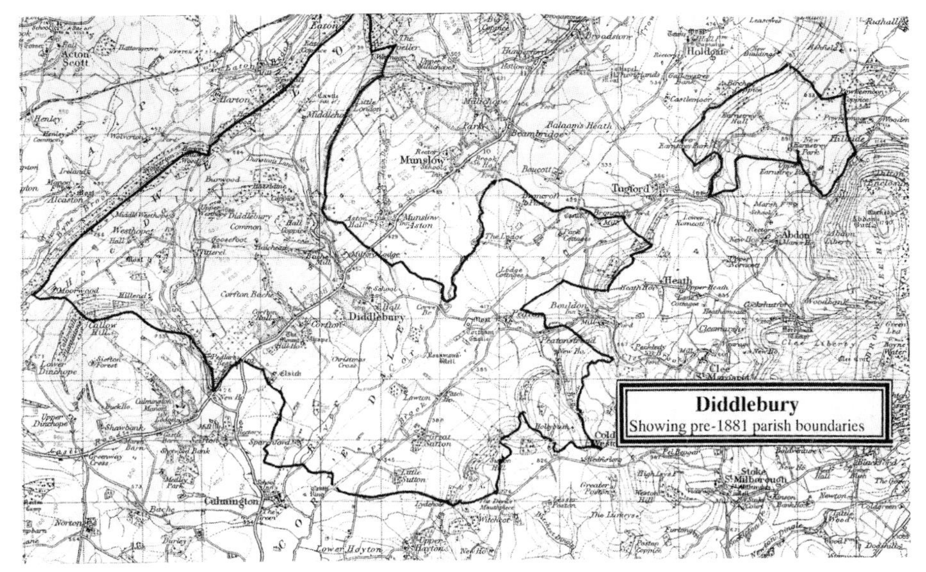

Fig. 2 Map showing the extent of the historic parish of Diddlebury, taken from Ordnance Survey New Popular One-Inch Map, sheet 129, (1947)

seen, these volumes contain a great deal of information not only about property, but also the lives of local people in the period. I have therefore attempted as far as possible to give as much coverage as possible to the medieval period.

A book represents the author's state of knowledge at the time it reaches the printer, and it is almost inevitable that valuable material will emerge at the point when it is too late to make any changes. There can never be a definitive parish history, but it is hoped that this book will contribute to the greater understanding of a rural community of which I am fortunate to be a member.

1 The Land

The Natural Landscape

The parish of Diddlebury is largely comprised of the valley of the River Corve, bounded on its eastern and western sides by upland areas. These are the limestone escarpments in the west, and the sandstone foothills of the Clees in the east. The origins of the landscape date from the Silurian period, some 445-395 million years ago, when the whole area was mostly under the sea. At the start of this period, Shropshire was situated south of the equator, and the shallow warm waters were the home to many corals, the fossilised remains of which are a feature of the resulting Wenlock limestone. There then followed a period of muddy waters which produced the lower Ludlow shales, followed by another period of clear water in which was formed the deposit of Aymestrey limestone now known as the Bringewood Beds. The final development was a period when the southern part of Shropshire was on the margin of the sea, with sediment collecting in estuaries and lagoons to form shales and sandstones. The eastern boundary of the Corvedale is formed by the sandstone foothills of the Clees, which were originally thought to have been laid down in the Devonian period that followed the Silurian, but which have subsequently been reclassified as Upper Silurian. At the end of the Silurian period earth movements on a massive scale caused an upward tilting of this series of rocks, which weathered over succeeding periods to form the typical landscape of parallel escarpments (Fig. 3).[1]

The escarpment of Wenlock Edge forms the westernmost boundary of the parish, following the 750 foot contour for the whole of its length. Behind, the

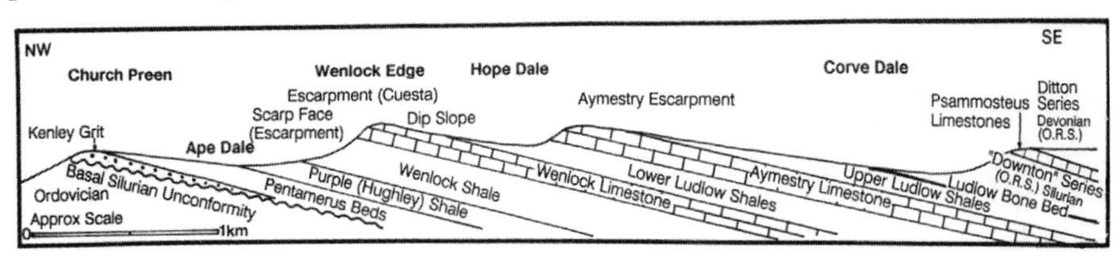

Fig. 3 Cross section through Wenlock Edge and Corvedale, from P. Toghill, Geology in Shropshire

dip slope descends gently into Hope Dale, which in this section contains the two settlements of Westhope and Middlehope. Above these rises the Aymestrey limestone escarpment. This attains a height of over 1,000 feet in three places: on Middlehope in the north; at Acorn Coppice above Upper Westhope; and at Callow Hill, where, topped by the tower erected by Benjamin Flounders in 1838, it marks the boundary with Halford and Culmington parishes. These three 'peaks' have been left by erosion, as the Aymestrey Limestone, which is much softer than the Wenlock, has been cut through by two streams, Seifton Brook and the Bache Brook, which drain from Hope Dale into the River Corve.[2] Hope Dale is a series of upland valleys or 'hopes' which are drained in this way. The steep-sided valleys are known as 'baches' in Diddlebury (Fig. 4).[3]

Fig. 4 Seifton Batch, one of the characteristic steep-sided valleys draining through the Aymestrey Limestone into the River Corve. Looking north from near Hill End

The long dip slope of the Aymestrey ridge falls down to the wide valley of the Corve, which runs north-east to south-west through the parish, before turning due south at Culmington eventually to join the Teme north of Ludlow. At the foot of the dip slope is a gravel terrace running parallel to the valley, a well-drained corridor which carried the main route from Bridgnorth and Much Wenlock to Ludlow, and provided the site for a number of settlements such as Aston Munslow and Corfton above the marshy lands of the valley bottom. In addition to the Corve, the valley was drained by the smaller Pye Brook, which rises in a number of streams on the southern slopes of the Brown Clee, and joins the Corve at Culmington (Fig. 5). A clue to the marshy condition of parts of the valley floor is found in the place name 'Marston' or 'Marsh Town', a long vanished settlement which probably lay between Peaton and Broncroft. To the north of this low-lying area, a ridge of Holdgate sandstone provided a site for the settlement of Broncroft.

The eastern boundary of the parish follows the line of the sandstone foothills of the Clee, from Wynett's Coppice in the north to Lyde Hole in the south at roughly the 750 foot contour. These slopes are cut at intervals by streams such as the Clee brook and the Strand Brook which drain into the Pye Brook.

It is difficult to conjecture the appearance of the area before it was settled and modified by man, though it may be deduced that the western uplands were heavily wooded. Certainly this was the case in the early medieval period, when the area formed part of the Long Forest, which was gradually, but only partially, stripped of its tree cover during successive centuries. It is, however, impossible to discover at what point in geological time the tree cover established itself. The fact that most of the settlements in the Corvedale were on gravel ridges suggests that the surrounding areas were predominantly marshy until drained. It is possible that the sandstone uplands of the eastern side of the parish were originally heathland, as the name of the adjoining chapelry of the Heath suggests.

Early Settlements

Like much of the Corvedale, Diddlebury suffers from what has aptly been described as 'the archaeological invisibility' of early settlers.[4] The sole prehistoric artefact from the parish is a Neolithic stone axe head found at Corfton in 1971,

Fig. 5 The Corvedale viewed from the Ox Pasture on the road from Diddlebury to Corve Bridge. Top: looking towards the Aymestrey Limestone ridge and Child's Hill. Lower: looking towards the Brown Clee from the same point

and now in Ludlow Museum.[5] There is certainly abundant evidence of the presence of Bronze Age inhabitants in the wider area, in the concentration of burial mounds on the Long Mynd, and the presence of a large prehistoric necropolis at Bromfield. This vast burial ground near the confluence of the Corve, the Onny and the Teme would appear to have been in continuous use for over 800 years from 1800 B.C., though there is also evidence of earlier Neolithic activity in the area.[6] It has been suggested that this burial ground was intended to serve a number of communities, some of whom may possibly have lived in the lower Corvedale, but this is pure hypothesis.

In the same way, the area has a number of fine Iron Age hill forts, including the Ditches and Norton Camp at the northern and southern ends respectively of Wenlock Edge, and three such structures on the Brown Clee. There is, however, no evidence of Iron Age occupation in Diddlebury parish, with the exception of a small enclosure which has been identified from aerial photography.[7] Roman sites are similarly absent, although three of the county's eight Roman villas lay within a five mile radius of Diddlebury, at Acton Scott, Rushbury and Stanton Lacy.[8] A putative Roman road has, however, been identified, following roughly the line of the B4368 through the parish.[9] Such evidence is very inadequate, and may indicate the inhospitable nature of the terrain, or equally that evidence has yet to be discovered.

Concrete evidence of settlement comes with the Anglo-Saxons, and, although the parish boasts a magnificent monument in the shape of St. Peter's church, most information about the period must be gleaned from place-names. These date entirely from the period of English settlement, and no trace of the Celtic names has survived, even for such a prominent feature as the Corve itself, whereas five miles to the west, Hope Bowdler parish has a number of names of Welsh origin such as the Cwms and the Gaer Stone. The name of the river derives from the Old English word 'corf', meaning a pass or valley, and is related to the modern word 'carve'.[10] This is an early usage, for it occurs in connection with the name Corfham, in which the 'hamm' element, referring to a piece of land surrounded by water, has been added to the name of the river. The suffix 'ham' is generally accepted as an early element, normally not later than the 7th century in date.[11]

At this time Shropshire south of the Severn, together with what is now Herefordshire, formed the kingdom of the Magonsaete, who take their name from the former Roman town of *Magnis* [Kenchester] near Hereford. The boundaries of this ancient kingdom are still preserved as those of the diocese of Hereford, and it has been suggested that the southern part of Shropshire may have been colonised by groups moving northwards from Hereford during the 7th century.[12] Following the conquest of the area by Penda, the pagan king of Mercia, who defeated the Christian Oswald near Oswestry in 641, the Magonsaete were ruled by his Christian son Merewalh. Merewalh's three daughters each founded religious houses, the most significant locally being Mildburgh, who founded the monastery of Wenlock, and was later canonised. It is possible that the concentration of pre-Conquest churches in the lower Corvedale may have some long-forgotten link to the influence of the early monastery at Wenlock.

It has been suggested that the Celtic inhabitants of the area and their settlements were absorbed rather than eradicated by the English settlers, and that the absence of Celtic place names in an area should not necessarily imply an absence of Celtic settlements.[13] Rowley quotes (but unfortunately does not reference) a study of local dialect which suggested that until the end of the 18th century the majority of inhabitants of Shropshire to the west of the Severn were the descendants of Welsh-speakers.[14]

The settlement names of Diddlebury are, however, uncompromisingly English in their origins. They may be divided into two categories, namely topographical and personal names, of which the former are by far the most frequent. Topographical names describe the location or prominent feature of a settlement. The use of 'hope' and 'bache' elements has already been mentioned, and other names related to physical features include Corfton (settlement by the Corve); Lawton (traditionally rendered as 'hill settlement', which is odd in view of its location in the valley bottom, and may suggest a different etymology); Sutton (south settlement, a very common name); and Marston (originally Merssheton or marsh settlement).[15] In two other examples the original name has undergone a slight alteration. Poston was originally Possethorne, referring to Possa's thorn tree, a possible boundary mark, similar to the Marked Ash at Blackwood in Munslow parish. Broncroft, until the 18th century more usually written Bromcroft, signified 'broom meadow'.

There are two, or possibly three personal elements in local place names. Peaton signifies the 'tun' or settlement of Peatta; Bouldon, originally Bolledon has long been accepted as 'the hill of Bulla', though Dr. Gelling has disputed this, somewhat unconvincingly in the opinion of this author.[16] The most significant example is, of course, Diddlebury itself. This has been accepted as meaning the 'burh' or dwelling of Dudela, a local chieftain of whom no other record exists. It is curious that although Corfham would appear to have been an earlier settlement, and was for much of the medieval period more important, that it was at the site of Dudela's 'burh' that the church was located.

An alternative rendering of Diddlebury is Delbury, which was once widespread, but now survives mostly in reference to the Hall and the adjacent farm. There is no occurrence of this usage before the last decade of the 18th century, and there is strong evidence to suggest that it was coined by the then vicar, Abraham Rudd. In a letter to Archdeacon Plymley in 1793, Rudd explained (quite erroneously) that he believed Diddlebury to be a misreading of the medieval 'de

Fig. 6 Middlehope from the air. The nucleated settlement around the former village green is clearly visible. The site of the castle (A), enclosed crofts (B), and ridge and furrow cultivation (C) may also be seen. (Photograph 89 MB 354 courtesy of Clwyd-Powys Archaeological Trust)

Delbury', and from this time onward the Delbury form is increasingly used.[17] If Byford-Jones is to be believed, use of the name Diddlebury marked one out as a stranger in the 1930s.[18] Delbury is, however, rarely heard today.

While the names of the settlements in the parish are of Anglo-Saxon origin, their present form does not necessarily date from that period, and the parish contains an interesting selection of settlement types. Many show evidence of considerable shrinkage, and in two cases, complete desertion. Corfham and Marston have completely disappeared, the site of the latter being a matter of speculation. Lawton and Sparchford have been reduced to one or two dwellings, while the Suttons, Peaton and Broncroft show signs of shrinkage (Fig. 6). Middlehope, which also shows evidence of shrinkage, is a classic example of a nucleated settlement* which is unlikely to date from before the 12th century in this form (Fig. 7a).[19] There is some evidence from the Tithe Award map to suggest that Great Sutton also had a nucleated plan, with field no. 246 representing a fossilised village green similar to that at Middlehope. Corfton, Bache Mill and Seifton Batch are all linear settlements along valley bottoms, and Diddlebury exhibits interesting evidence of migration from the original settlement around the church to Bache Mill. This pattern has been obscured since the 1970s by the gradual development of Mill Lane, but is clearly visible on the first edition Ordnance Survey map (Fig. 7b). This may well have been related to the need to capture passing trade on

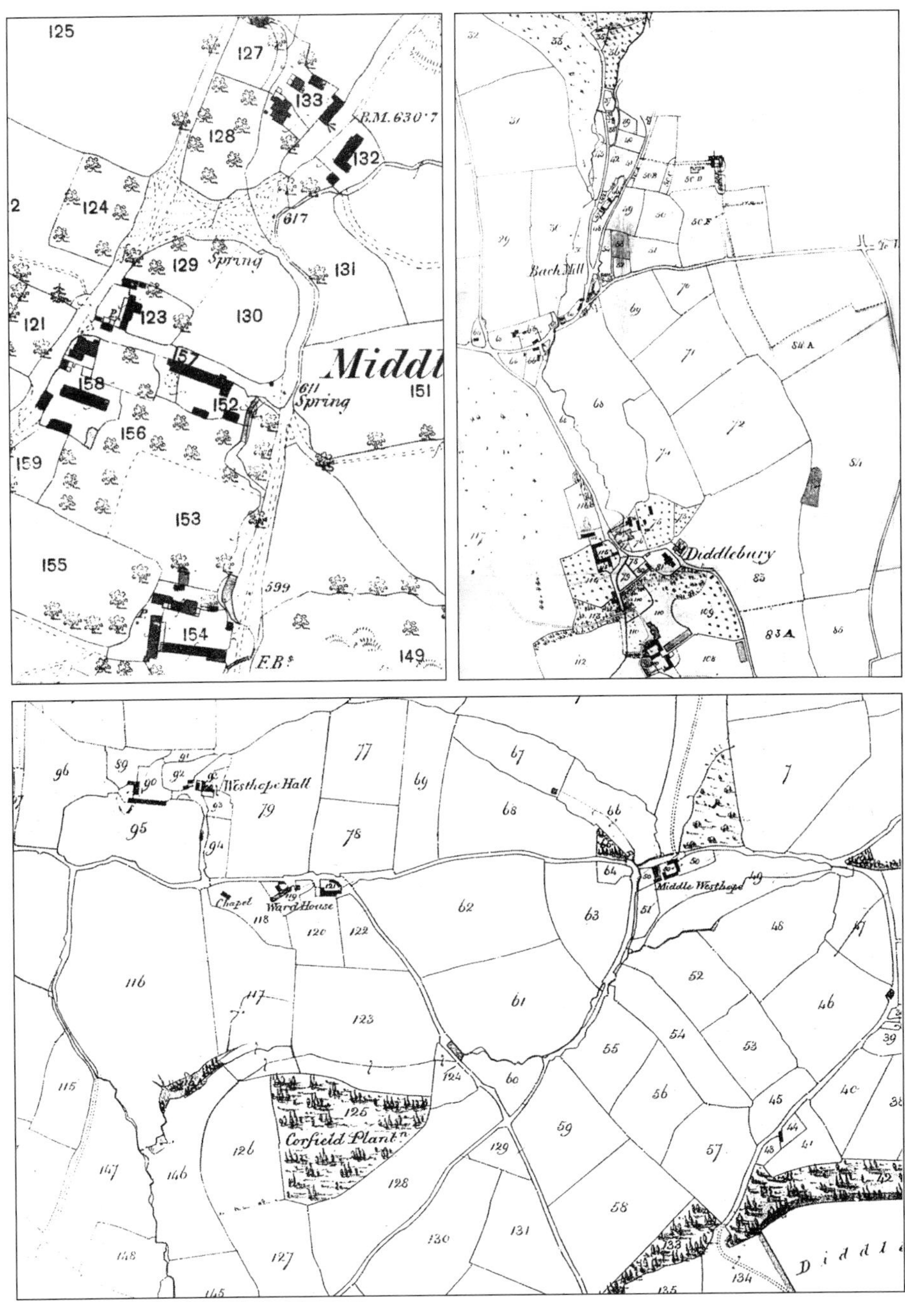

Fig. 7 *Settlement Plans*

(a) Middlehope, a nucleated settlement (from 1st edition OS 1:25 inch map, 1884)

(b) Diddlebury and Bache Mill, showing possible migration along the Bache Brook (based on Tithe Award map)

(c) Westhope, a settlement of scattered dwellings (based on Tithe Award map)

the main route from Bridgnorth and Wenlock to Ludlow. Westhope in contrast has always been a settlement of scattered houses, which is more typical of the western uplands (Fig. 7c).

LAND HOLDING

The Estates: 1066 to 1500

In many ways the history of Diddlebury is bound up inextricably with that of its estates. Until the second half of the 20th century virtually all land in the parish was owned by one or other of the estates, and even in 2006 much of the eastern side of the parish forms part of the estates of Lord Boyne, while in the western uplands Westhope remains largely intact as an estate which dates back a thousand years. The history of these estates has been a process of fusion and fission, with manors being amalgamated and subsequently split, often by the breaking away of former subsidiary estates which had developed within the parent holding. In many ways the great medieval estate resembled a present-day public corporation, continually involved in mergers and takeovers, and occasionally disposing of unprofitable or inconveniently located elements in a process of rationalisation. The metaphor may be carried further, for the baronial estate was essentially a commercial operation with a precise management structure, and controlled by accountants who were as powerful and demanding as any of their 21st century counterparts.[20] Here, however, the comparison ends, for the present day corporation is unlikely to have its assets seized by the crown for acts of treason, as happened with Corfham in 1155 and 1175. Nor were new estates normally acquired by purchase, certainly in the earlier part of the period, with marriage, inheritance, and royal grants being a generally more satisfactory means of achieving expansion.

THE KING

Roger de Montgomery, earl of Shrewsbury	Tenant in chief
Roger de Lacy	Undertenant
Herbert	Undertenant
Riding Man*	Undertenant

These all owed **military service** to their feudal superior from whom they receive land.

Two villeins*
Four Smallholders*
Four Slaves

These all owed **labour services** in return for their land.

Table 1 The Feudal Pyramid, based on the manor of Corfton

The start and end of the period currently under consideration were both periods of major redistribution of land. The first, following the Norman Conquest, was forced, with Anglo-Saxon landowners being dispossessed in favour of William I's followers, who required rewarding for their assistance in his conquest of England. The basis of all landholding was service, military service in the cases of the upper ranks of society, labour services in the case of the peasantry. This was the feudal system, which in its heyday provided a logical economic system for a society in which there was little money. Table I shows, in simplified diagrammatic form, how the Domesday manor of Corfton was organised.

The townships which were later to form the parish of Diddlebury had been divided between six landholders before 1066. The most important of these was the king, who had held the royal manor of Corfham. Almund, who had held Westhope, also had a portfolio of manors, mostly in the southern part of the county, but including Hodnet in the north. Wulfric, who had held Marston jointly with Camel, had an even greater selection of Shropshire manors, while Sutton and Poston had been held by Aelfric, who had possessed a smaller number of scattered manors in the south of the county, including Hatton, Gretton, Detton, and Aston Botterell. Adesi, who had held Corfton and Middlehope, had also possessed three other small estates in the area.[21] Thus before the Conquest all the manors in the parish area had been units in much larger and scattered holdings. After the Conquest all these estates were granted to Roger de Montgomery, earl of Shrewsbury, who held most of the land in the county, as tenant in chief of the crown.[22] The earl retained Corfham for his own use, and divided the rest between under tenants, who in turn rapidly did the same. This process, which is known as subinfeudation, will be discussed in more detail below. In this process of granting lands to a second tier in the feudal hierarchy, the manor of Westhope passed into the hands of Picot de Say, whose descendants obtained the lordship of Clun. Westhope remained thereafter linked with Clun, passing into the illustrious FitzAlan family of Arundel, in whose hands it remained until it was sold in 1561.

The detailed changes in the manorial holdings of the parish, and indeed the whole of Shropshire, were comprehensively chronicled by Eyton in the 19th century, whose findings have never been seriously challenged.[23] Instead of duplicating Eyton's work, the current study will attempt to consider two very contrasting estates, Corfham and Little Sutton.

The growth of the Corfham estate illustrates the importance of inheritance and marriage in the process by which landholdings developed, and shows how frequently such inheritances passed through the female line. Following the re-incorporation of the manor into the crown lands by Henry I, Corfham became linked with Culmington and Seifton, to form a block of land in the Corvedale which also included Earnstrey Park. In 1177 this was granted by Henry II to Walter de Clifford as a reward for services rendered, perhaps those of his daughter 'Fair' Rosamund, the king's mistress, who had died shortly before.[24] The Clifford male line died out in 1263 with the death of Walter III, a somewhat odious character who in 1250 had forced a messenger to swallow a royal letter and its seal. He was succeeded by his daughter Matilda, the widow of William Langspee, who subsequently eloped with or was abducted by John Giffard of Brimsfield. Giffard was another rather unsavoury character, who annexed the lands of Shrewsbury Abbey at Tugford, and stole corn from the Templars at Holdgate. Giffard died in 1299,[25] shortly afterwards followed by his young son, and the Corfton estate was ultimately inherited by his daughter Eleanor, who had married Fulk LeStrange[26] of Blakemere in north Shropshire. LeStrange also possessed other estates in Shropshire, Cheshire, Hampshire and Gloucestershire, and the marriage brought Corfham into the orbit of Blakemere, which was to be the focus of activity in the 15th century under the Talbots.

The LeStrange family was closely associated with the FitzAlans, the leading power in Shropshire between 1100 and 1400, and was renowned for its unswerving loyalty to the crown. John LeStrange and his son and heir Fulk both died within weeks of each other in 1349, almost certainly from the Black Death. The younger son John who succeeded them was married to Mary, the daughter of the earl of Arundel. At his death in 1361 his widow, always known as 'the Lady of Corfham' held the estate as dower* until her own death 35 years later. Her devotional excesses are mentioned in a later section. The descent of Corfham aptly illustrates one of the great problems of medieval inheritance, the extent to which dower could fragment an inheritance for many years.[27] After the death of 'the Lady' the estate again passed through a daughter, Ankaret, the widow of Richard, Lord Talbot, beginning a Talbot connection which was to last until the end of the 16th century. Under John Talbot, first earl of Shrewsbury (d.1453) the manor was further augmented by the Hallamshire lands based on Sheffield Castle, obtained from Talbot's first wife Maud, a co-heiress of the Furnivals. The increasing importance of Sheffield in the Talbot activities saw the gradual eclipse of Blakemere, and the ultimate disposal of the Diddlebury lands in the 16th century. This was certainly not contemplated in the time of the first earl, as he continued to augment his properties in south Shropshire by purchases, which included Middlehope, which he settled on Lewis and Humphrey, his sons by his second wife Margaret Neville, daughter of Warwick 'the Kingmaker'.[28]

This necessarily simplified account of the descent of the most important estate in the parish through three families does not indicate the role which the Corfham property played in the wider context of the holdings of these families. It is unfortunate that although the Talbot accounts are exceptionally detailed, they have not survived for two Shropshire manors, one of which was Corfham. A number of inferences may, however, be drawn from passing references in the Blakemere accounts. One point which is very clear is that in terms of rent income, Corfham was a relatively minor component of the Blakemere estates. In 1401-2

Corfham raised only £3 1s. 4d. out of a total income of nearly £295, the bulk of which was raised from Whitchurch, Dodington and Wrockwardine. Only Tilstock and Lyneal produced a smaller sum than Corfham.[29] It is also clear that grain was sent from the grange at Corfham to Blakemere, and there was a regular traffic of minor officials between the two places. Corfham was not on the route of the Talbot annual progress along the March from their estates in Cheshire to those in Herefordshire, and visits from the lord would appear to have been unusual. The comings and goings at Christmastide 1401, when 22 horses accompanied Thomas Neville, Lord Furnival (second husband of Ankaret Talbot and holder of the estates *pro tem.* in right of his wife) to spend the Epiphany at Corfham are very much an exception to the rule.[30]

While the subsidiary role of Corfham in the Talbot establishment cannot be denied, it must also be noted that it supplied the family with some of its leading officials. These included Richard Leggett, who entered the service of Ankaret, Lady Talbot and rose to the rank of receiver-general of all the Talbot estates in 1422, a position which he held until 1446. This post was roughly analogous to that of a chief executive of a corporation today, and much of Leggett's work was done in London, where Leggett's Place became the centre of Talbot financial business. He was followed by another Diddlebury man, Roger Stedman, whose ecclesiastical preferments are noted elsewhere [see p.49][31] Sir William Burley of Broncroft was a third local man who served the first earl in a number of capacities including legal advisor and seneschal of the Blakemere estate.

In this context it is worth noting that Broncroft was never run as part of the Corfham and Culmington estates, but had been held of the lords of Corfham for a sixth part of a knights' fee*.[32] From this Broncroft gradually developed into a separate estate in its own right, although as late as 1507 the manor of Broncroft was described as 'held of George, earl of Shrewsbury as of his manor of Corfham by service of one sixth of a knight's fee.'[33] By this time this was little more than a legal formality.

Corfham is a good example of an estate which was managed as a unit within a much larger collection of lands, and administered by a central bureaucracy. In contrast, the situation at Little Sutton showed how easily estates could by subdivided into a mass of sub-tenancies. Before the Conquest Great and Little Sutton and Upper Poston had been part of the extensive estates of the English thegn Aelfric. By Domesday, these holdings had been split, with Helgot, whose castle in Stanton Long gave its name to the village and parish of Holdgate, obtaining Great Sutton and Poston, while Little Sutton passed to William Pandolf, a follower of Roger de Montgomery. Most of Pandolf's 29 Shropshire manors were situated in the north-east of the county based on the lordship of Wem, and he appears to have reached some arrangement with the king whereby his outlying manors were taken back into royal hands and re-allocated.[34] In the case of Sutton, the manor was converted into a serjeantry, whereby the king's tenant was obliged to supply an armed escort to accompany the Sheriff to the Exchequer with moneys raised in the county. By 1207 the manor was held by the family of Sutton whose family continued to be tenants by serjeantry for several generations.[35] Between 1215 and 1245 Robert Sutton and subsequently his son Osbert began systematically alienating these lands (i.e. granting them to his undertenants). By 1246 the Crown had become concerned by the widespread alienation of serjeantries, particularly in Shropshire, and commenced a series of investigations. These revealed that the land which de Sutton held from the king had been sub-divided between no fewer than eight greater and five lesser subtenants.[36] Significantly, these tenancies paid a rent in money to the de Suttons, showing that by the first half of the 13th century, over a century before the so-called feudal crisis which followed the Black Death, cash had become the medium for conducting property transactions.

Such subdivision of estates had a number of consequences. It led to numerous legal cases such as a long-running dispute involving the daughters of Alexander the Chaplain, which meandered through the courts between 1249 and 1267, concerning a virgate (60 acres) of land in Sutton which their father had rented from Robert Sutton in 1225.[37] It also led to complexities regarding the feudal obligations owing to the king. Subtenants like William Cheles and Robert of Stanton Lacy were liable for the service of a thirtieth part of a knight's fee. It made increasing sense for the crown to commute these services to a money payment, and after the inquisitions of 1246 and 1247 Osbert Sutton's serjeantry was converted into an annual rent of 20 shillings to the crown, of which he paid two shillings, and the residue was met by the tenants. The liability for knight service was retained as the basis for tax assessment, so that for example in 1254 a knight's fee was assessed at 40 shillings, and the eight Sutton tenants each paid 18 pence on one thirtieth, while Osbert paid 9½ pence for the fiftieth share at which his serjeantry had been valued.[38] The complexities which are so graphically illustrated by the case of Little Sutton were addressed in 1290 by the statute *Quia Emptores*, which essentially sought to stop further extension of the feudal ladder, and gradually to reduce the number of existing 'rungs.'[39] It is clear that the process took a long time to operate, and in 1439 the Little Sutton estate was still parcelled into small portions, such as the half virgate (30 acres) which William Merssheton had held.[40] It was not until a century later, when Charles Foxe came into possession, that Little Sutton was united under a single landlord.

The examples of Corfham and Little Sutton have been discussed at some length as they illustrate two contrasting models of medieval estates. The remaining manors in the parish fell between the two extremes. Westhope, as has been noted, remained firmly in the hands of the FitzAlan family throughout the period. Corfton soon became divided into a number of sub-tenancies, but on nowhere near the scale of Westhope. It was united in 1486 under Sir John Savage from Cheshire, a kinsman of the Stanleys, whose duplicity towards Richard III at Bosworth was rewarded by Henry VII with extensive grants of land of former Yorkist supporters who had shown greater loyalty to the defeated king. Great Sutton remained with Holdgate, passing into the hands of the Burnell family who retained it until the 16th century. Middlehope, as already noted, passed into the possession of the Talbots in 1428. At the start of the 16th century the Talbots dominated landholding in Diddlebury. A century later none of the families who had held land in 1500 possessed so much as an acre in the parish.[41]

The Estates: 1500 – 2000

This complete change in land ownership occurred gradually, and was, directly at least, unrelated to the most striking cause of the redistribution of land in the 16th century, the secularisation of church land. Its most obvious feature was the growth of the Diddlebury estate from a subsidiary member of Corfham into the largest holding in the parish. This was matched by the break-up of the Talbot lands. The decline of the Diddlebury estate (or Delbury as it was then known) after 1845 was as striking as its rise had been. In the 20th century the short-lived activities of P.G. Holder, described below, were remarkable as one individual's attempt to reshape a pattern which had evolved over many centuries.

	1500	1600	1700	1800	1900	2000
Diddlebury	Talbot	Baldwyn	Baldwyn	Cornewall	Admin.	Wrigley
Peaton	Talbot	Stafford(?)	Stafford	Clinton	Atherden	Boyne
Middlehope	Talbot	Smith	Smith	Wright	Wright	Multi-owned
Broncroft	Littleton	Lutley	Lutley	Barnaby	Whitaker	Multi-owned
Earnstrey	Talbot	Briggs	Briggs	Mytton		
Corfton	Savage	Foxe/ Baldwyn	Baldwin	Roberts	Wood	Multi-owned
Westhope	FitzAlan	Dannett	Fleming	Dyer	Dyer	Dyer
Lawton	Baskerville	Lutley	Lutley	Cornewall	Admin*	Brick
Gt. Sutton	Witchcott	Foxe	Herbert	Cornewall	Admin*	Boyne
Lt. Sutton	Witchcott	Foxe	Herbert	Powell	Powell	Multi-owned

* estate in the hands of administrators

Table 2 Ownership of estates, 1500 – 2000

The above table shows the extent to which the breaking up of the Talbot estates changed land ownership in the parish. Diddlebury passed out of the Talbot estate into the hands of the Baldwyn family in much the same manner as Broncroft had become a separate estate in the 14th century. The Baldwyns had been loyal servants of the Talbots, and by1544 William Baldwyn was described as owning a capital messuage (the Hall), four tenements and two mills, together with 280 acres of land in Diddlebury, and a further 110 acres in Lower Hayton.[42] These were held for a nominal 7 shillings annual rent from the earl of Shrewsbury as of his castle of Corfham. It is interesting to note that this document mentions the creation in 1532 of a 'use' or trust designed to avoid the payment of succession duties to the crown. Thomas Cromwell's attempt to end this practice by the Statute of Uses in 1535 caused great opposition among the gentry. As loyal servants of the earls of Shrewsbury, the Baldwyns were rewarded by further grants of remaining Talbot property, such as that of 26 acres of wood on Whitehill Bank above Bache Mill made to Richard Baldwyn in August 1560.[43] In 1558 the earl sold Earnstrey Park to Oliver Briggs of Shifnal, followed in 1565 by his lands in Clee Forest. This left the Talbots with a small residual estate at Corfham, which passed by inheritance to the earls of Stafford shortly after the accession of Charles I.[44]

Independently of the break up of the Corfham estate and the growth of the Baldwyn possessions, significant developments were taking place at the opposite end of the parish. Charles Foxe, the second son of William Foxe of Ludford, is typical of the new class of landowner who emerged in the 16th century. A lawyer, Foxe spent much of his later life as secretary to the Council in the Marches, and established himself in the former priory at Bromfield in 1541. Even before this, Foxe had been accumulating property in the Ludlow area, and in 1532 had taken a 50-year lease of Sutton and Whitchcott, which he subsequently converted into a freehold. In 1561 he purchased the remainder of Sutton from the earl of Oxford.[45] During his long life, Charles Foxe accumulated a vast collection of properties in Shropshire, Herefordshire, and mid-Wales which were divided among his four sons at his death in 1590. The Bromfield estate, together with Sutton and Corfton, and other lands in Diddlebury, Munslow and elsewhere in the district were inherited by the eldest son, Charles, hereafter referred to as Sir Charles.[46] Shortly before his death, the elder Charles Foxe had greatly augmented his interest in Diddlebury by purchasing Corfton from Sir John Savage.[47]

The extent of the accumulation of property by Charles Foxe shows that the Baldwyns were operating on a very much smaller scale, and their approach was one of consolidation rather than expansion of their holdings. This was carried out in two ways. Firstly, a concerted effort was made to buy out the freeholders as their lands became available.[48] This necessarily gave the Baldwyns additional lands which were scattered across Diddlebury and Corfton, reflecting the parcels of land which had originally been held in the open fields. The next stage in consolidation was the conducting of a series of exchanges with Sir Charles Foxe of some of these pockets of land which straddled the two holdings.[49] In 1665 the Baldwyn family purchased the Foxe holdings in Corfton which had been held as dowry by

Lady Long, the widow of Sir Richard Foxe.[50] This meant that by the early 18th century the Corfton holding amounted to over 1,400 acres, which produced a rent of £276 7s. 9d. per year.[51]

The next augmentation of the Baldwyn estates, in 1709, also came about at the expense of the former Foxe holdings. After a prolonged legal dispute with the Corbett family following the death of Francis Foxe in 1636, in 1675 the Sutton lands were confirmed to the Herberts, as heirs of the Foxes.[52] In 1709, presumably as part of a rationalisation of the family holdings, the manors of Great and Little Sutton, together with Dowles in Worcestershire, containing 26 houses, a water corn mill and 1,220 acres, were sold by Henry Lord Herbert to Edward Baldwyn of the Inner Temple.[53] It would seem likely that the Herberts initially retained some land in Sutton, as in 1713 Lord Herbert granted a 99-year lease of some properties there to Rowland Powell of Little Sutton.[54] The Little Sutton estate would appear to have been carved out of the old Foxe lands by the Powells in the late 17th or early 18th century, but no documentary confirmation of this has yet come to light.

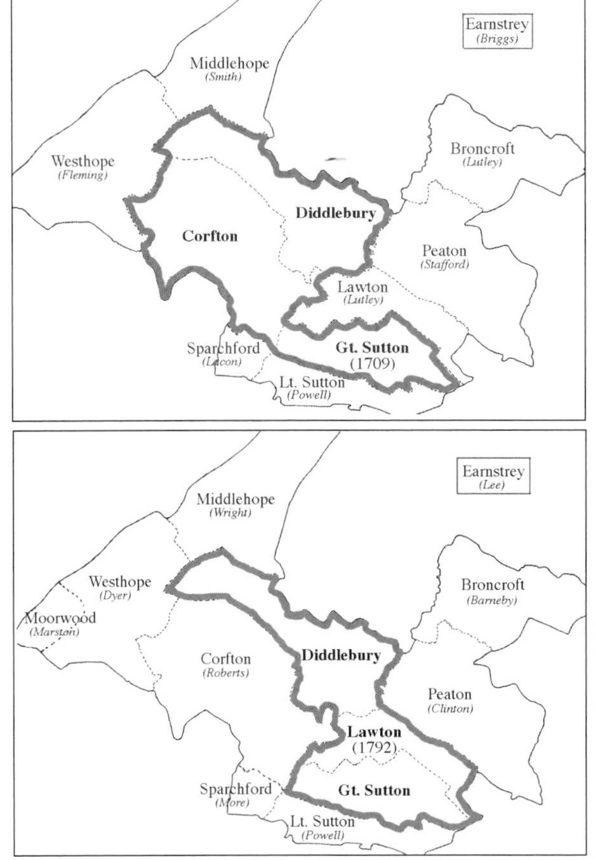

Fig. 8 The growth of Diddlebury Hall estate in the 18th century (a) The Baldwyn estates at their greatest extent c.*1720 (Baldwyn estates outlined in grey)*
(b) The position c.*1800 (Cornewall estates outlined in grey)*

By 1720 the Baldwyn estates in the parish comprised the greater part of the fertile valley bottom as indicated on Figure 8a. It would seem evident that within this concentration, Corfton was a separate entity in the hands of the descendants of Charles Baldwyn, who had moved from Elsich to Stokesay Castle (as tenant) in 1635. The family interests had become diversified by the middle of the 18th century which resulted in the disposal of their lands in Diddlebury. In

June 1752 the Diddlebury portion was sold by Edward Baldwyn to Frederick Cornewall of Ludlow for £9,854, who immediately began the rebuilding of the hall.[55] The descendants of the Elsich Baldwyns had acquired estates in Bockleton, Worcestershire and Aqualate in Staffordshire.[56] The interests of this branch of the family were gradually moving away from its original centre, and Charles Baldwyn, who in 1752 had married the heiress of William Lacon Childe of Kinlet, sold off Bockleton, Aqualate and, in 1779, Corfton. This was purchased by Wilson Aylesbury Roberts, the M.P. for Bewdley, who like the majority of landowners in the parish in the period 1750-1850, was an absentee.[57] The sale of Corfton marked the end of a link between the Baldwyns and the parish which extended back to the 14th century.

The Cornewalls, and particularly Folliott Herbert Walker Cornewall (d.1831), successively bishop of Bristol, Hereford and Worcester, lived in some style at Delbury Hall. The bishop would retreat to Delbury from his episcopal residences to hunt with his own private pack of foxhounds. In March 1787 he made the final addition to the Diddlebury estate by purchasing Lawton and some adjacent lands from John Barneby for £9,000.[58] Under Bishop Cornewall the estate was at its peak, and could well have continued to flourish but for the untimely death of his elder son, Frederick Hamilton, in 1845. Bishop Cornewall, fearing correctly that his elder son would not produce male heirs, had placed an entail upon the estate so that in that eventuality it would pass to the younger son, Herbert, and his heirs. Herbert, who lived in France, regarded the estate as a source of income, particularly in the form of collateral for raising money by mortgages. In order to pay the interest charges, the hall was let to a succession of tenants until its eventual sale in 1910. The complexities of re-mortgaging, and a damaging legal action in 1903 whereby the mortgagee sought to sell the property, meant that the Cornewall family ended up with nothing from the proceeds.[59]

The history of the smaller estates in the parish was less traumatic. Broncroft had been acquired by the Lutleys, a Catholic family from Staffordshire, in the 16th century, together with Lawton.[60] In the early 18th century the estate of Wolverton in Apedale was added to the holding. Estate accounts for the period 1756-64 show that the three estates were operated at least partially as an integrated unit.[61] The acquisition of the Barneby estate at Brockhampton in Herefordshire in 1735 gradually moved the family's focus away from Shropshire, and John Barneby, the last owner, sold Lawton (1787), Wolverton (1789) and Broncroft (shortly before 1807). Broncroft was owned by the Royds, a Lancashire family, until 1824, when it was bought by George Johnstone, whose son restored the castle.[62]

Westhope had been retained by the FitzAlans until 1561, when it was bought by the crown. In 1568 it was sold to Leonard Dannett, a Leicestershire gentleman whose ancestors had been tenants of Westhope. The Dannetts would appear to have been one of the few families in the parish with pronounced puritan sympathies, and the will of Sir John, proved in 1607, mentions a number of prominent divines including Robert Horne of Ludlow.[63] In 1655 Thomas Dannett's will instructed that the estate should be sold to pay his debts, in consequence of which it was purchased by Henry Fleming of Sibdon Carwood. The Flemings were, to say the least, colourful and their matrimonial problems are noted later in this work (see p.64). The line ended dramatically with the poisoning of Edward Fleming in 1773, and the subsequent death from drink of his heir, who was widely suspected of the crime.[64] The Westhope estate was subsequently sold to Sir John Swinnerton-Dyer, with the exception of 212 acres at Moorswood on the end of the estate, which was bought by Francis Marston of Cheyney Longville, and remained independent afterwards. Westhope is unique in Diddlebury in remaining in the hands of the same family that owned it in 1800.[65]

The 20th century saw a massive redistribution of land in the parish, much of which was occasioned by the actions of one man, P.G. Holder. Holder was a Tenbury solicitor who began systematically buying up estates in the Corvedale in 1910. Some of his purchases he subsequently sold, totally redrawing the map of property ownership in Diddlebury in the process. In 1910 Holder had purchased the Delbury estate for £40,000. He retained Great Sutton for himself, and sold Lawton and Delbury farms to their tenants. Delbury Hall and 154 acres were sold to Mrs. Wingfield-Stratford. In 1911 he bought most of the Corfton estate, excepting Sparchford Farm and the Sun Inn, at public auction in Shrewsbury.[66] In the same year Holder began to add the old Aston Hall estates, then owned by E.C. Wright of Kelvedon, Essex, to his portfolio. In 1911 he purchased Middlehope,

Fig. 9a Church Farm, Diddlebury which passed out of agricultural use at the end of the 20th century

Fig. 9b Hall Farm, Middlehope which also passed out of agricultural use at the end of the 20th century

Aston Hall and Bouldon, following this with the remaining 661 acres of Aston in 1914.[67] Aston Hall was almost immediately resold to J.I. Benson, and Middlehope was sold to V.S. Wrigley.

Vincent Shires Wrigley, a former Lancashire cotton manufacturer, had previously owned Eriviatt Hall near Denbigh. When the Wingfield-Stratfords, who would seem to have been unpopular, left Delbury in 1919, Holder created a new Delbury Hall estate for the Wrigley family out of the Middlehope lands.[68] In the meantime Holder had established himself at Corfton Hall, where he began to develop his experimental farming practices which will be considered below (see pp.34-35). No further lands were added until the purchase of Lesser Poston in the late 1920s. In the early 1930s Holder acquired first Peaton Hall, which he was to make his headquarters, and subsequently Sutton Court, following the premature death of the impresario Lionel Powell in 1932.[69] By this time Holder presided over an estate of his own creation amounting to some 4,665 acres. What he lacked was a son to succeed him, and in 1941 he bought Holdgate Hall with nearly 500 acres as a retirement home, and offered the rest of his estates to the Ecclesiastical Commissioners. After prolonged negotiations the Commissioners purchased the estate in 1942 for something less than Holder's asking price of £225,000.[70] As noted below, the lasting memorial to the Commissioners' period as landowners are the houses which they constructed for estate workers in Sutton, Bouldon and Peaton. The Church Commissioners did not remain the major landowners in the parish for any length of time. In 1953 Corfton was sold, mainly to its tenants, and in 1960 Peaton and Sutton, with the exception of Sutton Court, were bought by Viscount Boyne, recreating a block of estate land on the eastern side of the parish.

The break up of the Holder estate, despite Viscount Boyne's purchases (some of which in Bouldon and Poston were later re-sold), added greatly to the number of owner-occupiers farming in the parish. This was further augmented in 1995 and 1996 when almost 550 acres of the Middlehope estate were sold following the Lloyds' fiasco which had ruined many estates. In 2006 Westhope is the only estate to preserve any resemblance of its historic boundaries, and this, no doubt, is largely attributable to its remoteness.

Tenants, copyholders, leaseholders and freeholders

It is particularly gratifying to be able, in the course of a discussion of land tenures, to note that the greatest medieval authority on the subject had a close link with Diddlebury, Sir Thomas Lyttleton having married Johanne, co-heiress of Sir William Burley of Broncroft. Lyttleton's *Treatise on Tenures* adopted a classification which has been the basis for works on the subject since its first printing in 1481. The basis of feudal landholding has already been mentioned above (Table 1), and in the present context discussion will be confined to the lesser tenants, whose holdings were originally based upon the performance of labour services.

The main division was between those tenants who were free, and those who were not, who were known as villeins. In practise freedom and villeinage are extremely difficult to define accurately, though as a general rule it may be said that the free tenant possessed a greater freedom to negotiate the nature of his service with his lord than did his unfree counterpart.

As the economy developed, the free tenant was able to convert his labour services into a money rent, often known as a 'quit rent' as it released him from other services. Under Henry II the introduction of pleas of *Novel disseizin** and *Mort dancestor** enabled free tenants to take their disputes directly to the royal courts, by-passing the manorial courts, which might lack impartiality. The successors of the villein tenants, whose only protection had lain with the manorial court, became the copyholders* of the later medieval period.[71]

It is possible to learn more of the nature of these holdings from surviving records. A survey of Westhope in 1301 reveals that there was only one free tenant on the manor, Isabella de Acton, who held 2½ virgates (150 acres) for a rent of 2lbs. of pepper worth 2s. 6d. at Christmas. The other tenants were all unfree, of whom 20 of the 33 named in the survey had the basic ½ virgate (30 acres) which was regarded as the minimum viable peasant holding. Rents varied from 2s. 6d. to 7s., no doubt reflecting the quality of the lands, which would have been dispersed among the common fields of the manor. A further seven tenants had holdings of between a half and three 'nocks' or strips in the fields, which by themselves could not have provided a living. By 1301, holdings were being increased as parcels of the demesne land (which today would be called 'in hand' land, retained by the landowner for his own use) were rented out to tenants. Some half virgate men like Gervase, Richard's son and Richard the Clerk augmented their holdings with parcels of demesne meadow, while three holdings were comprised entirely of parcels of demesne of 12 acres each.[72]

In 1100 free tenants gained the right to inherit their lands on payment of a fee to their landlord, and the logical development from this was for them to be able to dispose of it to others. The complexities of the alienation of land have already been discussed above in relation to the Sutton estate, and the statute of *Quia Emptores* of 1290 partially addressed this problem by finally confirming the right of free men to sell their lands. This is an important stage in the development of the concept of 'fee simple', or freehold as it is more usually termed today. As these concepts had evolved during the 13th century there were many actions in the royal courts to decide who had been rightly *seized* of lands, and whether others had illegally deprived or *desseized* them. Thus in 1222 the Justices in Eyre (Assizes) in Shrewsbury heard six of these actions from Diddlebury, including an inquiry as to whether William Cheles was seized of eight acres of arable and an acre of meadow in Sutton when he died. This was an extremely complex action, brought about by the excessive sub-division of the Sutton lands.[73] The Assizes of 1256 produced a similar array of local disputes over seisin, and it is interesting to note that the parties involved were not averse to employing legal technicalities to gain their point. In one example Ingerith Spigh and Joan Corfton, who had featured in the Cheles case in 1221, claimed that the writ by which they were summoned by Roger Wain in an action over ten acres in Corfton had been wrongly made out, causing the action to fail.[74]

The 16th century began with a variety of forms of tenure operating on the estates in the parish, but a century later, there was a remarkable degree of uniformity. A Savage rental of 1532 for Corfton and Sutton shows that in each manor there were three types of holding: leaseholds, either for a life or lives, or a term of years; copyholds; and annual tenancies. Generally speaking, the larger properties were leased, and the smaller holdings, often single dwellings and a couple of fields, were rented annually. Thus in Sutton, William Heynes leased the main farm for the lives of himself, his wife and his son for 33s. 4d. per year. In contrast Richard Lellowe paid only 3s. 4d. for his house in Corfton.[75] The copyholders, the descendants of the old villein tenants, enjoyed what were in effect hereditary tenancies, the title for which was based upon entries in the manor court rolls. These tended to be medium sized holdings, which were becoming unpopular with landowners who sought either to create large farms by amalgamation or to raise rents. As copyholds were an obstacle to this, when they fell in they were generally converted into other forms of tenancy, though this process occurred at different times in different parts of the country.

Freeholds represented another barrier to the consolidation and development of estates. It is clear that by the end of the medieval period a number of the smaller freeholds in the parish had been bought up by several individuals to form larger holdings, the largest of which was made by the Stedman family, who had built up a block of lands in Diddlebury and Corfton. These were ultimately acquired by the Baldwyns who preserved the muniments of title for them, which in some cases dated back to the 14th century.[76] Diddlebury freeholders bought out by the Baldwyns at the end of the 16th century were Henry Normecott, Mr. Oliver and Mr. James. It is clear that the vendors took advantage of their position to charge over the odds for their rights. Thomas Baldwyn records that he paid Oliver the enormous sum of £420 for three houses in Diddlebury, which Oliver Briggs had purchased from the earl of Shrewsbury earlier in Elizabeth's reign.[77] By 1604 the position of Thomas Stedman had become so unusual that he was always referred to as 'the Freeholder'.[78]

It may be reasonably be asserted that by 1660 all the larger and medium-sized holdings in the parish had been converted to leaseholds, either for a term generally of 99 years, or for lives, or for both, whichever was the less. In many ways leaseholds had all the disadvantages of copyholds, as the rent was frozen, sometimes for a century. This led to the imposition of quite heavy entry fines when the properties passed to the next named 'life' on the death of the leaseholder. For example, what is now known as Hall Farm in Middlehope, leased to Francis Tippin in 1716, paid £4 rent annually (together with a cheese at Christmas), but the entry fine was £120. Another property in the same township paid £4 6s. 4d. in rent, but faced entry fines of £260.[79] The discrepancy between the value of these lands and the actual rents paid is shown clearly by a survey of the Carington estates made in 1733. Upper House Farm comprised 167 acres and was valued at £44 14s. 11½d., yet was leased at only £4 annually. Hall Farm, of 126 acres, was similarly valued at £36 11s. 9¼d., and paid four guineas in rent.[80] It is unsurprising that the leasehold system was recognised as unsatisfactory, and as leases came to an end they were converted into tenancies for much shorter terms of years. Thus by 1761 Upper House was being rented out at a more economic £36 10s., while Hall Farm was charged at £46.[81]

This process may be seen throughout the parish, and it is interesting to note that in Peaton (Corfham), an estate owned by another Catholic family, the earls of Stafford, rents for leaseholds tended to be proportionally higher than in Middlehope. It is also noticeable that the distribution of land between holdings is more equal in Middlehope and even in 1720 Peaton Hall has a far greater acreage than any other farm in the parish. The amalgamation of farms to form larger units was a process which was well underway in the 18th century, accelerated in the 19th, and the census of 1851 provides a snapshot of farm sizes before the onset of the agricultural depression after 1870. In 1851 Delbury Farm was the largest farm in the parish at 730 acres, followed by Broncroft Castle at 500, which at that time included Broncroft Parks. Unsurprisingly, all holdings greater than 300 acres were situated in the valley bottom. In 1912 when a comprehensive survey of all land was carried out in connection with Lloyd George's taxation proposals, there had been only minimal changes to the size of most farms in the parish since 1851 despite changes in tenant in most cases. The one exception was the result of the splitting up of the Delbury holding by P.G. Holder to create a smaller Delbury Farm and new holdings at Hale Farm and Church Farm.[82] This was to be a forerunner of later changes, the most significant of which were to be the result of Holder's operations. By 1941 nearly half of Holder's lands had been incorporated into one massive farm operation of 2,092 acres based on Peaton Hall.[83] This arrangement was ahead of its time, and the Church Commissioners soon returned to a system of smaller tenanted farms.

Peaton	**1720**		**Middlehope**	**1733**	
Name	Acreage	Rent (£)	Name	Acreage	Rent (£)
Alice Davies	529	80	Edw. Baldwyn	167	4
Thos. Amies	60	9	Wm. Down	126	4: 4:0d
Eliz. Benion	57	5	Eliz. Bird	135	4: 6:0d.
Edw. Jordan	51	8	Thos. Fosbroke	134	4
Fr. Keysall	48	5	Wm. Higgins	90	4
Wm. Halford*	30	5	John Downes	60	2: 6: 8d.
Edw. Jordan	30	5	John Taylor	28	1
Wm. Morris	23		Wm. Taylor	27	2
John Beamond	20	0:13:4d.	Edw. Fewtrell	16	1: 2: 4d.

* tenant at will

Table 3 Comparison of Holdings and Rents between Peaton and Middlehope (from 1720 Survey of Shifnal etc SA, 6001/2600; 1733 Survey of Carington estates, PRO C/103/164)

Acreage	**No. of Holdings**
500+	2
400-499	3
300-399	5
200-299	6
150-199	8
100-149	4
50-99	4
Under 50	4

Table 4 Size of Holdings from 1851 Census

The trend towards the creation of larger units was resumed towards the end of the 20th century when land came onto the market or tenancies fell vacant, and since 1980 many farms have ceased to exist as independent units, with their farmhouses, and often their outbuildings, becoming the homes of people with no links to farming. The example of Middlehope is most striking, with Hall Farm, Lower House, Green Farm, Burwood, and Wetmore passing out of mainstream agricultural use.[84] In Diddlebury itself, Delbury Farm, the Glebe, Church Farm and Hale Farm have ceased to operate in the same way, although the land is still farmed as part of other holdings. Holder's system has been vindicated in the long term.

A Living from the Land

It is no exaggeration to state that the land has been the basis of the economic life of the parish throughout its history, and that although today only a minority of its inhabitants may be engaged in agriculture, it remains the key occupation.

It is possible to make some conclusions concerning the state of agriculture during the earlier part of the medieval period, using Domesday as a basis. The area subsequently covered by the parish of Diddlebury may be considered in three sections at the time of Domesday. The first was the upland area, predominantly in the west, where settlements had been carved out of the forest, and were in the process of expansion. Earnstrey on the opposite side of the Corvedale was a similar area of upland forest. Most of the eastern side of the valley had been waste when its Norman landlords Pandolf and Helgot had taken possession, no doubt in consequence of the Welsh raids which were endemic at the time.[85] By 1086 Bouldon and the Suttons were on the way to recovery, with increased valuations, although Great Poston remained waste.[86] Between these lay the valuable former royal manor of Corfham, where agriculture was clearly in a more flourishing state than elsewhere in the area, though still not achieving its potential.

It must be remembered that the Domesday survey was a valuation concerned with assessment of tax, in this case the notorious Danegeld, rather than an agricultural survey. It does nevertheless give a clear picture of the type of farming practised at the time. The cultivation of arable land was the staple of the community, and in Corfham there were five plough teams on the demesne (in hand) land, but the potential for a further six. The villagers had a further three ploughs, with land for a further two, and there were a further two ploughs on the half-hide* which had been sublet to an unnamed knight.[87] The hide of land held by Shrewsbury Abbey also had the potential for three ploughs. Corfham was clearly in an advanced state of cultivation, with five hides under the plough.[88]

The upland townships of Middlehope and Westhope provide a clear contrast. The area was heavily wooded, and after the Norman Conquest became included in the Long Forest, a vast area which included the whole length of Wenlock Edge and beyond, with the woodland parts of Corfton and Diddlebury also being covered by its jurisdiction. The prime purpose of a royal forest was to provide hunting when required by the monarch, although certainly at a later date a degree of commercial forestry was undertaken (see below). Afforestation put a brake upon the expansion of cultivated land of settlements within the forest (assarting), which led to tensions. Assarts were either made illegally, which ran the risk of fines when the crown held periodic perambulations of the forest, or by purchasing licences. Few concessions appear to have been made before the end of the 12th century, but by 1209 Westhope was among a number of settlements which had been allowed to increase its cultivated land. By 1300 both Middlehope and Westhope had been disforested, along with most of the Long Forest townships.[89] The pressure for land in a time of expanding population had gained a significant victory.

Cultivation was carried out on common fields, in which inhabitants were allocated strips. The whole manor would have been run in effect as one farm, with the same crops being grown by everyone in each field, taking hay off the communal meadows according to each person's allocation, and grazing their stock on the commons. Middlehope alone of the medieval townships of Diddlebury would appear to have had the classic system of three open fields once

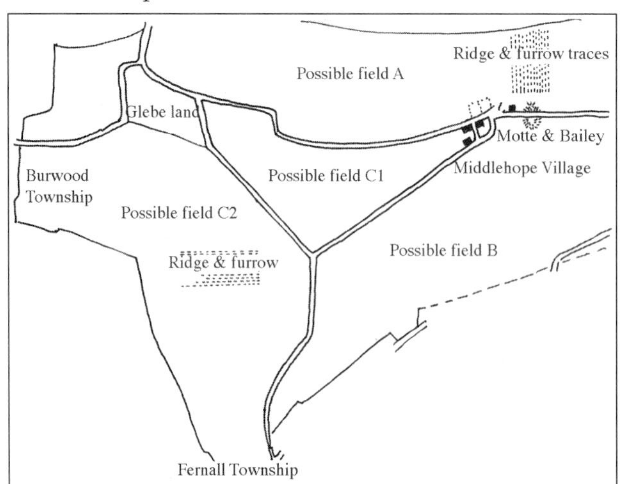

Fig. 10 (a) Conjectural reconstruction of the open fields of Middlehope, based on the Tithe Award map, 1843
(b) Early ridge and furrow near Dunstan's Lane shows up clearly in melting snow in March 1987

beloved of textbooks, although there is no documentary evidence to support this contention. The topography of the township is strongly suggestive of such an arrangement (Fig. 10a), and traces of medieval ridge and furrow which are visible in times of melting snow (Fig. 10b) supply a certain amount of corroboration. Other settlements would appear to have had so-called irregular common fields of varying number, as well as meadow land which were let out in proportion to each tenant in much the same way as strips were allocated in the arable fields.

One advantage of a parish which is composed of a number of estates is that an overall picture can be built up, with one estate's records compensating for deficiencies in those of another. In Sutton, for example, the survival of records of mearing (i.e. surveying the boundaries) of the meadows of Great Sutton in 1633 clearly demonstrates how this system operated before enclosure. There were three meadows, the Upper Meadow, the Mill Meadow and the Marsh Meadow, in which land was allocated, apparently semi-permanently, to individual houses in portions which varied from three acres to a single pole. Plots in the Upper meadow were generally larger than in the other two. Boundaries were fixed according to clearly defined procedures which merit quoting in part:

> We begin to meare the marshe at a meare stone that is hard by the carrying glatt [gap in the fence] of the right hand the way and we come into the meadowe, and soe carry the poule through upon a stone wych lyeth in the middle of the meadow hard by the way side that goeth from Lytle Sutton to Sparchford, and when wee are come to that stone we must go over Pyebrooke and stand under the hedge of Mary Jordan's leasowe under the Crosse ...[90]

This procedure would doubtless have been carried out in each of the various townships of the parish for many centuries prior to 1633.

The common fields of Corfton are the best documented due to the survival of so many records of medieval property transactions in the Baldwyn archive. This is to some extent offset by the tendency of many of the early grants to refer to 'lands in the fields of Corfton' without further identification. Specific references become more common in the 16th century, when the common fields were rapidly becoming enclosed. The renaming and use of alternative names for fields also places obstacles in the way of identifying the open fields, even when their names have been preserved to some extent in later field names. With these qualifications in mind, it is possible to make a conjectural reconstruction of the Corfton fields. Dogsitch, which lay to the west of the lane from Christmas Cross to Sparchford was known by that name since at least 1336, when it was also referred to as Carwardine, a name which vanishes from the records after that date.[91] Of similar antiquity is Sharpenhale Field, which had become Sharpstall by 1600, but had disappeared by the time of the production of the tithe award in

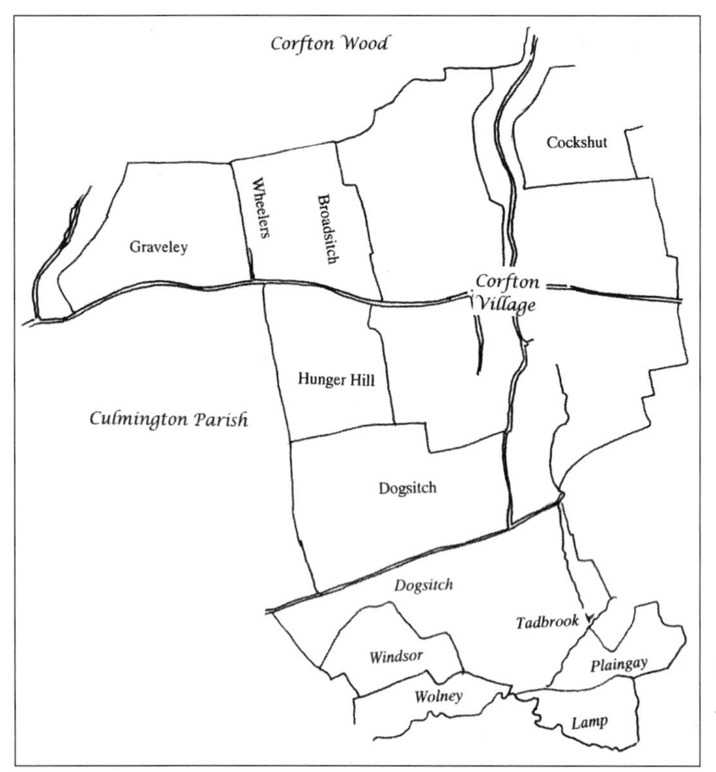

Fig. 11
Map showing the conjectural extent of some of the medieval fields of Corfton. Fields named in medieval documents are shown where their name occurs on the 1846 tithe award map. Meadows are named in italic script; other fields were arable. The pattern contrasts with the regular common fields conjecturally identified at Middlehope (Fig. 10a)

1846.[92] Graveley and Whichways lay on the north side of the 'Portway', the road from Wenlock to Ludlow, though the latter had apparently been subdivided into two fields known as Wheelers and Broadsitch by the early 17th century. Cockshut field was probably 'the field between Corfton and Diddlebury' in which lay four ridges which were granted by William Hyde to Richard Child in 1408 (Fig. 11).[93]

On the other side of the valley floor, Corfham (Peaton) would appear to have had four common arable fields: Graypit, Winslet, Lawton and Marsh Fields. These were partly surviving in 1720, although it is difficult to locate any other than Winslet by reference to the tithe award map.[94]

It is difficult to obtain much information on the type of agriculture practised in the parish during the medieval period, but a lengthy court action in the mid-13th century gives some idea of the stock of a prosperous peasant of the time. Herbert of Corfton claimed that William son of John of Holdgate had stolen eight oxen, six sheep, five wagon loads of corn, six bushels of wheat flour and a quantity of cloth, totalling in value £10.[95] This has been noted as evidence for the eight ox plough team, as well as providing an addition to the small volume of evidence for the ownership of sheep by the peasantry at this time.[96] Peasants at Westhope in 1301 are known to have kept goats, as pannage* for pigs and goats is mentioned in the survey of the manor.[97] An interesting sidelight on medieval cultivation is provided by an unique reference to the carting of lime from Corfham to Dodington in 1342 for use as fertiliser in conjunction with marl.[98]

Cultivating strips in open fields, as any allotment holder will attest, had many disadvantages, particularly when a bad tenant spread weeds and disease among his neighbours' crops. Turning cattle onto arable fields and hay meadows was a further nuisance, and one against which the manor courts were constantly battling. The manor court rolls of Corfham and Corfton contain frequent orders prohibiting the practice, and fines levied on offenders.[99] Enclosing strip holdings with hedges, particularly if they could be consolidated by exchanges with other farmers made for more efficient farming, and the process of piecemeal enclosure began towards the end of the medieval period. The question of enclosure became particularly emotive in the 16th century, particularly when arable land was enclosed and converted into grazing for sheep. This was most famously attacked in 1516 by Sir Thomas More, who, with a typical Londoner's expertise on agricultural matters, analysed the problem in his *Utopia*, in which he created the metaphor of sheep devouring men.[100] While this problem was most acute in parts of the east midlands and eastern England, Shropshire and other western counties were generally enclosed quite amicably, as when arable land was converted to pasture, it was normally for dairying rather than for sheep. Despite this, enclosure was one of the elements which underlay popular discontent throughout the century, and this prompted Tudor governments to undertake a number of generally ineffective measures to ease the problem. Initially Cardinal Wolsey established commissions to enquire into the extent of the problem. The first of these, in 1517, covered Shropshire, and the findings provide the earliest evidence of the practice in Diddlebury. It was reported that William Barker had enclosed 40 acres at Middlehope in 1505, and that six years later the earl of Shrewsbury had enclosed another 40 acres at Corfham, taking two ploughs out of cultivation.[101] According to the commissioners, these two ploughs would have would have provided a livelihood for 12 persons.

The process of enclosure may be assumed to have progressed steadily during the ensuing century, for by 1600 many parts of the parish contained a mixture of strip farming and enclosure operating side by side. An example of this is shown in the lease made by Charles Baldwyn of Elsich to Thomas Tege of Corfton in 1620, which included *inter alia* 'one parcel of arable of five acres set around with quicksett in Kirles furlong; also nine ridges or butts of arable butting upon Tanpit Meadows'.[102] This haphazard mixture of ancient and modern cultivation was obviously inefficient, and there is little reason to doubt the assertion of the Victoria County History that the exchanges made between the Baldwyns and the Foxes (see pp.14-18, and endnote 49) were intended to facilitate enclosure.[103] Official encouragement and enforcement of the process is seen in the Corfton court rolls with penalties of five shillings being levied upon inhabitants who 'tear or break any of the hedges within this lordship', or who failed to make sufficient hedges around their lands.[104]

By the early 18th century much of the parish was enclosed. There were no open fields under cultivation in Middlehope in 1733, and it is clear from the survey of that year that most of the holdings consisted of former strips which had been enclosed.[105] Most of Corfton had been enclosed, although in 1719 there were still a few small pockets of unenclosed land remaining, like the 'four parcels or doles of meadow lying dispersed in a meadow called Wolney' amounting to two acres, which Elizabeth Norncott assigned to her son with other lands in Corfton.[106] In Peaton (Corfham) the process was less advanced, with 177 of a total 830 acres of arable unenclosed in 1720, and a further 70 acres recently enclosed. The same survey noted that 80 acres of meadow were still farmed in common, and 91 had been recently enclosed.[107] By 1779 the only unenclosed land in the parish was the former Corfton Wood, consisting of 353 acres 39 perches which were enclosed by private act of Parliament in that year. With the exception of a central block of 50 acres allocated to the vicar, almost the whole of the area was granted to Wilson Aylesbury Roberts, the owner of the estate.[108] The landscape of large, regular rectangular fields in this part of the parish contrasts with the earlier piecemeal enclosures to the south and east, and also with the squatter settlements around the periphery of the former waste (Fig. 12).

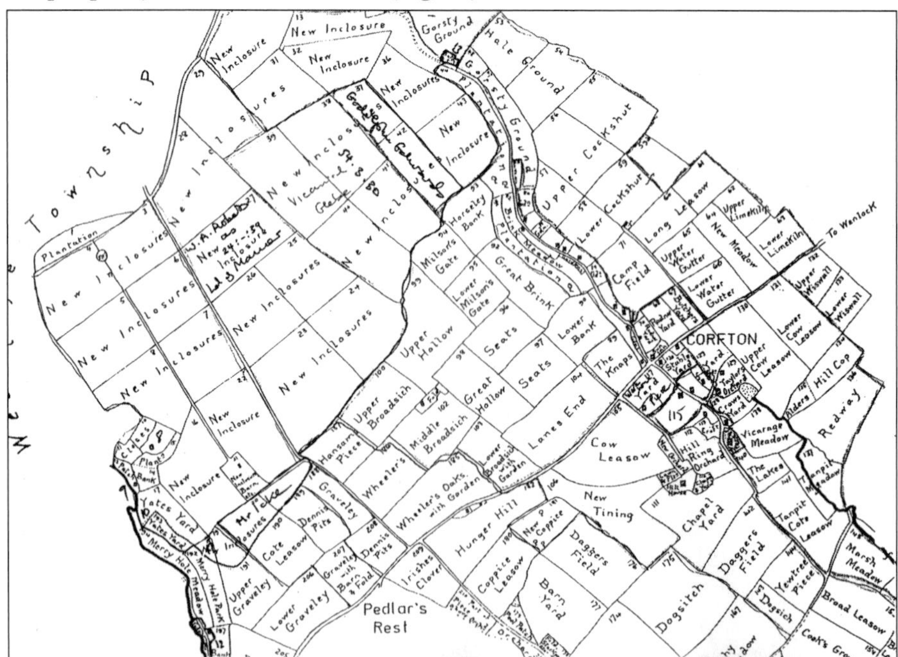

Fig. 12 Corfton Wood after enclosure in 1779. The map, based on the Tithe Award, shows the large rectangular fields typical of Parlamentary enclosure. On the eastern and western fringes may be seen former squatter cottages along Corfton and Seifton Baches

When considering the type of agriculture practised in Diddlebury before improved farming techniques began to be adopted at the end of the 18th century, it is clear that many of the smaller farms must have operated more or less at subsistence level. The 1720 survey of Corfham shows this disparity in its most extreme form. The Peaton Hall holding amounted to just under 530 acres, by far the largest in the parish. The remaining area, some 325 acres, was divided between nine farms, the largest of which was 60 acres and the smallest five.[109] Three of these holdings may be linked to probate inventories with reasonable certainty, and provide an interesting sidelight on the stock of smaller farmers of the period, particularly when they are compared with some of the wealthier farmers whose inventories have survived.

Richard Baxter, Earnestrey, 1683		**Thomas Keysall, Peaton, 1728**	
HRO, Box 36.		HRO, Box 62	
Three yoke of oxen	36 00 00	Six oxen	24 00 00
12 cows, one bull	36 00 00	Six cows and bull	21 00 00
Three mares, one colt	15 00 00	One fat cow	03 00 00
Sheep 'young and old', 180 approx.	23 00 00	Three three year olds	07 00 00
Four pigs	02 10 00	Four calves	04 00 00
Grain in barn and on land	20 00 00	Two horses and colt	07 00 00
		13 pigs	09 02 00
Total value of inventory	557 11 00	Seven sheep	01 08 00
		Poultry	00 05 00
		Implements	05 00 00
		Corn in barn	20 00 00
		Hay	03 00 00
		Barley, oats & vetches	12 00 00
		Peas	04 10 00
		Total value of inventory	169 10 00
Arthur Stedman, Broncroft, 1669		**John Meredith, Peaton, 1707**	
HRO, Box 25		HRO, Box 50	
22 cows and one yearling bull	34 06 08	12 cows & seven calves	26 00 00
Six oxen	32 00 00	Four bullocks	10 10 00
12 young beasts	30 00 00	Ten young beasts	16 00 00
11 calves	12 02 00	20 sheep & five lambs	03 00 00
One cade (orphan) lamb	00 05 00	Four pigs	02 00 00
Two mares, two colts	16 00 00	Corn on ground	06 00 00
15 pigs and three suckling pigs	12 00 00	Corn, malt & grain in house	05 10 00
25 geese & hens 12 ducks & other p'ltry	01 18 00		
Implements etc.	05 00 00	**Total value of inventory**	114 05 00
Fruit in orchard & house	01 00 00		
Corn, oats & peas in barn	30 00 00		
Hay	20 00 00		
Total value of inventory	337 19 08		

Richard Taylor, Great Sutton, 1684		**Timothy Benion, Peaton 1715**	
HRO, Box 38		HRO, Box 53	
Four oxen	13 10 00	Four bullocks	11 00 00
Five cows, one calf	13 10 00	Two cows	07 10 00
Nine cattle, one to three years	11 10 00	Three horses	10 00 00
One mare and colt	06 00 00	Four sheep	01 00 00
Nine pigs	03 13 04	Four swine	02 00 00
Six ewes & lambs, sundry sheep	04 10 00	Implements of husbandry	04 00 00
Corn on ground	08 10 00	Corn in barn and fields	10 00 00
Lent grain [spring sown]	10 00 00		
Implements of husbandry	08 11 00		
Corn and malt in house	02 10 00		
Total value of inventory	154 09 10	**Total value of inventory**	121 18 00

Table 5 Comparison of live and dead stock of six farmers

The three Peaton farms were small to moderate size, Benion's being 57 acres, Keysall's 48, and Beamond's a modest 20.[110] The acreages of the three larger farms at this time are not known, but in the case of Baxter and Stedman are likely to have been in excess of 200 acres. The six examples chosen are typical in that they illustrate the dominance of cattle at this period. Oxen (also referred to here as bullocks) were essential for ploughing, with horses not being used for the purpose until the end of the 18th century. Cattle would have been kept primarily for dairying rather than for meat, and many inventories, including some of the examples in Table 5, list young cattle by age. If the herds appear small compared to those of modern farms, it must be remembered that before the cultivation of turnips as a winter fodder crop, the number of cattle which could be over-wintered was dependent on the quantity of hay available, with many being slaughtered in the autumn.

Most households, even those without a direct connection to agriculture, kept pigs, and it may be assumed that the examples in Table 5 were largely kept for home consumption, with the exception of those of Stedman and Taylor. The greatest contrast between agriculture in Diddlebury at the start of the 18th century and three centuries later is the relative absence of sheep. Richard Baxter's flock of 180 was the largest to be found in any inventory, being nearly equally 50 years later by that of Francis Tipton (1730) who had 30 'feeding sheep' and no less than 148 stores.[111] The only other sizeable flock shown in probate inventories was that of Thomas Wall (1683), also of Earnstrey, and it is hardly surprising that sheep should be kept in larger numbers on the slopes of the Brown Clee. Discounting these three larger flocks, those inventories which enumerate sheep account for a total of 620 adult animals in 22 flocks over the period 1660-1760, giving an average size of 28 sheep in each flock. This compares very closely to the findings of Trinder and Cox in four north Telford parishes.[112] Compared with today's flocks, these appear very small. In 2006 Upper House at Middlehope, a mixed holding of nearly 200 acres dispersed in several blocks in and out of the parish, possesses a quota for a flock of 365 adult sheep.[113]

Statistics from probate inventories may not give a complete picture. Apart from their natural tendency to undervalue stock, individually they do not allow for seasonal fluctuations in stock numbers to be taken into account. Nor do they indicate that farming activities could extend far beyond the boundaries of the parish. The will of John Downe of Middlehope, proved at Canterbury in 1612, reveals the extent of one substantial upland farmer's network. Downe had cattle and sheep grazing on other farms at the time of his death, which included eight cattle with the vicar of Clun, three cows and 44 sheep at Edenhope in Radnorshire, and a further 64 sheep with Hugh Harries of the Cotchmore.[114] It may be presumed that other farmers from the parish also utilised the grazing lands of the Welsh foothills. Further evidence for the extent of the trading network of the farming community comes from the records of markets and fairs, though these are often fragmentary. In 1556 Edward Holland of Diddlebury was recorded buying two steers from David ap Evor of Montgomeryshire for 40s. at Leominster fair, which attracted buyers from as far afield as Aberystwyth and Cheshire.[115] Evidence from the toll books of the Wigmore fairs shows a number of Diddlebury farmers conducting business there on a fairly regular basis as both buyers and vendors. In July 1686, for example George Egerley of Lawton bought 38 lambs at 3s. 10d. each from John Strutty of Dilwyn, while at the same fair in 1694 Edward Pile of Sutton sold 20 lambs for £2 18s. 6d.[116] The same records include the sale of a cow and calf for £3 5s. by Francis Langley of Diddlebury, and the purchase of a bull for £3 2s. by Richard Davies. Three other transactions relate to horses, and horse sales appear to have been the most permanently documented livestock sales. It is clear from the records of the Ludlow horse fairs that Diddlebury farmers, as might be expected, were usually present, generally as vendors rather than buyers. During the period 1686-1695 a total of 25 individuals from the parish sold horses at the Ludlow fairs, 20 of whom did so on only one occasion, and none sold horses more than twice. This suggests that the sale of horses was a by-product of the main farming enterprise rather than a key element, though on occasions a hard bargain could be driven. While most of the horses sold fetched between £2 and £4, a few made much higher prices. On 17 September 1694 Richard Millichap from Earnstrey sold a grey nag to Richard Roads of Dudley for £6 7s. 6d., while in April of the same year William Wellens of Corfton charged Mary Bowen from Llanbister no less than £9 1s. for a brown mare with a brown muzzle and seven white saddle marks.[117] These may have been exceptionally good horses, although it is possible that canny vendors were exploiting a 'townie' and a gullible Welsh widow. It is interesting to note that the summer fairs in Ludlow attracted a regular contingent from Warwickshire, mostly from Bedworth and Solihull. It is hardly surprising that Diddlebury farmers made use of Ludlow for their trading, and no doubt it is where they bought and sold many of their sheep and cattle, for which no records have survived. Bridgnorth appears to have been used far less frequently.[118]

The latter part of the 18th century saw the beginnings of agricultural improvement in the parish, which accelerated in the early years of the following century. The process of piecemeal enclosure which had taken place since the 16th century had created a landscape in which the fields of different holdings were often mixed haphazardly. This is shown clearly by a survey of the Lutley lands at Lawton which was made in 1778 by J. Stone, and is one of only two pre-19th century maps of lands in Diddlebury to survive.[119] The total holding of just over 500 acres was divided between six farms, the most dispersed of which was that of Thomas Yates which consisted of 121 acres, most of which was comprised of islands of land surrounded by other estates. Here, as elsewhere in the parish, the consolidation of holdings into larger and more logically arranged blocks of land was a priority if more efficient farming was to be achieved. In Lawton this probably occurred after the estate passed into the hands of the Cornewalls in 1792, and by the 1851 census Lawton Farm was one holding of 400 acres farmed by William Cox. The process may be seen in its most extreme form at Peaton, where between 1769 and 1789 the seven farms on the estate had been amalgamated into one vast holding of over 800 acres based on Peaton Hall.[120] This was subsequently divided back into three farms.

As an area of mixed farming, the larger farms of the Corvedale were particularly suited to the adoption of 'high farming' practices in the 19th century. This system integrated cereal growing with the keeping of sheep and cattle, with the use of artificial fertilisers and oilcake to increase the production of both meat and cereals. The enriched dung improved grazing, and again increased production.[121] While this practice did not receive universal approval, with one local farmer, Henry Tanner of Aintree, Stanton Lacy, suggesting the conversion of arable to grassland as an alternative, a significant number of the larger farmers in Diddlebury adopted them enthusiastically.[122] Agricultural gentry became as obsessed with the genealogy of cattle as many of their clerical neighbours were with the pedigrees of local families and Norman earls. A very detailed account of the trials and triumphs of a scientific farmer is contained in a letter from George Johnstone of Broncroft to his uncle in 1849, which essentially comprises an account of his stewardship as a prelude to a request for an injection of money.[123] The letter mentions the dependence on turnips as winter fodder, and also the cultivation of vetches, a traditional fodder crop which is no longer seen. Johnstone also noted that 'all the farmers here use Guano', suggesting that it should also be used at Broncroft to supplement the dung from the farm.[124] Stone land drains were being laid at 27 feet intervals on land at the Parks, which was being farmed with the castle at that time. Among the problems being experienced was pneumonia among the cattle and tuberculosis in the sheep in the main farm. Interbreeding among the sheep was seen as a cause of weakening of the stock.

The agricultural statistics collected in 1854 by the Poor Law Union on behalf of the central government show a clear contrast between the level of stocking on the improved farms of the valley and the less intensively stocked upland farms. At Peaton Hall the 313 acres of permanent pasture (out of a total acreage of 436) supported 96 cattle of various descriptions, 265 sheep and lambs and 50 pigs. The neighbouring Peaton Lodge, with 240 acres of permanent pasture contained 70 assorted cattle, 223 sheep and lambs, and nine pigs. The Johnstone farm at Broncroft with 274 out of 428 acres under permanent grazing, had 102 cattle and over 500 sheep. By contrast, Earnstrey, which had boasted the largest flocks of sheep 150 years previously, carried a far lower level of stock. William Hanson, who farmed the largest holding, had 185 acres of pasture which supported a mere 24 cattle and 55 ewes and lambs, compared with more than three times as many sheep in 1683 (above Table 5). John Hanson at North Park, with 120 acres of grazing was somewhat better stocked with 19 cattle and 81 sheep, though the stocking rate was still quite low.[125]

The effects of the agricultural depression which took place after 1870 are not always easy to detect. There is no abnormal increase in the changes of tenancy, and a number of those which did take place can be explained by the death or retirement of long-established tenants such as the Keysalls at Little Sutton and the Bowens of Corfton.[126] In addition, many of the farmers who moved into the area between 1870 and 1900 became established over a long period, including Robert Hayhurst at Lawton and Morgan Jones at Delbury. No doubt the specialisation in cattle production and the relatively little corn which was grown enabled the farmers of the parish to avoid the worst effects of the depression. The decline in the number of farm labourers in the parish from 165 in 1871 to 98 in 1901 (see p.110, Table 14) may indicate a contraction in farming activity, although the decline had begun two decades before the start of the agricultural depression. The appearance of so many estates on the market after 1900 may be a significant indicator, with all except Westhope changing hands at least once in the period between 1900 and 1930. The First World War undoubtedly affected agriculture with greater controls, the pressure to increase production, and a drain of manpower to the services, and on the credit side increased profits, but there are remarkably few documentary records which have survived, compared with those for the Second World War.

The depression which hit farming after the Great War was to a certain extent offset by the activities of P.G. Holder. According to Holder's former farm pupil, John Cherrington, who later became a noted agricultural writer and broadcaster, his mentor's fortunes were made in property speculation, as his understanding of the economics of agriculture was very unsound.[127] Holder was ahead of his time as an agricultural improver, operating on an intensive scale, and making changes like the removal of hedges, which were to become commonplace after 1960 but which were regarded as revolutionary at the time.[128] The intensive pig unit at Peaton, and the dairy herd of over 400 cows, accommodated in a vast purpose-built shed described as 'one of the wonders of British farming',[129] which he established with the help of Cherrington, were pioneering, if short-lived ventures. The dairy herd succumbed to brucellosis, and the pig unit was requisitioned by the Ministry of Aircraft Production early in the Second World War.[130] Even so, the tally of livestock and employees on the farm in 1941 is most impressive. On 1,400 acres of permanent grazing, Holder accommodated 1,126 cattle, 15 sheep and 485 pigs. In addition a further 1,500 acres of grazing in the valley were let to J. Mellings, a Ludlow grazier.[131] A total of 39 men and boys and three casual women were employed on the farm.

War in the 1940s brought many changes to farming, and to the parish as a whole. Holder's cattle sheds became the basis of a factory manufacturing aircraft components, bringing skilled metal workers from Birmingham to supervise local labour. Sutton Court was requisitioned for an enigmatic body called the 'British Laundry Machinery Company', which a former owner believes to have been used in connection with undercover operations.[132] A massive army depot was established in the park of Delbury Hall, while Corfton Hall became a hostel for the Women's Land Army, whose members increasingly replaced male farm workers who had been conscripted into the forces.[133] Perhaps most controversially, it placed farming under the control of the War Agricultural Executive Committees, popularly known as the 'War Ag.', which attempted to increase production through stringent controls. The ploughing of grassland was nearly always contentious, and often led to acrimony. P.G. Holder seems to have acquiesced in the conversion of 300 acres of his grazing into arable, but others were less amenable.[134] The most colourful opponent of the 'War Ag.' was C.E. (Charlie) Edwards of Seifton and Elsich, a self-made auctioneer, race-horse owner and farmer, with a taste for publicity, who refused to pay a £20 fine for refusing to plough up some land, and was gaoled in consequence for a brief period. In 1945 he stood as an independent candidate for the Ludlow division in the General Election, largely on agricultural issues, and polled 989 votes.[135]

However controversial or unpopular the 'War Ag.' may have been at the time its farm surveys have provided a valuable insight into the state of farming in the early 1940s. Table 6 shows the main acreages of crops grown during the early wartime period, though the overall impression may be somewhat misleading due to the effect of the Holder enterprise. Thus 293 of the 551 acres of oats were produced by Holder, as were 75 of the 192 acres of roots, which included

Crop	Wheat	Oats	Barley	Mixed	Roots	Beans	Orchard
Acreage	459	551	88	80	192	13	106

Table 6 Crops grown in 1941 (PRO, MAFF 32/622/104)

a massive 64 acres of main crop potatoes. The amount of orchard is interesting, as again over three-quarters of this was on Holder's land, much of it at Corfton. There is now (2006) no orchard fruit grown commercially in the parish, although soft fruit is cultivated at the Pinstones. The Holder effect can be seen when the individual acreages are examined. Of 27 farms which produced wheat, no fewer than 19 grew less than 10 acres, and the same is true of 12 of the 20 growers of oats. Fifteen farms, mostly but not entirely smallholdings, grew no crops other than grass.

While not all farms grew grain, all kept livestock, and the totals in the surveys give a vivid picture of the extent of livestock farming in the parish. All 41 holdings kept cattle and sheep making an average herd of 63 cattle, and an average sized flock of 108 sheep. Once again, the figures for cattle are distorted by the Holder herd, for if the 1,126 Peaton cows are removed from the total, the average herd size becomes 35. The figures for sheep were not distorted in this way, as Holder possessed only a flock of 15 of these animals, though the 485 Holder pigs do disguise the fact that for the remaining 34 holdings which kept pigs, the average number was three, which suggests that most were kept for domestic use. All holdings kept poultry with an average flock size of 85 birds, many of which would have been housed in moveable sheds. While this figure seems ridiculously small in an age of intensive rearing of poultry, it does stress the importance of poultry at the time, when eggs were a luxury, at least for town-dwellers. Perhaps the most important statistic is the number of horses, which were kept on 33 holdings. The horse was still the main source of power on Diddlebury farms in 1941, but tractors were beginning to appear. The survey revealed that there were 13 tractors in the parish, of which all but two were Fordsons. Not unexpectedly, five were owned by Holder, though it should be added that he also possessed the largest number of horses. Possession of a tractor seems to have indicated an attitude to farming rather than merely wealth. While three of the larger farms, Lawton, Broncroft Lodge and the Hale, each possessed a tractor, so did three smaller units, Upper House at Middlehope, Batch Farm, Westhope, and Burwood Farm.

One final aspect of the survey which is worth examining is its comments on the state of the farms in the parish. These are often very forthright — e.g. 'widow inexperienced in farming; just existing, no idea of farming' (104/28); 'this

Stock	Cattle	Sheep	Pigs	Poultry	Horses
Totals	2,564	4,449	600	3,505	155

Table 7 Stock on Diddlebury Farms, 1941 (MAFF 32/622/104)

man has very little idea of farming. He is a shady customer' (104/84) — but also provide interesting comments of the terrain. Ward Farm, Westhope, (104/22) is described as a 'very banky farm' of poor quality soil on blue clay, while Hill End (104/3) nearby was plagued with rabbits and moles. The farms of Middlehope were dismissed as poor, with the best land only rated as fair. While Mr. Rowson of Upper House was noted as farming a very poor farm well, the Wetmore (104/17) was rated as 90% poor land, heavily infested with thistles. The valley farms were generally given a high approval rating, which was not confined to the larger holdings. The 24-acre holding at the Sun Inn (104/6) was described as 'a useful small farm, farmed well by an ambitious young man'. In several cases, all in the western uplands, mention was made of a shortage of labour due to lack of cottages (Ward Farm, Pinstones, and Green Farm, Middlehope).

Mention is made elsewhere of the amalgamation of holdings in the half century after the end of the Second World War, and of the rapid decline in the number of agricultural employees. Undoubtedly mechanisation played a part in this, and the handful of tractors noted in 1941 were the advance guard of a range of ever larger and more sophisticated farm machinery which continues to be employed. The 1960s and 1970s saw, as elsewhere, a greater use of chemicals and the removal of hedgerows in a drive for even greater production. One legacy of the war which has continued to grow unabated has been government control, with the European Union adding an additional element of bureaucracy to the farmer's burden. It is interesting to note that at the start of the third millennium, the pendulum is beginning to swing slowly backwards. Government grants are now being made for the reinstatement of hedges which had been removed in previous decades, and although organic farming accounts for a small, if growing sector of the industry, it is encouraging to see that this is actively promoted on the farms owned by the Westhope estate.

Fig. 13 Following the Second World War, mechanisation proceeded rapidly on farms in Diddlebury. Here a Fordson tractor is being used with a binder at Hale Farm c.*1950*

Brief mention should also be made of two occupations closely related to agriculture, which have both been significant in the parish over a long period. These are forestry and milling.

Forestry

The disafforestation of the Long Forest in 1301 was a change of legal status rather than of physical or economic aspects, and the woodlands which remained were to play an important part in the lives of the inhabitants of the various manors in which they were situated. Initially the primary purpose of the forest, as far as the crown and its chief tenants were concerned, was hunting, and licences were regularly issued permitting hunting by tenants. Thus in 1264 William son of William Middlehope was granted licence for life to 'hunt with his own dogs the hare, the fox, the [wild] cat and the badger in the forests of the County of Salop', and in 1280 John Giffard received a similar grant of 'the run of the king's forest called "la Longforest" and through the king's woods therein, for the purpose of hunting and taking his own deer, started by his own hounds in his free chase of Corfham'.[136] While hunting no doubt remained an important pastime, it is clear from the accounts of the foresters of Earnstrey that by the end of the 14th century this particular forest was being managed on commercial lines. The first set of accounts covers the period from Michaelmas 1385 to Michaelmas 1387, when William Lee was forester for Mary le Strange, the 'Lady of Corfham'.[137] Revenue was sought assiduously from all possible sources. Pannage* and agistement* were rented out to local farmers, and beasts which had strayed illegally into the forest were sold, such as the eight bullocks who raised 13s. 4d. in this way in 1386. Underwood, the inferior timber cleared from around the trees not destined for short-term commercial felling, was sold to the local inhabitants, and also sent to fuel 'the Lady's' fires at Corfham. In addition to money rents, poultry and eggs were received in large numbers as rent, with 163 hens and 1,405 eggs being received at Easter 1386. Accounts were rendered by tallies, the notched sticks used by medieval accountants, with 112s. 4d. being delivered on one occasion by three tallies containing 52s. 4d., 40s. and 20s. On some occasions cash payments were delivered to Eleanor, presumably a trusted maidservant, in the porch of the chapel of Corfham.

Lee died in 1390, and was replaced by John Jurden, whose accounts show that underwood was sold in parcels at 13s. 4d. per acre. As well as parcels of underwood, individual timbers were sold, sometimes at surprisingly high prices. A charge of 16d. for one branch of an oak tree sold to Thomas Skeddar seems excessive, while 4d. for an elder tree, sold to Adam Doughty, seems exorbitant in view of the well-known poor burning qualities of that wood. It is possible that the commercial exploitation of the woods on this scale had come to an end by the time of the next set of accounts, drawn up by Edward Cleobury for the period 1473 to 1480.[138] Only one example of the sale of underwood appears in this period, and the renting of grazing land features more prominently, with mention being made of various 'enclosures about the Park at divers places'. It would appear from references to the making of posts and rails for inclosing the park, and repairing the lodge, that part of the old forest had been retained for hunting and enclosed with a ring fence, while the remainder had been converted to agricultural land. This process was also noted by Rowley at Corfton.[139]

By the 16th century there was considerable commercial pressure to fell ancient woodlands. Enclosed agricultural land produced a respectable rent, and timber could be sold in large quantities to meet the demands of industry. The first major clearance was begun in the reign of Mary I by George, Lord Talbot, who employed surveyors to measure Diddlebury Wood.[140] After the initial felling, the land was sold to Richard Baldwyn in 1560. Other landowners followed Talbot's lead, and in 1575 William Savage sold all the timber in Corfton wood except for saplings. Leonard Dannatt of Westhope cleared his woods for glass making,[141] and in 1598 Francis Smith made great clearances in Middlehope, Aston and Over Millichope. Baldwyn alleged that Smith had cleared his woods on the pretext of coppicing*, but had in fact illegally converted the greater part into arable and pasture. It is significant that at this time the Smith family were establishing an iron furnace on their lands at Bouldon, which would have required quantities of charcoal.[142] The consequence of these actions was that a great proportion of the land on the dip slope of the Aymestrey limestone ridge had become denuded of trees in a matter of some 50 years, and there appears to have been some recognition of the need to conserve the surviving timber stocks.

This timber shortage may lie behind the acrimonious lawsuit between Baldwyn and Smith which began in the common law courts in 1580, and finally ended with judgement for Baldwyn in the Star Chamber 18 years later. It is likely that a good deal of personal ill-feeling fuelled the dispute, but it is clear that the right to take timber was jealously guarded by the landowners against all comers. George Mason, a Smith tenant who claimed the right to cut wood as a commoner, had been denied this on the grounds that as the impropriator of the tithes of Diddlebury he was an ecclesiastical person, and could not claim common rights. Other instances of close control of rights to timber were also quoted by Baldwyn.

In view of this extensive Elizabethan clearance, it is somewhat surprising to find so much woodland still surviving in the parish. It is clear that the areas which were converted to farmland between the 16th century and the enclosure of Corfton Wood in 1779 were on the gentle south-east facing dip slope of the Aymestrey ridge, and well suited to arable farming. Much of today's woodland is in the uplands of the west of the parish, and owes its survival in great part to shooting interests, whose role in the conservation of woodlands is often overlooked. The commercial planting of conifers has taken place on the Delbury estate, but on a fairly small scale. The estate yard at Bache Mill was closed in the 1980s, and houses erected in its place. The Westhope estate still employs a woodman and his assistants, and is actively engaged in partnership with English Nature in replanting the woods on the estate with native species.

Milling

The milling of corn was (and is) an essential adjunct of arable farming and it is not surprising that the fast-flowing streams of the parish supported a number of mills from an early date. Each manor normally possessed its own mill at which tenants were obliged to have their corn ground, some of which remained in use for a long period.

The Bache brook, which rises above Middlehope, fed a number of mills along its course. The earliest reference to a mill at Middlehope occurs in 1272, when Peter de Vaux and other dependants of John le Strange were brought before the forest assize charged with illegally killing a stag near Middlehope Mill.[143] A water-mill at Middlehope was also mentioned in the inquisition *post mortem* of Joan Tyrell in 1345, when it was out of repair.[144] It is also included in that of her son John in 1360, and it is likely that these references are to the mill at the eastern extremity of the township, which has been known as Fernalls Mill since the 17th century, after the family who tenanted it from at least 1637 to 1715.[145] Although there is evidence to suggest that the mill had ceased operation by 1717, an election canvas return in 1766 lists William Taylor of Vernalls Mill as a 'milner'.[146] The original cruck-framed building has collapsed, but the 18th-century house of the Taylor family still survives.

Fig. 14 Bouldon Mill. A mill existed on this site in 1611, but the present structure dates from the 18th century. It ceased working in 1934, but still preserves its mill wheel

The present mill at Bache Mill was erected shortly before 1817 by Joseph Cooke of Munslow, who, 20 years later, also built a windmill above the property by the side of the road to Middlehope. The two were run in conjunction, but the windmill appears to have fallen out of use some time after 1870.[147] It is likely to have been a tower mill, similar to the disused mill at Much Wenlock. The watermill was operated by James Rooke of Aston Munslow from 1894 until his death in 1916, after which time it appears to have ceased working. The other mill in the historic parish[148] to have worked into recent times was at Broncroft. A mill existed here as early as 1344, when a third share was owned by Joan Tyrell as dower, but records relating to the existing building date only from 1770.[149] Although the mill appears to have ceased working for a time in the middle years of the 19th century, it had resumed by 1881, and worked from then until some time after 1922.[150] The mill building subsequently became the laundry for Broncroft Castle, and was later converted into a dwelling.

Other mills are known from passing references, although their sites cannot be located. Before 1192 a mill at Lawton had been acquired by the preceptory (house) of the Knights Templar at Lydley in Cardington, though there are no further references to this.[151] The archives of the Dean and Chapter of Hereford refer to the 'mill stream of the mill of the two rectors' in a deed which dates from the late 13th century, but there are no further references to this.[152] An extent of the manor of Diddlebury in 1544 lists two watermills, but it is impossible to identify these. One may well have been the mill at Bache Mill.[153] At least some of the Diddlebury millers lived up to the reputation for dishonesty which attached to their calling. In 1256 Nicholas Preke, the miller of Diddlebury, William Millar and two others were outlawed, having absconded under suspicion of theft,[154] while in 1284 William son of Walter Molendarius of Diddlebury spent five days in Ludlow church hiding from bailiffs.[155]

A watermill existed in Corfton in 1294, and was still noted in a rental of 1620.[156] The field names Mill Yard and Mill Meadow mentioned in the rental are to be found on the tithe award map for Little Sutton rather than for Corfton, and it is possible that this mill at Corfton is the same as Sparchford Mill, which is noted in a marriage settlement of 1613.[157] In the reign of James I, Thomas Baldwyn claimed that he had refused to allow George Parcell to take timber from Diddlebury Wood to repair his mill at Corfham, but again there is no indication as to its location. A mill certainly existed at Westhope in 1301, as the FitzAlan survey notes that all tenants were required to cast millstones for the mill when required.[158]

The decline of the country miller in the early 20th century was virtually inevitable in the face of competition from industrial-scale milling operations like that of Marstons of Ludlow, which opened in the 1890s. Ironically this state of the art milling operation was destined to have a life of less than a century, falling prey to even larger competitors. The country miller is now virtually extinct in Britain, the few surviving working mills generally being tended by middle-class refugees from the 'rat race', while the farmers who would once have taken their grain to the local miller to be ground into animal feed are now served by travelling equipment. Woodhouse Brothers' massive German-made mobile feed mill is a common sight in the lanes of Diddlebury, and may be considered as the 21st-century expression of the most ancient of all rural industries.

2 Religion and Church Life

For most of the period that there has been a community in Diddlebury, religion and religious practice have been at the heart of most peoples' lives. For the majority of this time the focus of this religious life was the parish church of St. Peter, although in the medieval period, and to some extent after, this was shared with the dependent chapels in the parish, and for a relatively brief period in the 19th and 20th centuries, Methodism provided a flourishing alternative. It is, however, true to say that the history of religious life in Diddlebury has centred firmly upon its parish church, and in that it differs little from most rural parishes in the county, and indeed in much of England.

The survival of records has been crucial to the understanding of various aspects of parochial life. Few parishes have been as fortunate as the handful of places such as Morebath in Devon, Long Melford in Suffolk, or in Shropshire, Much Wenlock, where diaries and notebooks have left a vivid picture of religious life and worship on the eve of, and during the 16th century Reformation.[1] A greater number of parishes possess information from wills and pre-Reformation churchwardens' accounts which provide almost as comprehensive an impression of the worshipping life of the church community. Diddlebury possesses none of these sources, so that our knowledge of the practice of religion by clergy and parishioners before the 17th century is largely in the form of vignettes gained in passing from other sources. There is, however, a considerable compensation for this shortcoming, as, largely in consequence of a prolonged medieval dispute over the advowson* of the parish, there is a great deal of information on the legal and financial organisation of the benefice,* and it is this which provides a convenient starting point from which to approach the topic of religion and church life.

Benefice, Tithes and Glebe

The Benefice

The evidence of the fabric of Diddlebury church, which will be discussed later in this chapter, has generally been interpreted as dating from before the Norman Conquest, though there is considerable disagreement as to how long before that event the church was built. It may be significant that it is located in Diddlebury itself, for by the time of the Domesday survey in 1086, both church and settlement had become subsidiary elements in the great manor of Corfham, where presumably a new church would have been erected was one not already in existence.

Much may be learned about the organisation of the church in Diddlebury in the period after the Conquest, and by inference before it, from the protracted dispute which arose concerning the advowson. This arose because Earl Roger of Montgomery had granted this to the abbey of Shrewsbury, and also inadvertently to that of Séez in Normandy. In 1236 the abbot of Séez had surrendered the advowson to the bishop of Hereford in return for a pension of 10 marks out of the tithes of the parish. In 1237 Bishop Ralph Maidstone undertook a pastoral reorganisation of Diddlebury which endowed six vicars choral in the cathedral out of the revenues of Diddlebury. However, in the bitter feuding which erupted between Ralph's successor, Peter de Aquablanca, and the dean and chapter, the latter body successfully took over Diddlebury and a number of other parochial endowments, which were confirmed by a papal grant in 1246.[2] The dispute simmered for some years, until after high level arbitration the bishop finally renounced his claims in favour of the dean and chapter.[3] In 1269 the original grant of 1237 was confirmed by the new bishop, John le Breton.[4] In 1282 the controversy entered a new phase, with the abbot of Shrewsbury claiming title by virtue of Earl Roger's donation, and also a compromise which had been agreed between the respective abbots as long ago as the 1140s.[5] This meant that the dean and chapter were aligned with the abbot of Séez, who stood to lose his pension, against the powerful abbey of Shrewsbury. Eventually the matter was put to the arbitration of Bishop Swinfield of Hereford, who found for the dean and chapter, and compensated Shrewsbury with the living of Stottesden.[6]

This lengthy series of disputes reveals a number of points about the organisation of Diddlebury. In 1236, the church had been served by two clergy, Osbert the rector, and William the vicar. These were to retain their positions, but to surrender annually to the dean and chapter ten marks (£6 13s. 4d.) and 100 shillings respectively, for the endowment of two priests and two deacons to serve as vicars choral in the cathedral. On the deaths of Osbert and William, their successors were to pay an additional 20 marks (£13 6s. 8d.) to endow a further two sub-deacons as vicars choral. This endowment of the choral work of the cathedral amounted to £25 annually from the revenues of Diddlebury, which indicates the great wealth of the living. The dean and chapter subsequently reduced the number of clergy to one vicar, who lived in the former rectory at Corfton, as did all his successors until the building of a new vicarage in Diddlebury in 1883.

This reduction in the number clergy left the former residence at Diddlebury vacant, and it apparently remained in this state for some considerable time. In 1315 the parishioners petitioned the dean and chapter that 'the repairs in the building of their court house at Diddlebury with their stone roofs will cost 60 shillings; and six wooden arches intended for a lavatory are uncovered and their timber is rotting.'[7] A further petition of 1355 reiterated the charges, suggesting that the building had been neglected for nearly a century after it had been vacated by the vicar.[8] This building, called the 'court of the two canons of Duddelbury' in a document of 1334,[9] was clearly substantial, as witnessed by the mention of the six crucks from the uncompleted *lavatorium*, and may well represent the residence of an early college of priests who served a wide area.

This hypothesis is somewhat supported by the profusion of chapels in the parish. In addition to the castle chapel at Corfham, which may be considered as a necessary requirement of a residence of such importance, there were chapels at Westhope, Middlehope, Corfton, Mershton and both Great and Little Sutton. Whether or not these originated as dependencies of the parish church is not clear, although Corfton was always regarded as such. Certainly in 1397 the parishioners complained that the vicar was not providing a chaplain to say mass in the chapel of Middlehope on Sundays, Thursdays and Saturdays, as well as solemn feast days.[10] By this time, however, the other chapels in the parish would appear to have been regularly staffed with their own clergy, with the chaplain of Mershton even claiming, unsuccessfully, in 1335, the status of rector in an action against the dean and chapter.[11] Mershton would appear to have retained some form of extra-parochial status, as it is listed among the properties of Johan, widow of Sir Thomas Littleton of Broncroft in 1505.[12] Whatever the origins of these chapels, their existence is not inconsistent with a possible early collegiate organisation.

The organisation of the parish in the mid-14th century may therefore be summarised thus. The parish church was served by a single vicar, appointed by the dean and chapter, who resided in the rectory at Corfton. The chapels, with the exception of Middlehope, were served by their own clergy, who were probably appointed, and at least partially financed by the local landowner. The appointment of the vicar has remained in the hands of the dean and chapter until the present day, with the exception of the Commonwealth period, when the chapter was dissolved and its estates sold.[13] The Reformation, however, brought about a significant reduction in the number of clergy, with the disappearance of the surviving chapels, except those of Corfton and Westhope. This situation continued until the end of the 18th century, when Corfton fell out of use. Westhope has remained in use, having been rebuilt in 1728 and again in 1892, but since 1775 has been regarded, certainly by the Swinnerton-Dyer family, as the private chapel of the Westhope estate, although the exact legal status of the chapel is somewhat problematical. From 1891 until 1926 the benefice was described as 'Diddlebury with Westhope' by *Crockford's Clerical Directory*. In 1926 Bouldon, which had been transferred from Holdgate to Diddlebury for civil purposes in 1881, was incorporated into the ecclesiastical parish, which became known as 'Diddlebury with

Bouldon.' Bouldon possessed a chapel of ease* constructed of corrugated iron, which had been built in 1873, and which remained in use until 1981.

Parochial reorganisation became a necessity with falling attendances at all churches during the 1960s and 1970s, and the process began in 1972 with the joining of Munslow and Diddlebury. Tugford and Holdgate, temporarily linked with Stokesay, were added in 1977 and in the same year Abdon, formerly grouped with Stoke St. Milborough, was incorporated into the new Corvedale group of parishes. The new group was served by one incumbent, generally with the help of a retired clergyman, but retained their individual Parochial Church Councils. The right of presentation to the living remained with the dean and chapter of Hereford.

Tithes and Glebe

The dean and chapter had made a good bargain in the 1237 settlement, having, as has been noted, gained an annual endowment of £25 towards the provision of vicars choral. The revenues of the parish were made up of two elements, the profits of the glebe land of the parish, and the tithes which were paid on agricultural produce for the maintenance of the clergy. The glebe land consisted of some 125 acres of land distributed among the fields of the parish, which approximates closely to the hide of land (120 acres) possessed by the church in Domesday.[14] Tithes were a levy of one tenth of agricultural produce, and were divided into greater tithes (of corn and hay), which went to the rector, and lesser tithes, on other produce, to which the vicar was entitled. When the dean and chapter received the advowson, they assumed the role of rector, but in practice allowed the vicar to collect the rectorial tithes of Corfton for himself.

Tithes

Rather than manage these sources of income directly, the chapter chose to lease the revenues to third parties, who would collect them in exchange for a fee, retaining any profit for their own use. Thus for some time before 1286, the revenues of Diddlebury, together with those of Stanton Long, had been farmed by the prior of Wenlock for an annual fee of 35 marks.[15] On other occasions individual clergy leased the rights to the parish, such as John de Bromfield and his brother Reginald, who in 1309 took a three year lease of the revenues of Diddlebury and Stanton Long for a rent of £53 6s. 8d., and Hugh de Preston, the vicar of Diddlebury, who took out a six year lease of the revenues of his own parish and those of Stanton Long in 1333 at an annual rent of 90 marks (£60).[16]

Towards the end of the 14th century the dean and chapter seem to have begun splitting the two elements of the Diddlebury revenues, leasing the glebe lands separately from the tithes. By 1395 the glebe lands were being leased for life at an annual rent of 14 shillings, while the great tithes appear to have been leased at a rent of £24 per year from as early as 1422.[17] This rate appears to have been operating over a century later, when William and Thomas Mason leased the great tithes for 39 years.[18] By 1536 the value of the living to the vicar was calculated at £12 1s. 3d., making it in the middle range for the deanery between the extremes of Ludlow at £19 12s. 6d. and Cold Weston at £2 7s. 8d.[19]

By the 17th century a great deal more is known about the administration and yield of tithes in the parish. A terrier of the parish drawn up in 1637[20] shows that the vicar was entitled to the tithes of corn and grain (normally reserved for the rector) in the townships of Corfton and Sparchford, and in the home closes (small fields immediately adjoining houses) in other parts of the parish. In all townships except Ernestry Park, the lesser tithes were no longer collected in kind, but had been replaced by fixed money payments, normally known as *moduses*. It is possible to calculate the yield of these tithes as Nicholas Proude, who was vicar during the later part of the Interregnum, kept detailed accounts.[21] These show that in 1657 the tithes yielded a total of £24 13s. 4d., Great Sutton being the township with the greatest yield of £4 3s. 1d. The greatest individual sum paid in the parish was £1 7s. 4d. from William Pulley of Peaton Hall. In addition to the proceeds of tithes, Proude received Easter Offerings of 2d per adult, totalling £2 3s., and surplice fees (for burials and churching of women) of £2 18s. 6d. In cash terms the living was worth about £30, to which must be added payments of corn in kind totalling 53 thraves* from Corfton and Sparchford. The living was modest, particularly compared with Proud's previous and subsequent status as a

Fig. 15 The Tithe Barn, shown here in 2000, before its conversion to a dwelling

pluralist in Ireland, but his lot was much better than that of most dispossessed Anglican clerics.

In Diddlebury as elsewhere, tithes provided an ongoing cause of contention between the clergy and their flocks, with a steady stream of actions reaching the diocesan courts in Hereford. These sought to prove that certain pieces of land were exempt from tithe, such as the case between the vicar, William Fosbroke and William Filcox of Harton in 1683, over liability for a piece of land called the Ryes at Harton. Here the issue was complicated by the fact that the farm straddled the parish boundary between Eaton and Diddlebury. Interestingly, Proude's book was produced in evidence in this case.[22] These actions continued through the 18th century, and were such a problem that in 1731 a bill was introduced into Parliament 'to prevent suits for Tythe, where none, or any Composition for the same have been paid in a certain number of years.'[23] The issue was finally tackled by Parliament in 1836, when an Act was passed commuting tithes to a rent charge on land, which was fixed by Commissioners following a detailed survey of land ownership, occupation and usage.

The table shows how the tithes were apportioned between the vicar and the appropriators, who rented or managed the greater tithes on behalf of the dean and chapter. It is noticeable that in all townships except Corfton, where histori-

Township	**Vicar**	**Appropriators**
Broncroft	£27	£47
Corfton	£119: 13s: 2d.	£3: 8s: 5d.
Diddlebury	£35	£84: 7s: 0d.
Ernestry	£20	£33
Lawton	£21	£30
Middlehope	£20	£44
Peaton	£30	£76
Gt. Sutton	£26	£35 15s. 0d.
Lt. Sutton	£11 11s. 0d.	£22
Westhope	£25	£82 4s. 0d.
Total	**£315 4s. 2d.**	**£490 14s. 5d.**

Table 1 Summary of tithe apportionment by township 1836-1851

cally the vicar had collected the greater tithes, the vicar's share was always the lesser.

The value of the living fluctuated somewhat, but was never great. During the incumbency of R.C. Bolton (1907-1916) the notional value of the tithes was £344, with the total value of the living, including fees etc. being £402.[24] In 1925 tithe income was paid directly to Queen Anne's Bounty, from which the clergy were paid a salary, and in 1936 the tithe rent charge was finally abolished in favour of annuities which were to be completely redeemed by 1996. Thus a source of clerical income which had for centuries been a bone of contention between the clergy and their flocks was finally ended.

Glebe

In the wholly agricultural society of rural England in the middle ages, the clergy were allotted glebe land which they could cultivate for their own maintenance. So in Diddlebury, as elsewhere, there was both vicar's and rector's glebe. From a comparatively early date these were leased out to tenants, who in their turn sub-let various parts of the estates. This appears to have been the case since at least 1548, when the dean and chapter leased the glebe for 29 years to William Burghill.[25] From at least 1628 the Baldwyn family leased the glebe lands, which they retained until 1732. In 1650, following the dissolution of cathedral chapters by the Cromwellian government, the Diddlebury glebe had been bought by William Walcot, who four years later sold the freehold to Samuel Baldwyn, who held the lease. There may have been some tacit understanding that if happier times were restored the cathedral would get its property back, for in 1667 the Baldwyns appear once again as leaseholders from the chapter.[26] Detailed terriers of the glebe lands exist in both these documents, and also in the Cathedral Archives at Hereford. They show small parcels of land scattered through the fields of Diddlebury and Corfton, together with a small farm at Burwood in the township of Middlehope. Most of these were relics of the old strip system, which had been enclosed on a piecemeal basis.

Considerable continuity is shown by both the leaseholders of the Glebe and their tenants. Thus the Baldwyns, who had leased the lands since at least 1628 continued to do so until 1732. John Wolley and his descendants then held the lease until 1836. In 1885 the leasing system was ended when the Church Commissioners took over administration. There was similar continuity among the tenants who actually farmed the lands, with the Wilcox family occupying the Glebe from 1725 until 1829, and Walter Watkins and his son, also Walter, holding it for most of the ensuing period up to the latter's death in 1889. After the farmhouse had fallen into some neglect at the start of the 20th century, the Glebe was finally sold by the Church Commissioners in 1913.

THE CLERGY

One of the great contrasts between the situation in Diddlebury before and after the religious upheavals in the middle of the 16th century may be seen in the numbers of clergy employed there. Whereas after 1550 the parish tended to be served by one clergyman, the vicar or, for much of the period from 1740 to 1840 a curate, for most of the pre-Reformation period there were, in addition to the parochial clergy, several chaplains serving the various chapelries; clergy in secular employments; and those who never progressed beyond the four minor orders, but where nevertheless still legally 'clerks'.

Before the Reformation

Relatively little is known about the medieval clergy who served Diddlebury, often barely more than their names. Unlike a wealthy and prestigious parish such as Ludlow, where the living was often given to royal officials as a reward, Diddlebury, particularly after being shorn of the bulk of its endowments in 1237, was a fairly typical country living whose clergy rarely achieved much in the way of advancement. Significantly, the exceptions to this rule were in fact the two clergy who were in office at the time of the 1238 settlement. William de Ros, the last rector, had been clerk to Bishop Hugh Foliot (1219-1234), and may well have been put into the living to oversee a smooth change. Towards the end of his long incumbency, he was appointed Treasurer of Hereford.[27] His colleague Alexander became rural dean, and is generally referred to as 'the dean' in documents.[28]

It is possible to trace some of the movements of medieval vicars of Diddlebury from the bishops' registers. There were, for example, a number of straight exchanges, such as that in 1384 when Richard Lodelawe, the vicar, exchanged livings with John Davys, the chaplain at Corfham castle.[29] In a similar manner William Asturley, vicar of Stokesay, exchanged his living with William Brompton of Diddlebury in 1413.[30] Four years later Asturley made a further exchange with Richard Piers, the rector of Manafon near Welshpool.[31] At least two of the later medieval vicars are known to have died in office (John Sutton 1408; Richard Langley 1475). There are also two examples of clergy retiring with a pension. In 1420 John Peers resigned with a pension of six marks (£4), while in 1515 the retiring vicar, John Butler, was empowered to negotiate with his successor to secure a 'super annuate pension' for himself out of the revenues of the living. Butler had previously successfully applied to Pope Alexander VI for dispensation to hold another benefice in plurality with Diddlebury.[32] Another pluralist was Thomas Slade, who in 1508 was authorised by Pope Julius II to hold a living while under age. Two months later he was presented to the parish of Onibury by a relative, and remained vicar there until his death 60 years later. In 1515 he acquired Diddlebury on the retirement of Butler, and retained the living until after 1536.[33] These were not particularly bad cases of pluralism, and services would no doubt have been taken in the absence of the vicar by one of the many chaplains in the parish.

The chaplains are even more shadowy figures than the parish clergy, often being known merely from a name appended as witness to a deed. Names of known chaplains are included in Appendix 1. The status of chaplains clearly varied greatly. Some chaplaincies, such as that of Corfham castle, were clearly desirable livings in their own right, or as stepping stones to a parish. Others were clearly served by clergy who were distinguished from their peasant neighbours only by their rudimentary education, and who must have had little hope of promotion. It is interesting to note that in 1327 there were no less than three clergy resident in the township of Westhope, all of whom were bondmen.[34] At the opposite end of the social scale, Richard de Beck, and his successor Robert de Theme, chaplains of Mershton, were involved in a prolonged and expensive lawsuit in which they attempted to deprive the dean and chapter of Hereford of two-thirds of the tithes of the chapelry. They were clearly acting with the backing of Robert de Beck, a knight and relative of Richard, who attempted to pressurise the chapter by appealing to the royal courts in 1335. The initial judgement was in favour of the dean and chapter, and cost the plaintiffs a massive £20.[35]

Some chaplains succeeded in gaining promotion to a parish living. John Sutton, presented to the parish in 1396, and Edward Janyns, who held the living of Diddlebury for only a few months in 1465, were both chaplains prior to their appointment.[36] Others no doubt received parishes out of the district, but the majority of chaplains must have continued to exercise their lowly ministries for the whole of their lives. For some clergy, secular employment provided an alternative living. Holy Orders were the route to literacy, and to other benefits, not the least of which was immunity from punishment by the secular courts. One particularly unpleasant beneficiary of this was David Walshman, a chaplain who in 1479 was convicted of raping Eleanor Huddleston of Peaton, to whom he had been called to administer the last rites. Convicted before the king's justices, he claimed clerical immunity and escaped with little more than a reprimand.[37]

For most, however, the church provided a means of social and material benefit, which could be considerable. Probably the most striking example from the parish was Roger Stedman, whose career was largely spent administering the estates of John, Lord Talbot, whose receiver general (roughly equivalent to the chief executive of a modern company) he became in 1447. Before this he had worked in the Talbot administration since at least 1410, enjoying a number of Shropshire livings including Munslow and Culmington as additional rewards.[38] Similarly successful was Richard, son of Osbert of Diddlebury, who was a married cleric who served as steward, and possibly also chaplain, to Roger Sprenchose of Longnor between 1296 and 1327. Sprenchose had been an important local official, acting as Sheriff of Shropshire and Staffordshire, an assessor and collector of the fifteenth (tax), and bailiff of Stretton. In these functions, and in the management of Sprenchose's estates in Wales, he was assisted by Richard.[39] The Clerk family, as they became known, established their residence on an existing moated site in Longnor, which became the site of the later medieval Moat House.[40]

The marital status of Richard son of Osbert demands some explanation. While the church authorities had long attempted to eradicate the practice of clergy marrying, it remained deeply rooted, and there are a number of references to Diddlebury clergy and their families during the middle ages. Some of these may have been in minor orders, where marriage was permitted, but others were certainly priests who were married either legally or otherwise. A good example of this is Alexander the chaplain of Sutton, whose daughter was involved in precisely the sort of dispute over land that clerical celibacy was intended to avoid (see above, p.12).[41] References to children of the clergy appear from time to time, such as that to John son of the chaplain who was drowned while dragging a net in the Corve in 1256,[42] or Robert le Vickaresone, chaplain, who, along with several other clergy and laymen, was sued for trespass by Lawrence de Ludlow in 1352.[43]

Reformation and after *c.*1550-1850

The religious upheavals of the 16th and 17th centuries inflicted rapid and bewildering changes upon the people of England and their clergy, but in Diddlebury, as in many parishes, one vicar remained at his post throughout the period of most dramatic changes. Richard Normecott, a member of a prosperous local yeoman family which included the vicar of nearby Tugford among its number, accepted the living shortly after 1539 and retained it until 1569. There is no evidence to show how he viewed the move from the reformed Catholicism of the latter years of Henry VIII to the full-blown Protestantism of his son, the return to Rome under Mary I, and the compromise settlement achieved under Elizabeth. The continuity which he provided must have aided the acceptance of the changes by the parish, and indeed continuity of clergy is a pronounced feature of the first century of this period.

Normecott was succeeded by the first of two father and son incumbencies. John Habberley (1569-1599) was followed by his son Thomas (1599-1642). The younger Habberley was in many ways typical of a new breed of parish priest. One of the great aims of the 16th-century reformers had been to improve the educational standard of the clergy, and it is likely that Thomas Habberley was the first university graduate to serve in the parish. He had studied at Corpus Christi and New College in Oxford, and began a pattern whereby all vicars of the parish until 1958 were Oxford or Cambridge graduates. The final legalisation of clerical marriage after 1558 also began a trend whereby clerical dynasties became established. Just as Thomas Habberley followed his father's profession, so his own son entered the church and held two livings successively in Breconshire.[44] Thomas Habberley was a pluralist, who also held the livings of Shobdon in Herefordshire, and Cardeston in the far north-west of Shropshire. He was known to have had a curate, William Churchman, serving Diddlebury in 1637.[45]

The continuity provided by the Habberleys was dramatically broken by the turbulence of the Civil War. Thomas Habberley was ejected from Diddlebury following the fall of Ludlow to parliamentary forces in 1646, and was replaced by a Presbyterian minister, John Bryan. It is likely that Habberley was able to continue his ministry in the relative obscurity of Cardeston, which he appears to have retained until his death in 1661. In 1647 Diddlebury had been placed in the short-lived Sixth Classis or district into which parishes had been grouped, to replace the destroyed system of deaneries. In just over a year the system was abolished following 'Pride's Purge' of the Presbyterians in parliament.[46] While Presbyterian worship may not have been to the taste of the parish, and particularly its leading families, the church was well served in that Bryan was a Cambridge graduate who had previously been a chaplain to the Earl of Stamford. Many parishes were increasingly subjected to the ministries of ill-educated former tradesmen who had been installed by the parliamentary army.

Such was Bryan's eminence that he was destined to higher positions, and in 1652 took charge of Shrewsbury Abbey (to 1659), and subsequently St. Chad's, which he held until ejected for nonconformity in 1662. He then became minister to the Presbyterian congregation in the High Street, Shrewsbury, which finally gained legality in 1689. His successor at Diddlebury is unusual in that he was an Anglican of some prominence. Nicholas Proude had graduated from Cambridge in 1629, and had risen in the Irish church, becoming Archdeacon of Cashel in 1640. A few months later he was forced to flee the Catholic rebellion, and ended up in Shrewsbury in 1644, where the Royalist administration appointed him vicar of St. Mary's and also Meole. The fall of Shrewsbury a year later led to his ejection, and in 1652 he was appointed to Diddlebury, possibly due to the influence of John Walcot, who had purchased the living in 1650.[47] Proude remained vicar of Diddlebury until 1662, when it was safe to return to Ireland, where he resumed his archidiaconate and three other livings, including the deanery of Clonfert.[48] As vicar of Diddlebury Proude was meticulous in keeping a record of his tithes, and this provides an important record of many aspects of the parish at a time when few records are generally available.[49]

The four clergy who held the living for the succeeding century came from fairly modest backgrounds. The fathers of Richard Shepheard (1662-1676), Hugo Wishaw (1726-1730) and Robert Watkins (1730-1781) were all described as 'plebs' (*i.e.* not gentry or clergy) in their university matriculations, while William Fosbroke (1676-1726) was a member of an established family of yeoman farmers in Diddlebury. Shepheard was certainly not a wealthy man, as his probate inventory is valued at a mere £24 8s. 8d., and it is obvious from the livestock and other agricultural equipment which it includes that he farmed at least some of his own glebe.[50] Fosbroke leased an 'estate in Middlehope' (Lower House Farm) which remained with his descendants until 1830.[51] He was a pluralist, and was vicar of

Acton Scott from 1679 until his death. It is known from his will that he kept a curate at Acton Scott, and that he resided in each parish by turns.

Robert Watkins was also a pluralist, and after having been made vicar of Kinlet in 1736 resided there for the rest of his life. This began a period which continued until 1839 in which the vicars of the parish were non-resident and the bulk of the work was carried out by curates. Abraham Rudd, who was vicar from 1781-1794, lived in Ludlow, but appears to have taken some services at Diddlebury. Job Walker Baugh (1794-1839) was a member of a prominent local gentry family, and a kinsman of Revd. Dr. Cornewall, the squire of Diddlebury and successively bishop of Bristol, Hereford and Worcester. In addition to Diddlebury he held the livings of Moccas in Herefordshire (1797-1812) and Ripple in Worcestershire (1812-1838), and was also a prebendary of Hereford Cathedral, and Chancellor of the diocese of Bristol. With these responsibilities he had little time for Diddlebury, and preferred to reside at his wife's parental estate in Clapham.

Fig. 16 Houses of the clergy.
(a) The Glebe Farm, a 17th-century building on the site of the medieval vicarage
(b) The new vicarage of 1883

Curates thus performed an important role in the parish in the century before the accession of Victoria. Many are shadowy figures who served for no more than a few months, though some achieved more prominence, generally by virtue of their subsequent careers. One of the most unusual to hold this post was John Powell of Sutton Court, who appears to have done the lion's share of work in the parish from 1764 until 1799, and to have assisted intermittently for a further five years.[52] This is unusual because in addition to being a landowner of some substance and a Justice of the Peace, he was the absentee vicar of Pennington in Lancashire for the period when he was curate of Diddlebury. In 1793 he was also acting as curate of neighbouring Cold Weston, where he took Morning Prayer each Sunday.[53] Two successive curates in the early 19th century, Charles Taylor (1805-1808) and D'Arcy Haggitt (1808-1809) combined the office with the headmastership of Ludlow Grammar School. Taylor is an interesting example of upward social mobility. His father was an Oxford college servant, who had been cook at Balliol and Manciple (purchaser of provisions) at Magdalen. Charles Taylor was a chorister at Magdalen, educated at Magdalen College School and at the College, who ultimately became headmaster of Hereford Cathedral School and chancellor of the diocese.[54] Haggitt, whose father was a Northamptonshire clergyman, like other members of his family both before and after him, fell out with his employers, the Ludlow Corporation, and was forced to leave his post in 1809. He subsequently became vicar of Pershore, where he served for 25 years until his death in 1850.

Two other Diddlebury curates from this period are of more than passing interest. Thomas Hill Peregrine Furey Lowe succeeded Haggitt after an interval of nearly four years during which time the vicar, J.W. Baugh had to do duty. Lowe was the son of a landowner from Court of Hill, Burford, who had been intended for the law before entering the church. He served as curate at Diddlebury from 1812 until 1826, although by then he had acquired the livings of Tugford Second Portion, and Grimley with Hallow in Worcestershire. He subsequently moved to Exeter, where he became Dean in 1839. The last curate of the period, Thomas James Rocke, was also a member of a local landed family, though his father was an official of the East India Company. Rocke joined the Company after leaving Westminster School, and became a subaltern in the Bengal Native Infantry. In 1826 he resigned his commission, and entered Cambridge to train for the church. In 1831 he became curate of Diddlebury, where he remained until the death of vicar Baugh in 1839. He then moved to Exeter, where he stayed until his retirement in 1877. It is interesting to note that in 1828 he had married the eldest daughter of Thomas Hill Lowe. It might appear strange that these well-connected young men should have stayed so long in their curacies, but in fact in the absence of the vicar they lived in the elegant parsonage house at Corfton, being vicar in all but name and income.[55]

Victorian revival and its aftermath 1850-2000

The incumbency of Thomas Underwood (1839-1860) ushered in a period in which all vicars resided in the parish, which lasted until the removal of the vicarage to Munslow in 1967. There appear to have been no more curates in the parish from this date onwards, and there are many signs that the spiritual awakening in the Church of England was beginning to make itself felt in Diddlebury, though there is no evidence to suggest that any Victorian vicars deviated from

Central churchmanship. The clergy began to be more active, particularly in the field of education, with Thomas Underwood beginning the process of securing the sale of the parish house in Ludlow with the intention of using the proceeds for the improvement of the school. (For the purchase of this house in 1720, see page 118). This was only partially achieved, and his own efforts and those of subsequent vicars to extract the meagre capital sum so raised from the clutches of the Charity Commissioners were uniformly unsuccessful.[56] During the elder Underwood's incumbency the restoration of the church was commenced, initially by the rebuilding of the south aisle.[57]

Thomas Underwood's son Charles succeeded on his father's death in 1860, and served for 10 years. He was followed by Philip Edgar Pratt, an energetic young man who oversaw the building of a new school to replace the hopelessly inadequate room in the churchyard. At the opening of the school in 1873 the Dean of Hereford (admittedly hardly an unbiased commentator) noted that for the last 34 years 'the patrons of the parish had sent them a very good lot of vicars' and in proposing Pratt's health commented that 'he could not wish him to be more loved than his two predecessors.[58] Pratt, who had taught briefly at Ilminster School earlier in his career, began the active involvement of clergy with the school, on occasions standing in for the headmaster during his illness.[59] In 1880 he moved to Madley in Herefordshire, where his predecessor, Charles Underwood, had died.

Andrew Pope (1880-1890) was also a man of great energy and a conscientious parish priest, and is more widely known as the great friend of the clerical diarist Francis Kilvert. He completed the restoration of Diddlebury church in 1883, with the exception of the tower, which was left to his successor. He also instituted services on major saints' days, which were attended by the school children. His successor, Sidney Scarlett Smith (1891-1907) was a very active priest, in whose time the parish magazine became a mine of information about the life of the parish in its widest sense.

It is interesting to note that after Thomas Underwood, few clergy spent more than ten years in the parish before moving on or, in a few cases retiring or dying. W.A. Timmis (1928-1939) and N.F. Tripp (1945-1958) both ended their ministries at Diddlebury, and enjoyed satisfactory periods of retirement in Ludlow. Both R.C. Bolton (1907-1916) and J.A. Jones (1939-41) died unexpectedly while in office. Goodwin Purcell (1922-27) postponed this fate by moving to a less strenuous parish in Berkshire as a result of heart trouble, though having retired to Shropshire, he fell victim to the harsh winter of 1947 after delivering communion to a sick man in heavy snow.[60]

The second half of the 20th century brought increased pressure on the clergy, with falling congregations necessitating the merger of parishes. The brunt of this process was borne by Rev. J.G. Ellis (1965-1972), who also had a rather turbulent relationship with his parishioners, many of whom found his advanced ideas on matters such as infant baptism difficult to accept. In 1972 he left for a more congenial parish in west London, where he remained for over 20 years. His successor, Lionel Hunter, found the 'constant increasing work put on him by the diocese and the lack of communication from them' too much to bear, and resigned after only two years to take up a post in Canada.[61] It is possible that the failure of the diocese to provide a new vicarage in Diddlebury to replace the inadequate St. Michael's House in Munslow may have also been a contributory factor. The process of enlarging the group of parishes continued under Stuart Morris (1977-82), and the long incumbency of his successor I.E. Gibbs (1983 to date) has allowed the arrangements to become established. Ian Gibbs has held the living longer than any other priest since the death of J.W. Baugh in 1839. It is possible, that, given the tendency towards team ministries based on centres such as Ludlow and Wenlock serving a dozen or more parishes, that the present arrangement will not survive the current incumbent's retirement.

Recusancy and Nonconformity

While the pre-Reformation church undoubtedly had many faults, its greatest virtue was probably its universality. There was one Christian community in the West to which all belonged and those who, like the Lollards, expressed dissent were never more than a tiny (and often persecuted) minority. The Elizabethan settlement of the church, whether by accident or design, achieved a middle way between the extremes of Catholicism and Protestantism which the great majority of English people increasingly accepted. There were however minorities who wished to return to the old ways, some of whom were prepared to defy the law by absenting themselves from their parish church, and, whenever possible, employing the services of Catholic priests who operated illegally and in peril of their lives. These recusants, as they were known, were largely confined to the landowning classes, and were quite numerous in Elizabethan and later Shropshire.

At the other end of the spectrum were those who had wished for a more radical church settlement, more in line with continental Protestantism, who became known as puritans. In Shropshire they tended to be found more in towns than in the country, and gradually made their presence felt during the 17th century. These puritans, from whom sprang the 'older' nonconformist churches such as the Presbyterians, Baptists and Congregationalists, had little support in the conservative rural areas such as Diddlebury, and it was not until the advent of Methodism in the area in Victorian times that Protestant Nonconformity became a factor in the history of the parish.

Recusants

As stated above, many of the Shropshire landowning families remained Catholic. The Smiths of Aston Hall in Munslow, who had acquired that estate, which also included Middlehope, in 1542, were firmly recusant, as were their successors the Wrights of Kelvedon in Essex, who owned the estate from 1758 until its sale in 1911. The impact of this was limited, and there is no evidence that the family's religious position was adopted by their tenants or employees, and indeed several members of the family were buried in Munslow church. A lesser landowner in the parish, George Crowther of Sparchford was included, along with his wife, in an official list of recusants compiled in 1591-2.[62] The Littletons of Munslow, who were also proprietors of Broncroft, were initially Catholics, who gradually conformed, like so many of their co-religionists. The Luttleys, who purchased most of the Broncroft and Lawton estates from the Littletons at some point in the 16th century, remained loyal to the old faith for much longer, with 'Mr. Lutlowe of Bromcraft' (*sic*) appearing as a Catholic in a list of Shropshire justices in the time of Charles II.[63] In 1685 the churchwardens presented six people in the parish as popish recusants, including Thomas Luttley, his wife and his mother.[64] Other Catholic landowning families were absentees, namely the earls of Shrewsbury and Stafford, who successively owned the Peaton estates. While the Shrewsbury family, like most other English nobles, became reconciled to the Church of England, the Staffords remained loyal both to Rome and to the Stuart cause, with Henry, earl of Stafford following James II into exile in 1688. The final claimant to the title was deprived of his lands as an alien after the 1745 Jacobite rebellion, and his lands given to his sisters.[65] Despite this, there is no evidence that by the 18th century there were any Catholics resident in the parish, and in 1767 both vicar and curate were able to assure the bishop that there was 'not one Papist or reputed Papist within the parish of Diddlebury'.[66]

Protestant Nonconformity

There is little evidence of early Puritanism in the parish. Will preambles which use the fairly standard Calvinist formula of 'trusting/hoping to be numbered among the elect' are quite rare, though this may indicate the influence of the vicar, who often drew up the document. The two Habberleys appear to have been mainstream Anglicans, and certainly were conscientious in carrying out their obligations in encouraging those on the point of death to make a will. Puritan formulae, when they do occur, would therefore indicate the deeply held opinions of the testators. Certainly Thomas Downe of Middlehope (1632) included a lengthy preamble of highly Calvinist sentiment, while Thomas Mynton of Lawton (1621) expressed the same sentiments in fewer words.[67] Even more telling is the bequest of ten shillings made by William Bellamy of Westhope (1625) to whoever would bury him 'soberly and with least show of vanity' and secure the services of a 'godly preacher ... for the edifying of the congregation.'[68] Clearly the godly preacher was unlikely to have been Mr. Habberley. Puritans such as these were almost certainly always a small minority in the parish.

Protestant nonconformity did not affect the parish until the 19th century, with the penetration of Methodism into the area. The 18th-century Church had emphasised class barriers by consigning those who could not afford to rent their own pews to conspicuous open benches, which in Diddlebury were situated at the back of the church. This arrangement was hardly inviting to the poorer parishioners, and by 1840 small groups of Primitive Methodists were meeting in private houses at Sutton Hill and Bouldon, under the leadership of Samuel Hammonds, a local stonemason.[69] This predominantly working class branch of Methodism had been founded in Staffordshire by Hugh Bourne in 1807, and had reached South Shropshire via missions from Darlaston during the 1820s.[70] The Wesleyans had also been meeting in Diddlebury since 1816, in premises provided by Mr. Downes of Milford Lodge, and about 100 people had attended morning worship on 30 March 1851, the day appointed for the Religious Census.[71] This meeting was held under the lay leadership of William Hince, a butcher from Corfton Bache. It is perhaps significant that in the previous year the annual visitation return to the bishop of Hereford had noted that few of the younger people of the labouring class were communicants at the parish church, and that this group was generally literate.[72]

The rapid growth of support for both branches of Methodism saw the building of chapels in the parish. In 1873 a Primitive Methodist chapel, the last to be erected in the Ludlow circuit, was opened at Peaton Strand, midway between the existing centres at Sutton Hill and Bouldon. It became the basis of the Peaton Strand Circuit which served the Diddlebury, Clee and Craven Arms areas, before once more amalgamating with Ludlow in 1932.[73] A house was provided for the minister adjacent to the chapel, but ministers seem to have moved between the various centres on the circuit. An indication of the popularity of the chapel is the number of baptisms performed there, some 800 between the foundation of the congregation in 1867 (which predates the church building) and the outbreak of the First World War.[74] Candidates for baptism were drawn from a much wider area than Diddlebury parish, though labourers from the east of the parish featured prominently. It is worth noting that a number of families came regularly to Peaton for baptism from Seifton Batch and Westhope, although there was another chapel served by the same personnel much closer to them at Golden Plackett, a few yards into Culmington parish.

In 1880 the Wesleyans also opened their own chapel at the settlement known as Birmingham in Bach Mill (then in Munslow parish), on land given by John Overton, a stonemason from Corfton. The event was marked by a special service and a tea for 80 people. It is worth remarking that two leading Anglican landowners, Mrs. Powell of Sutton and T. Lloyd Roberts of Corfton Hall, had donated the hymn books and building sand respectively.[75]

A great strength of the Methodists at this time was the extent to which they engaged the support of the laity. Tea parties were a regular event, and an incentive to children to join the Sunday Schools. In 1877 over 300 people attended an anniversary tea at the Golden Plackett chapel, followed by no fewer than four addresses in an adjacent tent.[76] These tea parties were a constant irritant to the headmaster of Diddlebury (church) school, as they were held on weekday afternoons, and drew children away from school in considerable numbers. For adult worshippers there were opportunities to become Local Preachers, and to take part in leading the worship at the chapels in the circuit. George Lewis, a 20-year-old agricultural labourer living in Corfton Bache in 1861, and Thomas Partington of Sutton Hill, another agricultural worker, who appears in the 1871 census, are both examples of working people who had risen to the position of local preachers in the area. With Methodism offering working people the chance to run their own chapels and hold positions of responsibility, it is no surprise that Methodists became increasingly involved in radical politics, and it is noticeable that members of the Peaton Strand chapel formed the backbone of the attempt to remove the farming group from the newly-formed parish council in 1894 and 1896 (see p.141).

The rapid expansion of Methodism in the parish in the years prior to 1914 was followed by a marked and steady decline in the years following the First World War, shown by the rapid decrease in the numbers being baptised at Peaton Strand. Lacking the historic endowments which at this time still protected the Established Church, Methodist congregations had to pay their way or close. In 1964 the Wesleyan chapel at Bache Mill (Fig. 17) closed its doors, to be followed by that at Peaton Strand 20 years later. Methodists in the Corvedale are now served by the chapel at Aston Munslow, probably the most attractive architecturally of all Methodist buildings in the area.

Fig. 17 The Wesleyan chapel at Bache Mill was opened in 1880, and converted into a dwelling after its closure in 1964

Parish Life

Any attempt to depict the richness of religious life in Diddlebury before the Reformation is hampered by the lack of documentation. There are no surviving churchwardens' accounts before the 17th century, and only a handful of wills, all of which date from the very end of the period, when Henry VIII's legislation had already begun to weaken the fabric of traditional religion. As a result, the picture is a series of vignettes, often taken from documents whose main purpose was unconnected with religion or the life of the church. Notwithstanding these limitations, it is possible to gain some impression of the life of the parish before 1550. To see how this relates to the greater whole, it is necessary to consult Eamon Duffy's monumental work *The Stripping of the Altars.*

The parish church, and to a lesser extent the various chapels, was the centre of the spiritual life of the laity, and it is likely that many from all social groups would have attended Mass on a daily basis, although for most receiving of communion was an annual event at Easter, after they had been absolved of their sins. Unfortunately alterations and restorations since the Reformation have almost completely removed all trace of the medieval furnishings from the church, and there is little documentary evidence with which to fill in the gaps. In addition to the High Altar there was almost certainly a Lady Altar, as in 1543 Richard Lewys of Westhope bequeathed 3s. 4d. to the High Altar, and a further 6s. 8d. and a suit of vestments to 'our Lady service in the parish Church of Diddlebury.'[77] One precious aretfact survives as a reminder of the ceremonial of the medieval church. This is the cover of 12th- or 13th-century censer (incense burner) which was discovered in the parish in 2004 by a metal detectorist (Fig. 18). This was recorded by the Portable Antiquities Scheme (ref: HESH-8FC8F6) and subsequently returned to the finder.

In addition to attending Mass regularly in the parish church or one of the chapels, some of the wealthy, particularly women, began to follow increasingly strict regimes in their own homes. In 1389 Bishop John Trefnant advised Adam Asturley, the confessor to Mary LeStrange, the Lady of Corfham, to persuade her to reduce her commitment to excessive vigils, offices and psalms which were damaging her health.[78] For such personal devotions a private oratory was a desirable facility, and one which carried social prestige, as oratories were licensed by the bishop, and these licences were not freely given. The licensing of an oratory in the house of Edward Cleobury, the forester of Earnstrey, in July 1481 must have conferred social prestige as well as spiritual nourishment upon the family.[79]

The church had an important legal role in society, and for much of the pre-Reformation period, as mentioned above, clerical status carried immunity from prosecution in the secular courts. This was gradually eroded, as it was misused by malefactors who wished to pursue a life of crime rather than religion. An

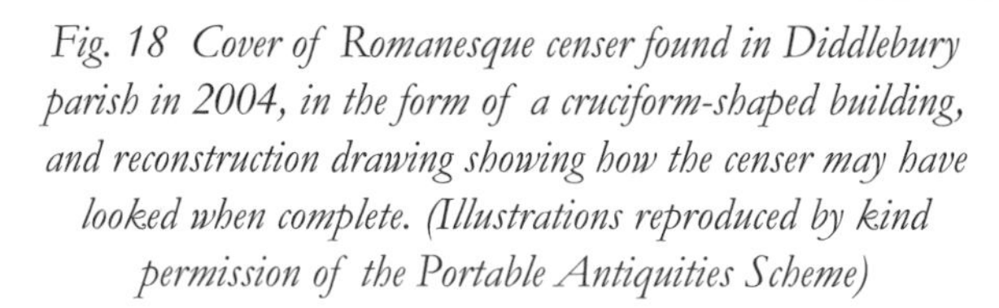

Fig. 18 Cover of Romanesque censer found in Diddlebury parish in 2004, in the form of a cruciform-shaped building, and reconstruction drawing showing how the censer may have looked when complete. (Illustrations reproduced by kind permission of the Portable Antiquities Scheme)

associated feature was the right of sanctuary, for which there are a number of examples concerning Diddlebury. In 1272, following a fight in Ludlow in which John de Hethe had struck John de Brewynoc with a sword and killed him, Hethe spent eight days in Diddlebury church, before being snatched from sanctuary by followers of the powerful John fitz Alan of Clun.[80] Similarly in 1293 William, son of Walter Molendarius (Miller) of Diddlebury sought sanctuary from the bailiffs in Ludlow church before giving himself over. He was fortunate enough to be acquitted.[81]

The church courts exercised considerable jurisdiction over the lives of ordinary people, which they managed to retain at the Reformation thanks to a bargain struck between Convocation, the body representing the clergy, and Thomas Cromwell. They alone could grant probate of wills, and they were active in attempts to control immorality. Proceedings in these cases give a fascinating glimpse of manners in medieval communities. The Visitation Return made in 1397 contains a catalogue of sexual misconduct alleged against parishioners. Allegations include several instances of fornication and adultery, such as that of William Laurens, the lord of Corfham's cook, who was fornicating with Matilda 'whom he keeps', or William Polley who had abjured Joanna, daughter of John Leys, on pain of marriage, but afterwards had two children by her. There was also one case of clandestine marriage, and another of marriage while betrothed to another.[82]

Cases like these were hard to detect in the absence of official registers, which were not required until 1538. There is, however, evidence that some Diddlebury clergy attempted unofficial record keeping. This comes from Inquisitions into proof of age, which themselves were necessitated by the absence of baptismal records. Two deponents in the inquest into the age of Katherine, daughter of Hugh Child (1371) mention that the baptism had been recorded in a missal or a psalter, while the same practice was also noted by a witness to the age of John Baskerville of Lawton a year later.[83] These inquisitions contain some charming vignettes of medieval religious life. Thomas Cressett testified that Katherine Child had been baptised in Diddlebury church on 26 March 28 Edward III, and that 'John de Paunteley, Katherine de Upton and Cecily de Perton lifted her from the font,' presumably in their role as godparents.[84] In an inquisition into the age of Hugh Tyrel in 1364, one Henry Corviser stated that on the date of the baptism in question he had begun his pilgrimage to Compostella, while another, John Robarts recalled that his son William had celebrated his first mass at Neenton on the same day.[85]

This pattern of worship and parish life was dramatically ended by the Reformation. The physical appearance of the church would have been radically altered, with the destruction of screens and images, and the replacement of the altar by a wooden communion table.[86] There is no record of the process at Diddlebury, but enough evidence from elsewhere to enable us to conjecture fairly accurately what took place. Instead of the mass, the main Sunday services were Morning and Evening Prayer in English, with the Communion celebrated every quarter. Behind this lay radical theological changes, with many of the underlying beliefs of the medieval church jettisoned. No longer did the elements mystically transform themselves into the Body and Blood of Christ at the Consecration, while Purgatory, was rejected as a 'fond thing vainly invented' (Article XXII), thus making redundant the complex bequests for the welfare of souls found in wills such as that of William Mynton.

The progress of religious change may be seen from the preambles to wills. It was usual until the death of Henry VIII in 1547 for the initial clause of a will to commit the testator's soul to' Almighty God, our Lady St. Mary, and the holy company of saints in Heaven.' Bequests made during the reign of Henry VIII generally included the provision of between two and six tapers, and sometimes torches, 'to burn while service is a-saying at my burial.'[87] By 1547 some testators were omitting this provision, though whether for theological or economic reasons is not clear.[88] Only one of the 14 wills which have been examined from the period

1540-1548 contains any provision for prayers for the testator's soul. William Mynton of Peaton (1546) bequeathed a cow to the vicar, Richard Normecott in return for prayers for his soul, and those of all Christians, and also made the bequest to his son of the lease of his farm conditional upon the performance of commemorative services. These were a solemn dirige, office and solemn Mass to be said every quarter for ten years for the welfare of his soul and those of all Christians. On each occasion, 3s. 4d. was to be distributed to the poor of the parish.[89]

The accession of Henry's son, the young Edward VI, brought about a gradual shift towards Protestantism under his first Lord Protector, the duke of Somerset (1547-1549), but the 1549 Prayer Book was sufficiently ambiguous to accommodate both Catholic and reformed interpretations. Under the influence of the duke of Northumberland, who ousted Somerset after the rebellions of 1549, the country was forced headlong into a more extreme version of Protestantism. It is odd that the only Diddlebury will dating from the period of Northumberland's rule, that of Thomas Wygley (1552) bequeathed two tapers to the 'hye altar of Dudylbury',[90] an aggressively traditional and largely meaningless gesture, as the high altar would by then have been replaced by a moveable wooden table. When the royal commissioners visited Diddlebury on 15 May 1553, a few weeks before Edward's death, all that remained of the church furnishings were a silver chalice and paten, and three bells in the tower.[91] Unfortunately the earlier inventory, which listed the furnishings and equipment which survived in 1552, has been lost. Whether the vestments and other goods had been destroyed, or, as often happened, placed in hiding, is not known.

The accession of Mary Tudor in 1553 brought about a return to Catholicism, and ultimately reconciliation with Rome, and the four wills from this period all use the traditional form of dedication. Only one, that of John Bowdeler (1555), includes a bequest of tapers for the high altar, though too much significance should not be read into this.[92] The death of Mary in November 1558 brought her half-sister Elizabeth to the throne, and although it was for some time unclear how religion would be settled, Diddlebury wills immediately adopted the politically correct dedication to 'Almighty God, my maker and redeemer.' The initial uncertainty, and the subsequent gradual acceptance of the Elizabethan church settlement has been lucidly covered by Professor Duffy, to whose work the reader is referred.[93] As the long reign of Elizabeth progressed and it became obvious that the old ways were not likely to be restored, the Book of Common Prayer gradually became part of 'traditional' religion, particularly to the rising generations who had no memory of anything else.[94] One curiously old-fashioned bequest to the parish of 'a diaper towel to the use of the communicants' by Thomas Posterne in 1585 is a reminder that sacramental worship still had a place in the Elizabethan church.[95]

The acceptance of the Elizabethan settlement and the Prayer Book was undoubtedly aided by the long incumbency of the two Habberleys, whose 75 years in the parish would have provided great continuity. It is significant that Diddlebury was one of the Shropshire parishes which sent petitions to Parliament in 1642 protesting against the abolition of the bishops and the Prayer Book.[96] While such a petition was undoubtedly the work of the clergy, it may be assumed that it represented the wishes of many if not all the parishioners. The Interregnum brought more disruption than simply the imposition of a Presbyterian system with its own service book, the *Directory of Public Worship*. In particular, marriage was removed from the jurisdiction of the church and made a responsibility of the Justices of the Peace. Some clergy like George Littleton of Munslow, who had conformed sufficiently to retain their parishes, conducted occasional, presumably clandestine marriages. Others who wished to be married by a clergyman did so in his home, in the presence of a Justice, who took no part in the proceedings. William Churchman, who had been curate of Diddlebury in 1637, performed a number of such marriages, as well as baptisms, in his house at Hungerford.[97] During the incumbency of Nicholas Proude, baptisms do not appear to have been performed at Diddlebury, but, rather oddly, his accounts of his surplice fees* in his Tithe Book record many instances of the Churching of Women.*

The Restoration in 1660 saw the gradual return to traditional Anglicanism, which was completed in 1662 by the expulsion of those clergy who refused to accept the Book of Common Prayer. The recovery of the Church of England after the chaos of the Interregnum was seen particularly in the reassertion of the power of the church courts, which had been abolished by Parliament. This was particularly true in matters of immorality, where the Church came down hard on offences such as fornication, adultery, and also defamation. Conviction in the diocesan court meant, in the case of fornication and adultery, the performance of humiliating public penance in front of neighbours. Thus in April 1669 Jane Pritchard, who had been convicted of fornication, had to stand for the whole of morning service near the reading desk in Diddlebury church 'bare headed and bare legged with her hair hanging over her shoulders and a white sheet over her wearing apparel, having a white rod of an ell length in her hand.'[98] Following the Nicene Creed, the penitent was required to make a public confession.

Defamation was another matter over which the courts sought to exercise renewed control. Actions of this sort frequently involved heated exchanges between neighbours, such as when in November 1690 Edward Wellings accused Thomas Burnell of trespassing in pursuit of game on his land, and called him 'the son of a whore and a whore's bastard.' Mrs. Burnell took this slight upon her honour to the diocesan court, where Wellings was ordered to do penance and pay costs of almost £6.[99] After 1690 these actions dramatically decreased in number nationally, perhaps as an unintended side-effect of the granting of toleration to the Dissenters.[100]

One area in which the Church retained its authority until 1857 was matrimonial matters, where the intention was that the courts should aid the restoration of marital relations, and where this was not possible, punish offenders. While divorce in its modern sense was not possible except by Private Act of Parliament, the diocesan courts heard cases of divorce (or more accurately, judicial separation) concerning Diddlebury parishioners on a number of occasions in the 17th and 18th centuries. While one of these was a relatively simple matter of a wife who had committed adultery while her husband 'went to live in remote places,' and was sued for divorce upon his return,[101] another involved most barbaric domestic violence committed by a leading landowner upon his wife.

John Fleming of Westhope had been the subject of an injunction in 1697 which prohibited him from beating, assaulting or misusing his wife, and which allowed her freedom to visit friends, manage the household and generally enjoy the 'privileges suitable to a mistress in her family.'[102] By 1707 it was clear that Fleming had long since ceased to comply, and his wife Elizabeth sued for divorce. A string of former servants testified to a series of assaults which had left their mistress bruised and bleeding about the face, and told how they had been forbidden to do anything for her on pain of dismissal, and how Fleming had attempted to imprison his wife, but had lost the key. It is worth noting that Mrs. Fleming obtained her separation, together with maintenance of £7 per quarter. It is interesting to note that in the 20 years prior to the breakdown of the marriage in 1697, she had borne no less than 19 children. Her husband died in 1716, and she lived for a further 12 years.[103] Curiously, the wife of a later Fleming, Edward, the grandson of John and Elizabeth, also had a tempestuous marriage, and was temporarily left by his wife in 1763, though subsequently the couple were partially reconciled. Ann Fleming died in 1770. Her husband was poisoned three years later, possibly by his son.[104]

Such episodes were, of course, exceptional, and for the majority of people contact with the Church took the form of regular attendance at Sunday services, and meeting with the vicar or curate as they went about their daily business. For the farmers there was the additional responsibility of parochial office holding, which will be discussed more fully under Local Government. The 18th century has traditionally been dismissed as a period of spiritual sterility between the turbulence of the previous period, and the Victorian revivals. This picture is gradually being modified, and the evidence from Diddlebury does not conform to the traditional picture of neglect. The parish is fortunate in possessing a comprehensive set of churchwardens' accounts from 1685 until 1870 which provide a great deal of evidence about the condition of the parish during the period.[105] Perhaps the most striking way in which Diddlebury differed from the conventional view of the period is in the frequency of celebration of Holy Communion. Until 1726 communion was celebrated 'according to ancient custom' at Christmas, Easter and Michaelmas.[106] The short incumbency of Hugo Wishaw (1726-30) saw the introduction of a monthly celebration. This would have appeared to have continued until 1759, after which payments for wine tend to become reduced. It would seem, however, that during the second quarter of the 18th century, sacramental worship played a more prominent role than usual in the church life of Diddlebury.

Worship in the 18th century, far from being staid and unchanging, required parishes to continually update their service books with supplements. The period was one of both domestic and international upheaval, with an insecure dynasty in the first half of the century, and almost continuous warfare in the second. Thus in May 1707 the parish bought a Book of Thanksgiving for the Union between England and Scotland, and also had to change the prayers in consequence. The following year there was a Solemn Fast, for the wars with France, and in most years there seem to have been fasts or thanksgivings to be observed, such as those for the coming of George I in 1714. Later in the century there were prayers against the Americans in 1776, and sometimes as many as five different forms of prayers were purchased in a year during the wars with France between 1792 and 1815.

The wardens' accounts also reveal a great deal about the musical life of the church. Throughout the period there are many references to the bell ringers, who received payment for ringing on national celebrations. These regularly included the anniversaries of the Gunpowder Plot and the Restoration of the Monarchy, but also other times of national rejoicing, such as George III's recovery from illness in 1791. In 1769 the church seems to have had a choir for the first time, as six shillings were paid for writing tunes and accompaniments. By the end of the 18th century there are regular references to the 'psalm singers', who were paid a guinea per year for their services. By 1828 they had been augmented by a band, whose instruments included a bass viol, a violoncello, four violins and a recorder. These instruments served the choir until the installation of an organ in 1855.

At the end of the 18th century Archdeacon Joseph Plymley made thorough notes as he conducted his visitations, and these provide an interesting comment on the state of the parish. In 1793 he noted that the vicar, Abraham Rudd, lived in Ludlow, but performed service twice on Sundays at Diddlebury in summer, and once in winter. He also took an afternoon service at Westhope once a month, paid for by a £5 a year legacy from the ill-used Elizabeth Fleming. The archdeacon commented that at Westhope there was a full congregation in good weather, but numbered no more than a dozen when the weather was poor.[107] Following the death of Rudd, a Mr. Fleming, the curate of Abdon and Clee St. Margaret, had been appointed by Sir John Swinnerton Dyer to serve the chapel once a month, walking seven miles each way, and paying the £5 salary to his mother's creditors.[108] A similar feat was performed, presumably on horseback, in 1793 by Revd. John Powell of Sutton, who did duty each Sunday morning at Cold Weston.

A snapshot of the state of the parish a half century later is provided by the Religious Census of 1851. On the morning of 30 March 1851, 102 persons attended morning worship at Diddlebury, with 49 children at Sunday School. This was claimed as below average due to the weather by the vicar, who estimated a normal attendance of 210. There was no afternoon service that Sunday, as there was a service at Westhope, which was attended by 43 persons, which was again claimed as below average. Mr. Underwood, like other Corvedale clergy, (e.g. Revd. H. Powell of Munslow) claimed that a third of his parishioners lived nearer to other churches. There was some truth in this, as for many years residents of Sparchford and Seifton Batch had attended Culmington church.[109] It should, however, be noted that less than 200 parishioners out of a total population in 1851 of 878 had been present in church on census day. This represents about 20% of the population, and even allowing for the 110 Methodists also worshipping in the parish, it is clear that about two-thirds of Diddlebury residents were unlikely to attend a place of worship on a regular basis.

After 1851 records of church attendance become more generally available, and provide a guide to the changing patterns of both worship and support. While Morning Prayer and Evensong remained the principal services every Sunday until 1966, it is clear that under Charles Underwood the clergy began to place much greater stress upon the regular reception of Holy Communion. Communion thereafter became celebrated after Morning Prayer on one Sunday each month, and subsequently on an increasing number of Holy Days. Underwood's record of communicants for the year from Advent 1864 to Advent 1865 reveals that this new emphasis was not shared by the majority of his parishioners. During the year, 92 individuals had received Communion. The only person apart from the vicar to do so on all 14 occasions when it was offered was, unsurprisingly, Thomas Edwards, the parish clerk. The other three who communicated ten or more times were all members of the vicar's family. Of the 92 communicants for the year, no less than 50 communicated only once, generally, though not exclusively at Easter. These included most of the gentry and wealthier farmers, and, surprisingly, Charles Cook, the schoolmaster, and his wife. It is also noticeable that only 23 of the 92 communicants were men.[110]

Associated with the greater stress on Eucharistic worship was an increase in the number of candidates put forward for Confirmation. In 1860, 14 candidates from the parish were confirmed at Munslow, with 26 at Culmington four years later. In 1872 confirmation was held at Diddlebury for the first time in many years, and not less than 41 candidates were presented. Between this date and 1907 (when the records cease), 124 candidates from the parish were confirmed.[111] This

Fig. 19 The Revd. Goodwin Purcell, photographed outside the Vicarage c.*1925, was probably the last vicar to use horse-drawn transport around the parish*

demonstrates one aspect of the revival of church life which was taking place in the second half of the century.

From service registers it is possible to chart the strength of support for the church by using the number of Easter communicants. This shows a slight overall decline during the 20th century. In 1909 at total of 90 people at Diddlebury and a further 26 at Westhope made their Easter communion.[112] In 1922 the number was 87, in 1923 it had risen to 123, and the number grew each year to peak at 167 in 1927. This undoubtedly reflects the efforts, and the great popularity of Revd. Goodwin Purcell. After 1927 the number of Easter communicants at Diddlebury averaged about 100, with significant increases in 1938, probably influenced by anxiety about the international situation, and in 1941, probably also reflecting the state of the war.[113] The 20 years after the war saw a gradual decline, with fewer than 70 communicants in five of the years. The number of Easter communicants is not an entirely accurate guide to the amount of support for the church in this period. Goodwin Purcell, alone among clergy who compiled the service registers, included numbers for all services during his incumbency. It is clear that at this time Evensong was the most popular service. A study of attendance for the month of April for each year between 1922 and 1927 shows that the lowest number at this service during the period was 69, with the highest (161) on Easter Day 1927. While Easter Day might be expected to produce above average attendances, in April 1926 and 1927 there was only one Sunday when less than 100 people attended Evensong. While fewer attended Mattins, attendances were rarely below 80 in the same period, though it may be assumed that many people attended twice each Sunday.[114] It is also noticeable that by contrast the 8a.m. celebration of Holy Communion consistently attracted between three and seven communicants, except on Easter Day, and on Sundays when Holy Communion followed Mattins, figures were similarly low (e.g. seven communicants out of 95 worshippers on 15 April 1923).[115] The reluctance of Diddlebury parishioners to communicate other than at the great festivals of the Christian year which was seen in the 1860s had clearly persisted into the 20th century, and it is possible that the replacement of Mattins by Parish Communion as the main Sunday service a week after the institution of a new incumbent in 1965 is not unconnected with the subsequent decline in attendance.

As in many parishes, this process became most marked in the last quarter of the 20th century. The Church electoral roll, which stood at 127 in 1973, had declined to 29 by 2000, and although this may in part have been influenced by fiscal considerations relating to the parish quota, it illustrates a real decline in active involvement with the church.[116] It is worth noting that this is not a specifically Anglican problem, with all the Methodist churches in the parish having closed during the same period. There may be various explanations for this decline. The period since 1970 saw the amalgamation of parishes, which reduced the number of services in each church. Whereas in the 1960s Diddlebury, like most churches had an early Communion, Matins and Evensong on a typical Sunday, there is now only one Sunday service, with a morning Eucharist alternating with Evensong. At the time of writing, average attendances are 16 at morning Eucharist and 9 at Evensong. The sharing of a clergyman between five parishes inevitably reduces the amount of time available in each, and contrasts with the earlier period when each parish had the undivided attention of 'its' vicar. The same period has also seen a considerable amount of liturgical revision, with various experimental services being lauded as the way forward before disappearing into obscurity. It is possible that these experiments caused the loss of some older worshippers, while the droves of young people which they aimed to attract failed to materialise. These trends were not unique to Diddlebury and are indicative of the transformation of England into a largely secular society. It would, however, be a mistake to dismiss Diddlebury at the start of the third millennium as a post-Christian community, for a very large number of parishioners have a deep and genuine attachment to the parish church, even if few regularly take part in its worship.

PLACES OF WORSHIP

St. Peter's Church

It is somewhat frustrating that although there is considerable, if somewhat puzzling, architectural evidence remaining from the medieval church at Diddlebury, there is virtually nothing in the way of useful documentary material. Apart from a number of fairly routine complaints in the 14th century that the chancel was in need of repair,[117] no references before the 16th century to the fabric of the building have been located. This contrasts with the fairly abundant documentary material relating to the appearance of the church (and also the chapels at Corfton and Westhope, discussed below) during the 17th and 18th centuries, of which virtually no physical evidence remains.

St. Peter's church has long been famous for the survival of extensive Anglo-Saxon work in the north wall, but there has been considerable controversy over

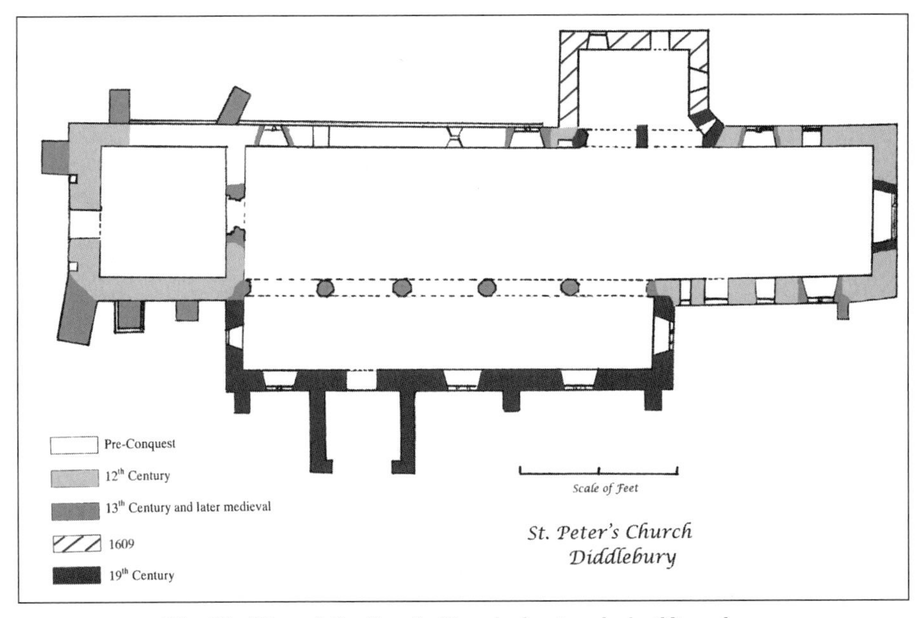

Fig. 20 Plan of St. Peter's Church showing the building phases

the nature of the pre-Conquest building, and also its date. The north wall of the nave is unusual in being faced internally with herring-bone masonry (Fig. 21a), but externally in large square ashlar blocks (Fig. 21b). The wall also contains a small and deeply-splayed window of unimpeachably pre-Conquest design, and a blocked north doorway with similarly characteristic heavy imposts (Fig. 21b)*. This combination of external ashlar and internal herring-bone is without parallel in England, with the exception of a somewhat similar arrangement at neighbouring Culmington, where two unquestionably Norman windows occur in the context of the herring-bone work. The use of herring-bone, normally regarded as a post-Conquest feature, has led a number of architectural historians to ascribe a very late date to the work, with the latest contribution to the debate suggesting that it could have been constructed by English masons working shortly after the Conquest.[118]

Diddlebury is also unusual in that there is incontrovertible evidence of a stone structure extending at least 13 feet to the west of the present nave. Any possible features to the west of this have been obliterated by the building of the Norman west tower, but it is most likely that this represents a form of narthex or western entrance similar to that at Deerhurst in Gloucestershire, which may have contained a gallery on an upper floor from which the landowner could view the service. It is likely that the original west door of the Norman tower, a great archway 14 feet in height and ten feet across, perpetuated this arrangement, until it was blocked later in the 12th century and the present much smaller doorway inserted

Fig. 21 Pre-Conquest work in the church.
(a) Interior of the north wall of the nave showing the herring-bone pattern.
(b) The squared ashlar masonry on the exterior of the wall, and a blocked doorway with characteristic pre-Conquest imposts

(Fig. 22). The presence of a capital carved with a much eroded animal figure, superficially resembling the work of the Herefordshire School of carving on the south side of this arch also strongly suggests a possible 12th-century date (Fig. 23a).[119]

The combination of two such unusual pre-Conquest features in one building will no doubt ensure that Diddlebury will be the cause of controversy among architectural historians for many years to come. The dating of the pre-Conquest features is particularly problematical, yet it would appear that so far no discussion has centred upon one crucial piece of evidence. Almost alone among architectural historians, the late Eric Mercer drew attention to the fact that Diddlebury was part of the important royal manor of Corfham, the *caput** of two hundreds in 1086. He suggested that the administrative decline of Corfham after 1102 saved Diddlebury church from comprehensive redevelopment in later times.[120] This theory is closely linked to the assumption that the church dates from the 'Anglo-Saxon overlap' period rather than an earlier date. This does, however, neglect the significant point that Diddlebury itself had become completely overshadowed by Corfham at the time of Domesday, being reduced to the status of a member or subsidiary part of that manor. It would therefore seem logical that if a new church was to have been built *c.*1050-1080, it would have been built at Corfham, rather than in the less significant settlement of Diddlebury. If an important church already existed at Diddlebury, there would surely have been less pressure to replace a serviceable structure with a new one a mile away. Thus a date earlier rather than later in the 11th century becomes more feasible. It is worth noting that the herring-bone masonry which has been regarded as the hallmark of a late date has been found in 10th-century work at Deerhurst, where timber samples from the western porch gave radio-carbon dates of 800 A.D. +/- 90 and 960 A.D. +/- 80.[121]

Later developments at St. Peter's are comparatively straightforward. The chancel was erected or

Fig. 22 Pre-Conquest work in the church. The blocked opening at the west end of the church, with the later inserted doorway. It is possible that this represents an open porticus or western porch

Fig. 23 Early carvings. (a) The south impost of the blocked western arch shows traces of an animal figure reminiscent of the Herefordshire School of the 12th century

Fig. 23 Early carvings.
(b) The sheila-na-gigs on the southern side of the tower.
Other examples may be found in the nearby churches of Tugford and Holdgate

extended in the 12th century — it is impossible to say which, because work to the east of the pre-Conquest masonry of the nave has been obscured by the building of the family chapel of the Baldwyns in 1609. It has recently been noted that those churches which possessed an ecclesiastical patron tended to be provided with much longer chancels than those under lay patronage.[122] This is true of Diddlebury, and the subsequent unwillingness of the authorities to maintain the structure has already been mentioned. The east wall of the chancel does show some 'long and short work', a feature normally associated with Anglo-Saxon masons, and the outlines of two blocked Norman windows, probably part of a three- or four-light east window. Several early 19th-century drawings by reliable artists such as David Parkes show a single Romanesque window in the east wall of the chancel. This may be the central light of the original Norman window. At this time the tower was begun, and around the corbel table are a number of grotesque animal heads similar to those found in Herefordshire at Kilpeck and elsewhere from the middle of the 12th century. On the south face of the tower is a pair of *Sheela-na-gigs** (Fig. 23b), a feature to be found in two other Corvedale churches.[123] At the end of the 12th century the large western opening discussed above was filled in, except for the much smaller west door which was created at this time. The tower has been heavily repaired and buttressed at various times during the medieval period, and it is tempting to suggest that the instability of the structure may have been due to the over-large opening in the west wall.

The church was enlarged in the 13th century by the addition of a south aisle of five bays, separated from the nave by a rather crude arcade of hexagonal columns on high and undecorated plinths. Later medieval alterations were largely confined to the insertion of windows in the Decorated style in the chancel and the east wall of the aisle, and a large Perpendicular window in the aisle.[124]

The post-Reformation period saw important developments in the internal arrangement of the church. In 1609 the Baldwyn family successfully gained permission to set up a 'chappell or chancell' on the north side of the church for their exclusive use.[125] At the same time the roofs of the church would appear to have been completely renewed, though all that remains from the work are the series of grotesque carved wooden corbel heads which were spared in the restoration of 1859-60. These show considerable affinity with other examples in domestic buildings in the area, most notably in Sutton Court (Fig. 24). An early 19th-century description mentions that the nave contained a 'singularly (*sic*) oak ceiling' while that of the south aisle was stuccoed.[126]

The most striking physical change carried out in this period was the introduction of pews, which were allocated to particular townships. This was accomplished by 1666, when a note of pew allocations was inserted into the churchwardens' papers. It is not clear from this document whether the whole church was pewed, and there is a possibility that pewing was confined to the nave and part of the chancel. It is clear that male and female servants of the Diddlebury and Broncroft estates were segregated in their seating.[127] In 1682 John Fleming of Westhope

Fig. 24 Carved corbel heads dating from the 17th century (a) from the south aisle of the church (b) from Sutton Court. It is almost certain that they are by the same hand

sought permission from the diocese to erect a gallery on the north side of the church to increase seating capacity. It was to be 13 feet in length, 7 feet in depth, and to stand 7 feet 6 inches from the ground.[128] The stairs were to be partly outside the church, and it is likely that they were situated in the long window opening next to the present vestry, the purpose of which has long perplexed antiquaries. The structure would have been similar to the elevated pew/gallery which survives at Croft in North Yorkshire. As it encroached partly in front of the Baldwyn chapel, it provoked a vigorous protest from Timothy Baldwyn, who protested that it would be 'very disgraceful to the Church, and prejudicial to our seates and others.'[129]

Baldwyn's protest was in vain, and the gallery was built. It appears to have undergone quite extensive repairs in 1723, when the churchwardens' accounts include haulage of timber from Ludlow, Hayton and Westhope for use in the gallery, and payments for mason's work and iron work there.[130] In 1763 a note in the flyleaf of the account book records that a seat in the gallery was sold to Revd. John Powell of Little Sutton for a guinea and a half.[131]

The churchwardens appear to have been reasonably assiduous in repairing and maintaining the church throughout the period of the accounts (1681-1838). Glazing windows was a regular expense, as was removal of rubbish from the tower, no doubt caused by birds. The roof was in constant need of repair, with fairly major efforts being made in 1761-2, 1767-8, 1777-8 and 1791-2. A surprisingly recurrent item of expenditure was for bell ropes, which were often renewed almost annually. A sample decade (1730-40) saw four new ropes purchased in 1734 and 1739, and two in 1730, 1731, 1733 and 1735. Ropes cost three shillings each including carriage, and it is surprising that they were so short-lived.[132]

Given the evidence of the churchwardens' accounts, it is somewhat surprising to find Archdeacon Plymley commenting in March 1793 that 'the floor of the Nave and ailes is bad; and the whole appearance of the Pews & Ch. slovenly.'[133] Shortly afterwards, the whole church was comprehensively re-pewed in accordance with a faculty, at a cost of £168 13s. During the course of this work, Dr. Cornewall, the owner of the Hall and dean of Canterbury, ordered the churchwardens to demolish the hated gallery adjacent to the chapel which his family had taken over from the Baldwyns when they purchased the Hall in 1752. This was done without consulting Mr. Mytton, the owner of the Sparchford estate, and proprietor of the four seats of the gallery. Mytton sought legal advice, but wisely decided not to take on the Cornewalls. Dr. Cornewall subsequently had his chapel comprehensively redecorated in 1806, with new oak wainscot, coloured walls, and chocolate painted doors.[134] The uniform pewing installed in 1794 remained until 1883, and several plans show the interior in 1860.[135]

The church underwent two restorations in the 19th century. The first, carried out in 1859-60, was relatively conservative and prompted by structural concerns rather than by ecclesiastical fashion. The church was completely re-roofed with Memel timber, and covered with blue tiles from Coalbrookdale. The wall of the south or Corfton aisle was taken down and rebuilt a foot lower than the original, with the east and south east windows replicated, and two new windows added in the Perpendicular style (Fig. 25). The work was carried out by two local contractors, Messrs. Overton and Pugh.[136] It would seem that the stripping of the walls

Fig. 25

(a) A view of the church from the south, drawn by the Revd. Thomas Lowe on the cover of the marriage register book c.1820. The 18th-century porch is clearly seen

(b) A view of the church from the south in 2006 shows that the rebuilding of the south aisle in 1859-60 largely reflected the previous structure

Fig. 26 The rebuilding of the tower in 1900. The structure had clearly been unstable for centuries, as shown by the addition of buttresses during the medieval period, and the rebuilding of the upper parts of the tower had been made possible by a bequest from Thomas Lloyd Roberts of Corfton

of their internal plaster took place at this time. While this revealed the enigmatic herring-bone work, the overall effect, particularly of the raised pointing, is less pleasing than plastered interiors. Although there is no mention in the specification of rebuilding the arcade separating the nave from the south aisle, a number of writers including Plymley and the 19th-century genealogist Hardwick mention that the pillars were out of perpendicular alignment, which is obviously not the case today.[137] Rather surprisingly, the classical porch, built in 1724,[138] was retained in the process, as were the box pews and three-decker pulpit in the church.

It is not surprising that the second stage of the restoration was undertaken by the energetic Andrew Pope. In September 1881 a meeting was held to consider proposals to reseat the church, raise the level of the chancel, convert the Cornewall chapel into an organ chamber, and other works. The diocesan architect, Thomas Nicholson was employed to oversee the works, which were essentially a re-ordering, with the exception of the rebuilding of the south porch. In the process, almost all trace of the 17th- and 18th-century work was removed. The box pews were replaced by oak benches, and the chancel was equipped with choir stalls. The old pulpit was retained for a short period, as its replacement had not arrived by the time of the official opening in the presence of the bishop of Hereford in August 1883. One of the most regrettable features of the restoration was the raising of the chancel floor, in the course of which a number of monuments, including a cast-iron heraldic slab to Mary Baldwyn of Middlehope (1659), were buried.[139] The one intended feature which was never installed was the chancel screen. For this restoration, the services of contractors from outside the parish were employed, namely Messrs. Jones and Sons of

Sedgeley. The whole cost of the work was £650, of which some £350 was raised by subscription.[140] The restoration of 1883 gave the church its current appearance, and the view of the interior in 1910 differs little from that today, except that most of the attractive paraffin lamps have long disappeared. The most notable recent alteration has been the formation of a Lady Chapel in the south aisle in memory of Canon Reginald Houghton (1910-1989) who had lived at Church Cottage since 1978, and assisted in the Corvedale group of parishes.

Westhope Chapel

Although there are documentary references to the chapel as early as 1255, nothing remains of the medieval building, which has been twice rebuilt. The first occasion was in 1728, when it was rebuilt by Richard Fleming as a result of a stipulation in the will of his mother, the much-wronged Elizabeth Fleming.[141] A drawing made at the end of the 18th century by Revd. E Williams (Fig. 27a) shows a plain brick-built Georgian building, and interior details are described by Plymley, who noted '3 large pews, desk and pulpit in the chancel, 9 pews & one open seat in the nave, all of neat oak wainscot'. The building appeared to Plymley to have been neglected, with many patches to the stucco ceiling, broken hinges on the pew doors, and a 'rather infirm' pulpit.[142]

In 1892 the chapel was again rebuilt, by the then proprietor, Col. Swinnerton-Dyer, as a brick structure with no division between nave and chancel, and an overhanging western bellcote (Fig. 27b). The windows were a simple late-Perpendicular design of two lights under brick hood-moulds, with the exception of the simple three-light Perpendicular east window. The chapel was originally furnished plainly without a screen, but after the First World War the interior was equipped in an Anglo-Catholic manner, and also provided with a wayside Crucifix, possibly of

Fig. 27 Westhope Chapel.
(a) As rebuilt by Richard Fleming in 1728, drawn by the Revd. E. Williams c.*1790*

Fig. 27 Westhope Chapel.
(b) Following its last rebuilding in 1892

continental origin, by the entrance path. Regular services ceased in 1974, and until recently Harvest Thanksgiving and an annual carol services were the only acts of Anglican worship held at Westhope. In 1997 the present owner of the estate, who is a Quaker, converted the chapel and the adjacent orchard into a centre for environmentally friendly funerals.[143] In order to make the surroundings more attractive to non-Christian clients, portable items of specifically Christian imagery were subsequently removed from the building. It would seem unlikely that it will be used again for Anglican worship in the foreseeable future.[144]

Corfton Chapel

While Westhope retains the fabric of its chapel, Corfton, the only other chapel in the parish to survive the Reformation, has disappeared almost without trace. Unlike Westhope, there was never any doubt as to the status of Corfton Chapel which was always attached to Diddlebury, with maintenance the responsibility of the vicar, as holder of the rectorial tithes. This responsibility was avoided whenever possible, and there are many complaints from 1315 onwards that the chapel was in need of repair. In 1635 commissioners inspecting the chapel had reported that it was 'in great decay and ruinous in the walls, roof, seeling (ceiling) and glazing and paving', and ordered the vicar, Thomas Habberley, to repair the chancel, and the inhabitants to take responsibility for the rest of the building.[145] It would appear that the Baldwyn family took charge, for accounts of five weeks work in the autumn of 1635 are preserved among the family papers at Stafford. Potter the mason and his four assistants, together with a tiler and a plasterer were

Fig. 28 Lost chapels:
Corfton, drawn by Williams about the time of Archdeacon Plymley's visit in 1793, when there had been no services for a decade

employed, and the total cost of the job was £12 1s. 10d. Included in the accounts is 6d. for the repair of a borrowed ladder which had been broken.[146]

By 1707 the state of the chapel had again deteriorated, to judge from a threatening letter from the bishop of Hereford to vicar Fosbroke, in which the bishop expressed surprise that the vicar could 'have any peace of mind to see it thus, & ye place once used and dedicated for ye service & worship of Almighty God so abused by your neglect.'[147] The bishop noted that workmen had offered to glaze 11 windows and repair the roof for £3 as a holding operation, which appears to have been a remarkably low price. By the time of Plymley's visit in 1793, less than a decade after the last service had been held, the windows were unglazed and the roof needed attention. Inside, Plymley noted a 'good reading Desk & pulpit, neat altar rails & 18 handsome regular pews made with oak wainscot'.[148] The rapidity of the process of decay was frightening, and when Hardwick visited the site in the 1840s little remained but the external walls, with three round-headed windows.[149] Today it is not possible to identify any meaningful features from the fragment which survives in an agricultural building.

Bouldon Chapel

Bouldon chapel was originally a detached portion of Holdgate parish which was transferred to Diddlebury for civil purposes in 1881. In 1926 the ecclesiastical parish of Diddlebury with Bouldon was formed, and from then until its closure in 1981, Bouldon chapel was served by the vicar of Diddlebury. It was a prefabricated structure of corrugated iron in the Gothic style with a small western bell-

Fig. 29 Lost chapel:
Bouldon, photographed shortly before its demolition in 1981

cote. This type of building was being manufactured in considerable numbers at the period, and many were designed for export to the colonies. Bouldon chapel was built by Croggon and Company in 1873, and was demolished shortly after 1981. A house now occupies the site.[150]

The Methodist Chapels

The three chapels which served the Methodists of Diddlebury were architecturally undistinguished, and in the case of the Primitive Methodist chapels at Peaton and the Golden Placket (just in Culmington parish), appear to have been influenced by the need for economy.

Both the Primitive chapels were of brick, with yellow brick detailing to quoins and window openings, with a much-altered manse adjoining that at Peaton. Both were entered from the gable end, with a central door between round-headed windows. Following closure the Peaton building was demolished to the height of the window sills, while the Golden Placket was converted into a dwelling.

The Wesleyan chapel at Bache Mill was a similar design to the other chapels, but somewhat wider, and without the use of yellow bricks. After closure in 1964 it ws also converted into a house.

3 Population and Society

Population

The extent to which the population of a parish has grown or declined over its history, and the reasons for these movements, are factors eagerly investigated by historians. The task is, however, complicated by the relative scarcity of information until the coming of the first national census in 1801 heralded the growth of a mass of officially-gathered data. For the medieval period, information is scanty and often provides little more than a basis for deduction. As the 16th and 17th centuries saw the development of more systematic keeping of parish registers, and taxation records become fuller and more frequent, it becomes more possible to make accurate estimates of population. Paradoxically, while the 20th century has carried the information gathering process to new heights, less information is available as most of the data is covered by limitations such as the 'hundred year rule' which limits access for a century after a document was produced. This makes it harder to be categorical about the most recent past than about the Victorian period. This section will first examine population trends over the period as far as is possible, to attempt to determine the population of the parish at certain specific times during its history. Certain specific features from the period after 1650 will then be examined in more detail.

Population trends: before 1550

The Domesday Survey of 1086 provides the basis for examining the population at the end of the 11th century. The purpose of the survey was a valuation of land for tax purposes, which *inter alia* provided information about the size of the workforce. For the eight manors which subsequently made up the parish of Diddlebury a total of 68 households were listed, which would suggest, on the basis of an average household size of between four and five people, a population in the region of 300. The largest concentration was, not surprisingly, in the manor of Corfham, which included Diddlebury, and, it may be presumed, Earnstrey, in its figures. The workforce here comprised no fewer than 10 ploughmen, three villagers and three smallholders, with the addition of a further two villagers and two serfs on land which was held by a man-at-arms as sub-tenant of Earl Roger, the tenant in chief. This would suggest a population of between 80 and 100, using the average household size of four or five members. By contrast, Little Sutton, the smallest settlement, had only half a hide of taxable land (60 acres) containing only two ploughmen and a smallholder, comprising a population of a dozen or so people.[1]

Domesday gives a useful snapshot of the community at a particular date for which few other records are available. The subsequent position is even less clear. It is generally accepted that the population of England as a whole expanded rapidly in the period between 1150 and 1300, possibly to three times that of Domesday,[2] and it may be reasonable to assume that the Corvedale as a whole, and the parish of Diddlebury which had taken shape by this time, shared in the process. It may equally be asserted, and supported with a certain amount of evidence, that the area subsequently experienced the decline in population associated with climatic change, epidemic diseases and other factors which afflicted the country from the middle of the 14th century.

There is good evidence to support these assertions. The manor of Westhope contained ten households in 1086. By 1267 there were 14 tenants,[3] and a survey carried out in 1301 lists no fewer than 34, of whom all but one were bondsmen, or unfree tenants.[4] This suggests that a considerable expansion of population had taken place, and the persistence of bondage may be accounted for by the remoteness of the manor, both physically and as an outpost of the FitzAlan lands, which in south Shropshire were centred upon Clun.

This growth in population may also be seen in Little Sutton, the smallest of the Domesday manors (with the exception of the tiny detached estate at Upper Poston). From the three households noted in 1086, the population and the amount under cultivation grew steadily until by 1250 its 180 acres (1½ hides) of land was divided among 16 tenants, whose names and holdings are listed in detail in the *Book of Fees* and the *Hundred Rolls*.[5]

It is fortuitous that these detailed examples come from two contrasting areas of the parish — the relatively remote and poor uplands, and the fertile valley floor. As the same trend can be seen in both manors, it is reasonable to conclude that it was broadly reflected across the parish. The Lay Subsidy Roll of 1327 lists six taxpayers for Westhope, of whom two are recognisable from the FitzAlan survey of 1301, which has been discussed earlier (see pp.19-20).[6] If we assume that the number of households had not changed much from the 1301 total of 33, the six taxpayers of 1327 may therefore represent about 15 to 20% of the actual number of households in the manor, which suggests that Westhope had a population of more than 100 in the early 14th century. The 1327 Lay Subsidy Roll is of considerable assistance in calculating the population of the parish on the eve of the Black Death, but suffers from limitations, the chief of which is the omission of the townships of Great and Little Sutton, Lawton and Middlehope. This may represent inefficiency on the part of the collectors. The 1327 assessment does, however, include Marston, which was left out of the 1334 assessment. Although the latter includes Lawton, Middlehope and Little (but not Great) Sutton, its utility is greatly reduced as it does not list persons, and groups settlements together for collective assessment.[7]

One point which clearly emerges from the 1327 Lay Subsidy is that Diddlebury had overtaken Corfham as the principal settlement, with 18 taxpayers listed compared with eight for Corfham. Similarly the valuation of Diddlebury was 34s. 4d., while that of Corfham was 18s., of which 5s. 3d. was the assessment of John LeStrange, lord of the castle. Of the other townships listed, Corfton had nine taxpayers and Mershton seven. If the situation which has been suggested for Westhope is typical, and taxpayers represent some 20% of the total number of households, then possible totals of 90 households for Diddlebury, 45 at Corfton and 35 at Mershton are suggested. If this is correct, it would seem that in the early 14th century the population of the parish may well have equalled or even exceeded the later peak of 987 reached in 1821.

Evidence for the subsequent decline is even more fragmentary and circumstantial. Diddlebury, like most parishes in the Corvedale and Brown Clee areas, can provide instances of settlements which have shrunken or even completely disappeared. The most striking example is Marston, which disappeared so completely, that even its location is not conclusively known.[8] Lawton has shrunk to a farmhouse and cottage surrounded by house platforms and other physical evidence of desertion. Corfham and its castle have completely disappeared save for earthworks, and other settlements such as Middlehope and Great Sutton contain house platforms as evidence of much larger settlements in the past.

Traditionally the desertion of settlements has been associated with the Black Death of 1348 and the subsequent recurrent epidemics of plague in 1361, 1370 and 1375. The effect of these epidemics, and particularly of the first outbreak, was undoubtedly catastrophic, but was also notoriously poorly documented. The only Diddlebury reference so far located is contained in the Inquisition *post mortem* on John LeStrange, Lord of Corfham, taken in August 1350. LeStrange held lands in Gloucestershire, Hampshire and Wiltshire as well as in Shropshire, where his principal seat was at Blakemere near Whitchurch. It is noted that in one of the Wiltshire manors all but one of the tenants was dead, and that the value of the manor of Whitchurch had been much reduced by 'the late pestilence', and that 'La Yeye by Corfham' (Earnstrey Park) contained a ruinous house, and was reduced in value from 30s. to 10s. 'with the present pestilence'.[9] The fact that Fulk LeStrange, John's son and heir, died six weeks after his father on 6 September 1350, suggests that both may have succumbed to the disease.[10]

While it may be assumed that the plague caused considerable devastation in other parts of the parish, it would be unwise to attribute the desertion of settlements to this factor alone. The neighbouring parish of Cold Weston contains classic features of desertion, with an isolated church surrounded by the earthworks of the abandoned village, but it was already described as a 'waste place' in 1340, before the onset of the plague.[11] Similarly the decline of Corfham may well date back to the later 13th century. In the Inquisition *post mortem* of John Giffard (1299) the castle and its buildings are described as being valueless and requiring 40 shillings annually for upkeep.[12] This suggests that the castle had been run down by the Giffards, and that its poor state mentioned in the LeStrange inquisitions of 1350 had nothing to do with the plague. This contention is also supported by the eclipse of Corfham by Diddlebury noted above.

There is also evidence to suggest that a reasonable number of people survived the epidemic of 1348 and contributed to the subsequent recovery of the population. A number of inquisitions to establish proof of age have survived from the later years of Edward III's reign, namely for Hugh Tyrel (1364), Katherine Child (1372) and John Baskerville (1372).[13] In each of these inquiries, which were necessary to prove when a young person had come of age in the period before the introduction of parish registers, statements were taken from older inhabitants concerning the date of baptism of the subject of the inquisition. The age distribution shown in Table 1 reveals the identity of 34, all of whom would have been adults when the plague struck. It may be assumed that these witnesses represent a small percentage of those who survived the catastrophe in the parish.

	Hugh Tyrrel	Katherine Child	John Baskerville
60+	3	1	1
50+	4	5	5
40+	5	4	6

Table 1 Ages of Witnesses at three Proof of Age Inquisitions

Evidence for population trends in the parish between the mid-14th century and the commencement of registers in 1583 is very sparse. However, a study of probate grants in the Court Books of the Episcopal Consistory of Hereford between 1442 and 1551 has produced evidence for years of high and low mortality during that period.[14] The figures for the parish of Diddlebury mirror the general trend noted in the article with remarkable consistency. Indeed in 1459-50, the year in which the highest number of probates in the period was granted (560), no less than 11 came from Diddlebury, the eighth highest figure in the diocese. Other years of above-average mortality in Diddlebury were 1453-4; 1529; and 1537-8, all of which were years in which the number of deaths in the diocese was higher than usual.[15] In 1454 and 1479 outbreaks of plague were noted in other parts of the county, with that of 1479 being the most severe and widespread. The high mortality of 1529 and 1537-8 may have been due to the sweating sickness, an infection which has not been conclusively identified, but which may have been a form of influenza.

Population trends 1550 – 1800

Although the amount of data which can be used in studying the population of Diddlebury increases rapidly during this period, it is nevertheless impossible to make an exact calculation of the number of inhabitants of the parish prior to the introduction of the census in 1801. Although the keeping of parish registers became compulsory in 1538, Diddlebury has been less fortunate than its neighbour, Munslow, which possesses a complete set from that date. The surviving Diddlebury registers begin only in 1583, and end in 1599. The series does not begin again until 1683, although the Bishop's Transcripts may be used to supplement the missing material from 1661. The record of tithes and Easter offerings kept by the vicar, Nicholas Proude, between 1657 and 1662 does, however provide a major source for the middle of the 17th century, and makes a convenient starting point from which to attempt to assess the size of the population at this time. The period from 1662 to 1672 is also well endowed with tax assessments, which can be used in conjunction with the parish records. Of particular use are the Hearth Tax returns of 1662 and 1672.[16]

Township	Proude 1661	H.T. 1662.	H.T. 1672
Diddlebury	12	23	21
Corfton	19	22	22*
Lawton	6	3	
Lt. Sutton	4	6	
Gt. Sutton	11	12	10
Middlehope	11	11	9
Westhope	13	17	15
Peaton & Broncroft	15	23	22
Ernestrey Park	1		
Sparchford	4		
Total	96	117	99

* the 1672 assessment includes Lawton and Little Sutton with Corfton

Table 2 Household numbers 1661-1672

Table 2 makes a comparison of Proude's book with the two Hearth Tax assessments. Although there is little more than a few months difference between the first two sources, it is noticeable that Proude includes far fewer households than the Hearth Tax. This may well be due to the fact that Proude was recording households which had paid their tithes, and it is clear that a considerable number were always behind with their payments. Proude also includes eight households who do not feature in the Hearth Tax assessment for 1662. Some of these may well have been exempted from Hearth Tax due to poverty, but this cannot have been the case with Edward Stedman and Widow Turner at Lawton, both of whom kept two servants.

The particular value of Proude's book is that it is possible to calculate the number of adults in each household from the amount of Easter dues paid. Communicants over the age of 16 were bound to pay an Easter Offering of two pence, and as offerings are usually recorded separately, it is usually possible to discover the number of adults in a household. The liability to pay tithes on servants, generally four pence for a female and six pence for a man, enables the number of servants to be estimated.[17] Despite the closeness in time between Proude's book and the 1662 Hearth Tax, only in the case of one community, Middlehope, is there complete agreement of both totals and names. This is fortunate, as it is possible with reasonable certainty to place six of these households into properties which still survive today. The largest number of adults (eight — which included no servants) was contained in the household of George Child (Hall Farm), while there was only one single adult household, that of Anne Butcher, widow. The total of adults in the township was 38, of whom only one was a servant. This is strange, as servants would have been expected in the household of the recently widowed John Baldwyn (Upper House) rather than that of Thomas Fernalls, a carpenter.

The evidence of Proude's book for Middlehope gives a total adult population of 38, or 3.4 per household. If this is extended to the whole parish as listed for the Hearth Tax, this would suggest an adult population of 398 for the parish in 1662. At first glance, the difference in household numbers between the two Hearth Tax assessments would suggest a decline in population, whereas in fact it shows that people were becoming more skilled in securing exemptions on the grounds of poverty. Certificates of exemption survive for 1670, 1671 and 1674, and list between 43 and 47 households, making a total of some 145 for the parish. At 3.4 adults per household, this would indicate an adult population of 493 in 1672. It is possible to calculate the total population, including children, by taking an average household size of 4.3, as taken by Gwyneth Nair in Highley for the same period.[18] This would give a total of 623 people in 1672.[19]

The next concrete evidence for population comes from the end of the 18th century, when that compulsive accumulator of data, Archdeacon Plymley, included in his 1793 visitation notes a detailed breakdown of the population of the parish by township and occupation. The source of Plymley's figures is not known, but appears to be accurate. He gives the total population of the parish as

749, contained in 138 families, which he calculates at an average size of 5.3 per household.[20] This raises some interesting questions. If Nair's figure of 4.3 per family was correct for 1672, then a modest increase in population had taken place in the ensuing 120 years. If, however, Plymley's figure of 5.3, which appears to have been based on accurate figures, is correct for 1672 (which is not unlikely), then there had been a very slight decline over the period, from a possible 768 at the earlier date. This would be consistent with the slight fall in the number of households from 145 to 138.

The picture is further complicated when the numbers of baptisms and burials during the period, for in every decade between 1661 and 1800, the former exceed the latter. Table 3 reveals that whilst in a number of decades the gap is quite narrow (1691-1700; 1711-1720; 1721-1730), the general trend is one of steady, and in some decades (e.g. the 1770s), substantial, growth. This would suggest that the parish should have had a much larger population at the end of the 18th century than that quoted by Plymley, so that other factors must clearly be taken into account. The most obvious of these must be migration of population, for which there is abundant evidence in the following century.

	1661-70	1671-80	1681-90	1691-00	1701-10	1711-20	1721-30
Baptisms	169	178	213	198	192	173	171
Burials	122	112	151	180	132	164	158

	1731-40	1741-50	1751-60	1761-70	1771-80	1781-90	1791-00
Baptisms	211	205	199	181	222	230	212
Burials	105	145	129	143	111	142	153

Table 3 Baptisms and Burials, total by decade 1661 – 1800

An examination of a sample of 18th-century marriages demonstrates that outward migration was indeed a factor of importance during the period. Marriages performed in the last year of each decade from 1701 to 1800 have been examined and, where possible, the subsequent careers of the couples have been followed. The sample consists of a total of 44 marriages, in all but six of which both partners were resident in the parish at the time of their wedding. Of these, no less than 25 couples made no further appearance in the registers, including, unsurprisingly, five of the six couples where the husband came from another parish. Of the 19 couples who feature in later entries in the registers, five appear to have left the parish after the birth of their first child, and a further couple left after the birth of the second. Eleven couples remained in the parish to raise apparently complete families, while another two had children baptised at a long interval after their marriage, suggesting that they had moved away but subsequently returned. If these samples are typical, it would suggest that only a quarter of couples who married in Diddlebury in the 18th century remained in the parish for all, or a substantial part of their married lives. This would correspond with the much more fully documented trend in the following century, which will be discussed in more detail below.

Population trends 1801 – 2001

Knowledge of population trends during this period is greatly enhanced by the availability of census data, although enumerators' returns are available only for the period 1841-1901.[21] Table 4 shows the totals for each of the censuses during the period, which shows the population reaching a peak in 1821, and thereafter declining steadily to reach a low of 526 in 1981, which may represent the lowest level of population for four centuries. It is interesting to compare these figures with those for baptisms for the period from 1801 to 1900, which are shown in Table 5. During this period there was an increasing trend for inhabitants of the western side of the parish, including Sparchford, Seifton Batch and parts of Westhope to use Culmington church, and entries for Diddlebury parishioners baptised there are included, as are Methodist baptisms conducted at Peaton Strand from 1861.[22] These statistics are somewhat puzzling, as the decades of high baptisms such as 1831-1840 and 1881-1890 are not paralleled by an increased population in the censuses of 1841 and 1891, though in the latter case there is an increase of eight over the preceding decade. The picture becomes even more confusing when burial statistics are examined for the same period. These show a remarkably steady death rate until 1871, though with the first decade of the century having a lower level of mortality than average, and the period 1831-1840 being much higher. The plummeting death rate after 1870 is most striking, and with the above average births and reduced mortality, the decade from 1881-1890 would be expected to be one of rapid population growth. That it was not must be explained in terms of emigration from the parish, a factor which is discussed in some detail below.

Twentieth-century developments show a pattern of gradual decline, with a temporary recovery in the decades 1911-1931, which is rather unexpected in view of the heavy losses suffered in the First World War, totalling 35 deaths from the parish. Baptismal records need to be treated with some caution after 1960, when the social conventions requiring children to be baptised were breaking down. Nevertheless, the sudden decline in the number of baptisms after 1960 also reflects clearly social changes which were taking place at the time. Not only were parents having fewer children, the lack of employment in the area was forcing a far greater number of young people to move further afield in search of work. During the same period, South Shropshire has become increasingly attractive to people who wish to escape from the urban areas, with the result that parishes like Diddlebury now contain significant numbers of households which consist of retired people, or those who live in the parish and commute to the towns of the West Midlands.

1801	1811	1821	1831	1841	1851	1861	1871	1881	1891
837	817	987	920	896	878	829	824	763	777

1901	1911	1921	1931	1951	1961	1971	1981	1991	2001
709	690	727	704	670	646	580	526	585	636

Table 4 Total Population from Census returns 1801 – 2001

Decade	1801-1810	1811-1820	1821-1830	1831-1840	1841-1850
Diddlebury	154	193	273	296	164
Culmington	7	23	18	18	21
Total	161	216	291	314	185

Decade	1851-1860	1861-1870	1871-1880	1881-1890	1891-1900
Diddlebury	230	201	197	248	168
Culmington	19	14	26	24	12
Methodist		7	32	24	14
Total	249	222	255	296	194

Table 5 Baptisms 1801 – 1980

Decade	1801-1810	1811-1820	1821-1830	1831-1840	1841-1850
Diddlebury	123	157	161	206	162
Culmington	4	18	19	28	25
Total	127	175	180	234	187

Decade	1851-1860	1861-1870	1871-1880	1881-1890	1891-1900
Diddlebury	168	158	101	88	89
Culmington	15	16	11	9	5
Total	183	174	112	97	94

Table 6 Burials 1801 – 1900

1900-10	1911-20	1921-30	1931-40	1941-50	1951-60	1961-70	1971-80
157	91	101	86	83	107	38	37

Table 7 Baptisms at Diddlebury 1901 – 1980

A breakdown of the 1991 census statistics compiled by Shropshire County Council shows how the profile of the parish had changed. While the population had fallen to 585, there were no fewer than 216 households, compared with 1831 when there had been 159 households and a population of 920.[23] The average household size in 1991 was 2.7, but this conceals the fact that over 43% of households were below this average. Only 73 of the 216 households contained children. By 2001 the number of households had increased to 238, while to population had risen to 636, reflecting new house building, and particularly the conversion of redundant farm buildings in the previous decade.[24] The average household size remained unchanged at just under 2.7. Thus Diddlebury is once more typical of many parishes at the beginning of the 21st century, with fewer people living in a growing number of houses, and an increasingly ageing population (21% aged over 60 in 1991). For the historian, this represents another in a long series of changes which have occurred in the development of the community. For the planners, and those who have to manage the effects of such processes on such matters as the provision of public services, the matter is of much more than academic interest.

Some factors in Population trends

Nineteenth-century Emigration from the Parish

In March 1899 Rowland Jones, headmaster of Diddlebury School made his annual lament in his log book about the annual exodus of labourers' children from the school at Lady Day.[25] His complaint of a migratory population was justified, for an examination of the school's admissions register reveals that few children completed their time there, mostly staying for no more than a maximum of three or four years, and in many cases little more than a few months.[26]

It is possible to gain information about the movement of farm workers by comparing the 1871 census return with the computerised index to that of 1881. In 1871, 133 agricultural workers were listed as Diddlebury residents. Of these, 44 had been born in the parish, 25 came from the adjacent parishes of Munslow, Culmington and Stanton Lacy, with a further 44 originating in other parts of Shropshire. A mere 20 or 15% came from other parts of the United Kingdom. Of these 133 agricultural workers, 84 have been traced in the 1881 census, of whom 44 were still living in Diddlebury. This represents just over 33% of the 1871 total, and contrasts with the position noted in the Warwickshire parish of Wellesbourne, where 59% of labourers (of a total of 143) were residing in the parish for at least ten years after 1871.[27] Of the 44 labourers who were living in Diddlebury at the time of both censuses, only 14 had been born in the parish, of whom six were also later buried there. The remainder came from the rest of Shropshire, with the exception of a Welsh shepherd and two men from the eastern counties.

The proportion who cannot be traced is quite high at 37%, compared with 11% at Wellesbourne. Six of the 49 were probably dead by 1881, having been aged over 70 ten years previously, and many were young unmarried men living in the house of their employer as farm servants. The striking feature about those whose movements have been traced is that 38 of the 43 had moved to another job within the county. Three of the others had moved to Herefordshire, one to Birmingham, and the last, an Irishman, had joined a group of his compatriots on a farm in Cheshire.

This would suggest that movement took place within a fairly restricted area, and this is confirmed when the places of residence of those who claimed in 1881 to have been born in Diddlebury are examined.[28] These make it clear that migration was very localised. Herefordshire, particularly the area between Ludlow and Leominster, proved the most popular destination for those who left the county, followed by Worcestershire and Warwickshire, with Birmingham not surprisingly dominating the latter county. This localised emigration is clearly shown from Table 8. It is strange that there was such a reluctance to move to Wales. Not one Diddlebury person appears in the returns for the adjacent county of Denbigh, and it is clear that the coalfields of South Wales held no attraction. Those few who ventured into Wales strayed only a few miles over the border, generally into the border towns of Brecon and Radnor, but this is hardly surprising as, outside the coalfields, Wales was generally poorer than Shropshire. Cultural and linguistic factors may also have deterred potential migrants.

Herefordshire	36
Worcestershire	11
Warwickshire	17
Wales and Monmouthshire	9
Greater London W.	10
Greater London E.	5
East Anglia	6
South West	Nil

Table 8 Places of residence of persons noted in 1881 census as born in Diddlebury

It is clear that those who moved into Herefordshire were not primarily labourers. Eight were women who had joined their husbands, while six were children who had been born in Diddlebury, but were essentially transients. Of the remainder, labourers (7) were slightly outnumbered by servants of both sexes (8), while there were two boarding house keepers, two governesses, a farmer and a solicitor. It is clear that labourers tended to move within Shropshire, and often only to parishes neighbouring Diddlebury. An examination of the index of Shropshire residents in 1881 who claimed to have been born in Diddlebury, shows that out of 415 individuals who have been identified, 105 described themselves as labourers, though this total includes general labourers, though not those specifically described as labourers on the roads or railways. Another 94 followed other occupations, which included 11 farmers and 33 servants,[29] while 216, of whom the overwhelming majority were wives and children, had no occupation. A large number of these households were headed by an agricultural labourer.

Of the 84 farm workers listed as resident in the parish in 1881, but who had not been born there, 61 were Shropshire born, almost entirely from parishes within a ten mile radius of Diddlebury. The largest group of the remaining 23 came from neighbouring Radnorshire.

From this examination of the 1881 census, it is obvious that the labouring population was very mobile, but within a fairly confined area. The extent to which the population as a whole was mobile is underlined by the fact that in 1881 only 34% (262) of the population of Diddlebury claimed to have been born there.[30] This shows a significant change since 1851, when 47% (412) had been born in the parish. An examination of the composition of the individual townships, as shown in Table 9 is instructive. This shows variations within the parish between townships in both the number of natives and incomers, but also graphically illustrates the growth in the population of Diddlebury and Bache Mill, the relative stability of Westhope, and the significant decline in the populations of Corfton, and particularly Sutton, in the 30 year period. The 1881 census records 18 unoccupied houses, though this does not always signify depopulation. The largest number (seven) was located in Peaton and Broncroft, where the fall in population was much less than in Sutton, where there were only four unoccupied dwellings, one of which had recently collapsed.[31]

1851	Born Diddlebury	Born Elsewhere	**1881**	Born Diddlebury	Born Elsewhere
Diddlebury	73	56		42	102
Middlehope	30	40		29	33
Peaton/Broncroft	59	81		39	90
Sutton/Lawton	60	83		47	53
Corfton	138	116		65	132
Westhope	33	55		28	55
Earnstrey/Poston	19	35		12	33

Table 9 Comparison of residents born in Diddlebury 1851 and 1881

Infant and child mortality

One factor which seems to have had a limited effect upon population trends is the number of deaths of infants and children. After 1717 the burial of infants was specifically noted in the registers, and from 1812 the ages of all deaths were recorded as a matter of course. From this it is clear that, as might be expected, deaths of those aged under 15 formed a considerable proportion of the total mortality of the parish during the 18th and 19th centuries. In only three decades between 1721 and 1870 did fewer than one in ten of those baptised die before the end of their first year.

Decade	Total infant deaths	Total Juvenile deaths	Infant deaths as % of baptisms	% of burials
1721-30	11		6	7
1731-40	41		19	39
1741-50	34		34	23
1751-60	32		32	25
1761-70	42		23	29
1771-80	20		9	18
1781-90	37		16	26
1791-1800	21		10	14
1800-10	14		9	11
1811-20	27	8	14	17
1821-30	31	18	11	19
1831-40	35	41	17	19
1841-50	34	23	15	21
1851-60	32	18	14	19
1861-70	34	15	17	21
1871-80	20	9	10	20
1881-90	15	16	6	17
1890-1900	15	6	9	17

Table 10 Infant and child deaths 1721 – 1900

It is also significant that whereas individual decades between 1721 and 1810 experienced marked fluctuations in the number of infant and child deaths, between 1811 and 1870 the number was remarkably consistent, as was the percentage of juvenile to total burials. The dramatic decline in infant deaths after 1870 is part of a general decline in the number of burials of people of all ages, and also conforms to the national pattern.[32]

An interesting feature of these statistics is the remarkable increase in the number of deaths of young people. The table is to a certain extent misleading in that it includes all children between the ages of one and 15, so that, particularly towards the end of the period, many of those included were under-fives. Nevertheless, there is a noticeable rise in the number of juvenile deaths in the middle years of the 19th century. This feature was repeated in Highley, although in that parish the peak was reached two decades before Diddlebury.[33] While there were factors present in Highley, such as a dangerous river and growing industrialisation, which would account for many accidental deaths, and which were absent from Diddlebury, the resemblance in trends between he two parishes is striking.

Poverty was undoubtedly a factor behind mortality among both infants and older children. In general the children of the labouring class were undernourished and poorly clothed, and lived in overcrowded conditions in damp and poorly-ventilated cottages. It is hardly surprising that epidemic diseases spread rapidly through the community, particularly when large numbers were concentrated in a single classroom at school. Despite a huge take-up of vaccinations in Diddlebury, occasional outbreaks of smallpox took place.[34] One of the most devastating cases of epidemic disease occurred in 1884 in the Hince household at Fernalls Mill, where in a period of 16 months the father and five of his children died from a variety of complaints. Scarlet fever, tuberculosis, whooping cough and influenza were normal features of life, while occasional outbreaks of typhoid struck, as in 1891. Ironically, compulsory schooling may well have increased the spread of infection, and by 1896 the Medical Officer of Health had taken to closing the school for long periods in an attempt to stem this. The decline of child mortality may well have been due at least in part to increased intervention by the authorities.

While poverty was an obvious factor in juvenile mortality, infant mortality was no respecter of persons. Some quite wealthy families, such as the Dawes of Elsich, lost three of their 10 children in infancy between 1764 and 1784. Morgan Jones of Delbury Farm, the second largest holding in the parish, lost two of his 14 children at the age of six, and a further two in early adulthood. By contrast, many poor couples seem to have raised large families without apparent loss. John and Sarah Beddoes of Corfton Bache, who clearly lived on the bread line, successfully raised seven children between 1829 and 1847 without any deaths.[35]

Longevity and Life Expectancy

If infant and child mortality had an effect upon population, so also did the number of people who survived to old age, though again, the picture is complicated. What is clear from Table 11 is that while the proportion of people who reached the age of 75 fluctuated somewhat from decade to decade, the position at the end of the century did not differ greatly from that in 1830. What is striking is the decline in the number of deaths in the 16-35 age group after 1850, and the similar if slightly less pronounced trend among the 36-55 group two decades later. By the end of the century the largest number of deaths was occurring in the 56-74 age range, suggesting that on the whole the population was living longer than had been the case a century earlier.

Age at death	1821-1830	1831-1840	1841-1850	1851-1860	1861-1870	1871-1880	1881-1890	1891-1900
16-35	25	25	29	15	11	15	18	17
36-55	15	21	24	10	24	20	18	13
56-74	30	25	25	36	25	34	43	41
75 +	34	28	22	38	41	30	19	28

Table 11 Ages at death by decade, 1821 – 1900 as percentages

Illegitimacy

The incidence of illegitimate births in the two centuries after 1700 conforms very largely to trends which have been noted in studies both in Shropshire and elsewhere in England.[36] During the first half of the 18th century there were few such births, with all but one decade failing to reach double figures. Thereafter there is a steady climb in numbers, which reaches a peak of 35 out of a total of 212 baptisms in the final decade of the century, a total of 16½%. A fall in the first decade of the 19th century was followed by a rapid rise in succeeding decades, peaking at 16.8% in 1841-1850. A moderate decline to 1880 was followed by a return to single figures for the last two decades of the century. This decline continued into the 20th century, when the concept of illegitimacy became increasingly irrelevant as the millennium moved towards its close.

It would be tempting to relate these figures to such factors as the absence of a resident vicar for much of the period from 1750 to 1850, but this would not explain the fact that the trend may be found in many other parishes. It is significant that Diddlebury to an extent conforms to the national pattern in other respects. There is a definite correlation between the rate of illegitimate births and the general trend in the population, but whereas the percentage of the former peaks in 1850, and is still 12¼% in 1880, the population of the parish reached its peak of 987 in 1821, and thereafter began a steady decline. On the evidence of other places more of a correlation could have been expected between these two trends. The link between years of high fertility and high rates of bastardy, and vice versa would also appear to be true in general, but with so many exceptions in both the 18th and 19th centuries its value is questionable.

The tendency for illegitimacy to run in families has been noted in other parishes, and Diddlebury was no exception in this respect.[37] There are many examples, of which the Dodson and Challenger families are fairly typical. Mary Dodson and Margaret Challenger were both mothers of several illegitimate children, and neither married. Thomas, the youngest of the three Challenger children, and a labourer by trade, who had been born in 1795, married Anne, Mary Dodson's elder child, in 1820. Five years previously Anne had produced an illegitimate daughter, Margaret, who would appear to have been absorbed into the Challenger family, which ultimately consisted of three sons and two daughters. One of the latter gave birth to her own illegitimate daughter in 1845. Similarly John Challenger, the elder brother of Thomas, and a stonemason, had married Anne Morgan who had no offspring prior to the marriage. Of the three daughters of this union, two produced illegitimate sons.

While the majority of mothers of illegitimate children baptised during a sample period from 1800 to 1830 were singletons (i.e. having only one such child), there were a number for whom the experience was repeated. The most striking of these repeaters were Martha Weale of Bach Mill and Mary Downes, who each

Fig. 30 The tomb of Charles Powell (1868) in the churchyard. The illegitimate son of the Revd. John Powell of Sutton Court, he inherited his father's estate in 1806

produced no fewer than four bastards. Martha's last child was fathered by William Beddoes of Sparchford, who had intended to provide for her by the bequest of a £20 annuity. Unfortunately he thought better of it, and reversed the bequest in a codicil to his will.[38] Other victims of a rich man's passion occasionally fared better. The Rev. John Powell of Sutton Court found a husband for his housekeeper by whom he had a son, and bequeathed her a house and a £30 annuity when he died in 1806.[39] It is interesting to note that the three illegitimate sons of gentry in the parish at this time, James Beddoes, Charles Powell and Thomas Lloyd Roberts all inherited their fathers' lands and were apparently fully accepted in society.

It is probable that some of the repeaters were promiscuous rather than unfortunate, but it would seem that in most cases, whether singletons or repeaters, the mothers were not only abandoned by the father of their child, but found it difficult to find a husband who was willing to take on another man's offspring. Of the 42 singletons examined in the 30-year sample period only nine are recorded as marrying within the parish. While it was normal for the unmarried mother and her child to live with her parents during the years of infancy, most seem subsequently to have left the parish never to reappear. Occasionally the child remained, like the grandson of John Challenger, who is recorded as living with his widowed grandfather in the 1861 census. If there was no support from the mother's family, most had to fall back on the parish. The numbers of illegitimate children being supported in this way were often high. In a sample month of February 1832, no fewer than 17 mothers and 21 children were receiving allowances of between 4 and 12 shillings.[40] The parish attempted, with a reasonable degree of success, to obtain recompense for this expense from the fathers, extracting either a weekly contribution of 1s 6d per child, or a once-for-all payment of £10 or £20.[41] After 1836 abandoned mothers with no means of support were forced to enter the Union workhouse in Ludlow. Throughout the 1850s the names of Sarah Haycox, Anne Farmer and Eliza Childe, and their miserable and increasing following of children may be seen in the workhouse registers, discharging themselves for a few weeks, and then seeking re-admittance when unable to support themselves in the outside world.[42]

From the analysis of the 1881 census it has been possible to trace the subsequent fate of 22 individuals who can be traced back to the parish registers as bastards. While most were employed in various labouring jobs, it is heartening to note that a number had made their way in the world despite their origins. Apart from James Beddoes, the most successful of the sample was James Bint, who at the age of 87 was living as an annuitant on his son's 265 acre farm at Chelmarsh. Two became publicans, Alfred Downes being the licensee of the Cottage Crown Inn at Cressage, while Mary Hince (née Leighton) had married a local butcher in 1832, and as his widow was running the Swan at Aston Munslow in 1881. James Downes was butler to Henry Cavendish Cavendish, D.L., J.P. at Claverley, the most exalted of those who had entered service. Two married women in addition to Mrs. Hince appear in the sample. There are undoubtedly others in the census, but it is generally impossible to identify them under their maiden names, unless they were married at Diddlebury. Only one of the sample appears to have fallen upon really hard times, namely John Pritchard, an unemployed farm worker who was an inmate of the Stretton Union Workhouse.

Diddlebury Society

There are a number of problems inherent in any attempt to analyse the nature of society in the parish, the most obvious of which is the availability of evidence. As noted elsewhere, while the landholding classes are relatively well documented from a comparatively early period, our knowledge of the poor is scanty until the authorities, for whatever reason, began to take an interest in their condition. In addition changes took place throughout the period which make the application of terms such as gentleman or yeoman difficult. While it is relatively easy (and accurate) to describe the Baldwyn family in the 16th and 17th centuries as gentry, they are in many ways very different from landowners at both an earlier and a later period. Recognising these difficulties, a fairly arbitrary classification of social groups has been made. These have been termed for convenience the higher classes; the middling sort; and the poorer classes.

The Higher Classes

As has been mentioned earlier, for most of the medieval period, and much later, much of Diddlebury was held by absentee aristocratic landlords, who rarely if ever spent time in their estates in the parish, which formed a comparatively insignificant part of their holdings. There is evidence that some of the larger landowners, such as the Tyrells of Broncroft, resided for at least some of their time in Diddlebury, as the birth of an heir to the estates, John Tyrell, at Broncroft is attested in a proof of age in 1364, and a similar document of 1372 records similar information relating to the Baskervilles of Lawton.[43] Corfham castle was used as a dower house for widows such as Mary LeStrange, whose devotional excesses have already been noted,[44] who lived for most of her 35 year widowhood there, and Ankaret, widow of Sir Richard Talbot, who also held the castle and manor for her life.[45]

In some parts of the parish there soon developed a lower rank of landholders, sub-tenants of the main landholder or tenant in chief, many of whom resided on their estates. An example were the family of Middlehope, who appear in the records at the start of the 13th century, and to whom frequent references were made throughout that century.[46] The Middlehopes clearly took an active part in the life of the community, with members of the family serving as jurors of the various assizes, and in positions such as coroner, verderer of the forest, and under-bailiff of the Munslow Hundred, in which office Thomas Middlehope was accused of corrupt practices in 1274.[47] The Sutton family of Little Sutton appear to have been a family of similar status, although, unlike the Middlehopes, the Suttons rapidly sub-divided their lands among under-tenants. Elias Sutton appears to have been employed in a judicial capacity by the king in the 1280s, where he was given a Commission of Oyer and Terminer in various cases including an assault on the archdeacon of Newcastle in 1284.[48]

It is clear that in addition to those families which had held land for several generations, such as the Middlehopes and Suttons, there were others who were rising through from ranks to establish what would later be known as some of the leading families of local gentry. There were two main methods of gaining upward mobility: by accumulation of land and wealth, and by service. Those who managed to combine the two were almost guaranteed success, and the family of Baldwyn provide a good illustration of the process of steady upward mobility.

The origins of the Baldwyn family are somewhat obscure prior to their appearance in Diddlebury, when John Baldwyn married Anne, the daughter and heiress of Richard l'Enfant, one of the more prosperous members of the parish community. During the 14th and 15th centuries they consolidated their position by further marriages to heiresses of a number of landowners in the area.[49] By the mid-15th century the family had established another branch in Munslow, where the family had acquired freehold estates. By 1497 John Baldwyn was in service as a Yeoman of the Crown and his inquisition *post mortem* in 1544 shows that by that time the family was in full possession of the Diddlebury estate. His son, William, followed him into the royal service as Cup Bearer to Mary I. The last member of the family to be involved in affairs of national importance was Thomas (1546-1614) who was agent to the Earl of Shrewsbury, and with him involved with the care of Mary, Queen of Scots. Perhaps as a consequence of this that Thomas Baldwyn spent a period of confinement in the Tower of London, where he left a graffito inscription in 1585.[50] By this time the Baldwyns had become established as the leading family in the parish, and had begun to establish satellite branches, most notably at Elsich.

The rise of the Baldwyn family has been dealt with in some detail as they are a classic example of continued upward mobility over several generations. The family of Burley of Broncroft owed their initial rise to royal service in the time of Edward III. By 1399 John Burley was in possession of Broncroft, and was employed as an official of the earl of Arundel on whose behalf he frequently presided alone over the Shropshire sessions of the peace.[51] He was Sheriff of Shropshire in 1409, and knight of the shire (M.P) in 1401 and 1412.[52] His son, Sir William, who also served as Sheriff in 1426 and represented the county in several Parliaments, was a barrister like his father, and served John Talbot, first earl of Shrewsbury as attorney and councilor, and also seneschal* of his main Shropshire estate at Blakemere.[53] He has been described as the 'most influential member of the Shropshire gentry, not only as a magistrate but also in many other capacities'.[54] His daughter and co-heiress married one of the greatest legal minds of the times, Sir Thomas Lyttleton, whom she survived by almost a quarter of a century, dying in 1505.[55]

By the 16th century it is possible to gain a much clearer picture of the distribution of wealth in the parish by use of the records of the Lay Subsidy for 1524-7.[56] This reveals that only four persons were charged tax on lands, the wealthiest of whom was John Lutley of Broncroft and Lawton, who was assessed at £8. John Baldwyn followed at £3, with two others, John Normecott and William Mason both being rated at 20 shillings. These entries represent the larger freeholders of the parish, suggesting that Lutley possessed estates worth £160 per year, and that those of Baldwyn were worth £60. In addition to those who paid tax on their lands, the lists of those assessed on 'goods' shows clearly the wealthier members of the community. These were headed by Richard Lewis of Westhope, whose goods were assessed at £12. It is significant that all but one of the rest of those whose goods were assessed at £5 or more came from the townships of Great and Little Sutton.[57] It is unlikely that any of these could have been considered gentry at this time, despite their undoubted wealth, and they will be discussed in more detail below.

The middle years of the 16th century saw an expansion in the number of those in the parish who could legitimately be regarded as members of the 'gentry'. In no case was this directly attributable to the redistribution of church land, though the large estate of Sutton and Whichcott was acquired in 1532 by Charles

Foxe, who later gained the lands of the dissolved priory of Bromfield. The most significant cause was the gradual process by which the earls of Shrewsbury sold off their holdings in the parish, which has already been noted (see p.9).

It is clear that by the end of the 16th century there existed in Diddlebury a small group of families who had precedence in the community. Baldwyn, Briggs, Lutley and Foxe were all prominent in the government of the county during the period, and the century which followed. The Smiths of Aston would also have been qualified for these responsibilities, but presumably their dubious religious and political loyalty excluded them. These families formed the upper echelon of society, below whom there was another level consisting of those who were regarded or regarded themselves as gentry, but who participated in the work of the community at a parish level, particularly by serving as churchwardens.[58] These divisions were not completely exclusive. Two members of the Baldwyn family, for example, also served as churchwardens, John Baldwyn of Middlehope, (1666-70), who gave the third bell to the church, and Edward Baldwyn (1723 and 1725). Somewhat surprisingly, John Fleming of Westhope served as overseer of the poor in 1708, though he probably employed a substitute. On the whole, however, the upper gentry avoided parochial office. Although the elder sons of this group quite naturally tended to marry the daughters of families of equivalent standing, the daughters and younger sons quite regularly married into families from the lower ranks of the gentry, or even the upper yeomanry. For example, Thomas Baldwyn, born 1659 who was later Recorder of Shrewsbury, had married the daughter of Thomas Minton, a Diddlebury yeoman, and other examples are noted by Mrs. Martin.[59]

Fig. 31 Folliott Herbert Walker Cornewall (1754-1831), squire of Diddlebury, and successively bishop of Bristol, Hereford and Worcester. Portriat by William Owen, courtesy of the National Portrait Gallery

Changes in the ranks of the leading families of the parish were generally accomplished by purchase or marriage, although it was still possible to rise through the ranks. An interesting case of purchasing concerns the Dannett or Dannatt family of Westhope. These had originated in Westhope in the 15th century, but accumulated estates in Leicestershire and Essex. When Westhope was put on the market by the Crown in 1568 it was bought by Leonard Dannett, whose family held it until 1655. The most significant change brought about by purchase was the sale of the Diddlebury estate in 1752 by Edward Baldwyn to Frederick Cornewall, which ended a 400 years link between the Baldwyns and the parish. The Cornewalls were a branch of 'an ancient and renowned family'[60] with seats at Moccas, Burford and elsewhere, and Frederick Cornewall, the purchaser of Diddlebury, was married to a daughter of the Herberts of Oakley Park. His third son, Folliot Herbert Walker Cornewall, raised the Diddlebury family to its greatest heights by becoming successively bishop of Bristol, Hereford and Worcester.

There is one significant example of rising from the ranks of the yeomanry to the 'county' during the 18th century. The Powell family of Sutton appears to have been descended from a Meredith Powell of Lydbury North, whose descendant Rowland Powell married Susannah, the widow of Thomas Harris of Little Sutton. The Harris family appear to have been freeholders, yeomen rather than gentry, and the Powells would seem to have augmented their property by purchasing lands from the Herberts.[61] Rev. John Powell, whose long curacy has been noted (above pp.32-33), served for many years as a Justice of the Peace, and his most memorable act was the committal for trial of the notorious Molly Morgan in 1789.[62] His natural son Charles Powell also served as a justice and a Deputy Lieutenant for the county. While the estate was never large, comprising some 480 acres in 1845, the Powells were definitely considered as 'county' gentry.

Probate inventories for the gentry of the parish, though few in number, give some idea of their wealth and lifestyle. That of Richard Baldwyn of Diddlebury (1639) contains detailed descriptions of the rooms of the old hall which was demolished by the Cornewalls, and the total value of the inventory was a fairly modest £214 16s. 8d.[63] That of his son John, of Middlehope, (1671) is interesting because it is one of the few inventories which can be linked to a house which is still standing (Upper House), totals a mere £152 5s. 8d.[64] This is markedly less than the valuation of a number of testators who were described as yeomen, including Richard Baxter of Earnstrey Park (1683) at £557 11s.; Arthur Stedman of Broncroft Park (1669) at £337 19s. 8d.; Thomas Wall also of Earnstrey Park (1683) at £371 11s. 5d.; and Adam Hanson of Broncroft (1675) at £194 18s. 4d.[65] What clearly distinguished the Baldwyns was birth and social standing rather than merely material wealth.

From the limited evidence of probate inventories of the 18th century, it would appear that the gap between gentry and prosperous yeomen was widening. The inventory of Bartholomew Lutley of Lawton (1717) was valued at £2,501, the largest sum so far noted, but it must be added that £2,100 of this was accounted for by debts owing to him.[66] The same is true of the other gentleman whose inventory survives from the period 1700-1750, John Dale of Elsich, who was in fact a tenant of the Baldwyns rather than a landowner. No less that £1,466 10s. of the total of £1,573 10s. was comprised of debts, and it would appear that by this time the local gentry were augmenting their income by money-lending on quite a large scale.[67]

By the end of the 18th century Bishop Cornewall and Revd. John Powell of Sutton were once again the only resident landowners,[68] but the following century saw a number of developments. The first of these was construction of a number of gentlemen's residences in the parish, beginning at the start of the century with Milford Lodge, built on a parcel of freehold land owned by the Downes family, who farmed over 600 acres at Aston Hall in Munslow as tenants. This was followed by the rebuilding of Broncroft Castle by Charles Edwards Johnstone some time after 1860, and the building of Corfton Hall by Thomas Lloyd Roberts at about the same time.[69] The close of the century saw the most ambitious of these projects, the building of Westhope Manor by Mrs. Swinnerton Dyer as a gift for her son. This augmented the ranks of the resident gentry, as did the increasing trend during the century for a class of tenant gentry to rent the country houses of absentee landowners. Delbury Hall was the most striking example of this, having been let out from the time of the death of F.H. Cornewall in 1845 until the eventual sale of the estate in 1910. A number of these tenant gentry were members of local families, such as Edward Wood, who rented the Hall in the 1860s before moving to Culmington Manor, or Captain Richard Pudsey-Dawson, who resided there with his family from the departure of Edward Wood until 1886. The administrators who took over the estate in 1886 followed a policy of short-term lettings, and many of the tenants appear to have been birds of passage who moved on to another house after a few years. Some played an active role in the community during their stay, and the Diddlebury *Parish Magazine* under the editorship of the Revd. S. Scarlett Smith contains many references to the works of Col. and Mrs. Wade of Delbury Hall, and Mr. and Mrs. Henry Champion, the tenants of Corfton Hall.[70]

The 20th century saw a breakdown in the traditional landowning structure in the parish, largely due to the redistributions carried out by P.G. Holder (see p.18). Delbury was purchased in 1922 by Vincent Shires Wrigley, whose fortune had been made in the Lancashire cotton industry, and whose grandson still resides there. Although the Swinnerton-Dyers had owned Westhope since 1782, the construction of the manor was financed by money earned in industry by Col. H.C. Swinnerton Dyer, who had been a director of the Armstrong Whitworth works at Newcastle. The premature death of Lionel Powell, the impresario, in 1931, brought to an end what had become one of the old 'county' families. Sutton Court became divorced from its estate and, like Broncroft which was similarly divorced from its original holdings, passed through a number of ownerships during the century. At the start of the third millennium, the Swinnerton-Dyers of Westhope are the only family who can claim over a century as resident gentry.

The Middling Sort

In many ways this is an unsatisfactory classification in that it encompasses a very wide spectrum of society, ranging from those whose wealth was equal to that of many of the gentry, to tradesmen and smallholders of very modest circumstances. The main criterion used has been the possession of a degree of economic independence which the wage labourers and servant class did not enjoy.

The group has always been fairly sizeable, and the number of legal disputes over property in the small selection of judicial proceedings from the 13th century which have been published indicated the existence of a numerous and active class of small property holders who were ready to use royal justice in defence of their rights. In 1221-2, for example, the Justices in Eyre* heard 13 pleas from Diddlebury parish concerning cases of disputed claims to land and houses, and allegations of *Novel disseizin.** It is interesting to note that when action was taken against members of the higher classes, the result was by no means a foregone conclusion. When Margery, the daughter of Richard of Tugford, sued a group which included the local landowner Robert de Furches and the vicar of Lindridge for disseizing her of five and a half acres of land in Lawton, she obtained her verdict, the defendants having unwisely failed to appear.[71] The existence of a class of prosperous peasants by the middle of the 13th century is illustrated by a lengthy case which dragged on from 1248 to 1256 concerning the alleged removal of a quantity of cattle and goods worth £10 from the house of Herbert of Corfton by William fitz John of Holdgate.[72] Herbert was clearly a man of substance, though very clearly of peasant rank.

The returns for the 1327 Lay Subsidy, even though they are incomplete, provide something of a roll-call of the more prosperous members of society in the parish at that time. Only two members of the higher classes appear (John Lestrange and Hugh Tyrel under Corfham),[73] and the remainder represent a cross section of society with assessments ranging from 6d. to 3s. It is clear that Westhope was the poorest of the six townships for which assessments have survived, with six taxpayers, the wealthiest of whom was assessed at 10¼d. This contrasts with Diddlebury, where 12 of the 18 taxpayers were assessed at 2s. or more, and Corfham where the same was true for five out of the eight assessments. Corfton and Mershton, were somewhat less prosperous at this time, but with no-one assessed at less than 1s.[74]

The Childs were clearly one of the leading families in the parish, and had been in Diddlebury since at least 1272, when William l'Enfant was bailiff of Corfton. Curiously, they would appear from the 1327 lay subsidy to have been among the second rank of taxpayers of the manor, with Richard being assessed at 18 pence, compared with the 2s. 6d. charged on Richard de Paunteley, and the 3s. assessment of Richard the Herdsman.[75] While little is as yet known of the family's lands in Diddlebury, they would appear to have been accumulating a portfolio of property in Ludlow, by means which would seem to have been rather questionable given the number of disputed claims in which they were cited as defendants.[76] Members of the Child and Paunteley families regularly witnessed deeds during the 14th century, and in addition to their names, those of the families of Russel and Pitchford also appear quite regularly, suggesting that these were all families of some worth and reputation.[77] While one branch of the Child family became absorbed into the Baldwyns, another seems to have continued as prosperous yeomen until the mid-19th century. Many of the taxpayers named in the 1321 assessment do not appear elsewhere, and nothing is known of them. There are five occupational names — John the Smith at Corfton; Richard Smith, John the Porter and William the Cordwainer at Corfham; Richard the Herdsman at Diddlebury — but these may be patronyms rather than evidence that these were actual practitioners of the trades named.

From the16th century onwards it is easier to obtain documentation about individuals, and the Lay Subsidy returns for 1524 and 1525 provide a clear indication of the distribution of wealth in the parish, even allowing for obvious inaccuracy and attempted under-valuation. Table 12 shows the distribution of wealth as illustrated by assessments taken on goods. By far the largest number of taxpayers were in the group whose goods were assessed at 40s. (or in one case, 46s. 8d.). Four of the wealthier inhabitants of Sutton can be identified from a rental of 1532 in the National Archives.[78] Three of these, John Wellens (£9), Ralph Posterne and William Jordan (£4) were copyholders,* while William Heynes (£7) held his land by a lease for three lives. It is noticeable that Heynes paid a far higher rent than the others (33s. 4d. compared with 14s. and 10s.), and illustrates why landowners were keen to replace copyhold tenancies with leaseholds.

Category	Diddlebury	Great & Lt. Sutton	Westhope	Middle-hope	Corfton	Peaton*	Total
£5+	1	4	1			1	7
£3+	1	2			1		4
40s.+	5	3	2	3	9	8	30
20s.+	2	2	1	2	1		8

* Peaton assessment for 1525, as 1524 return is damaged. The rest are taken from 1524.

Table 12 Distribution of Wealth according to Lay Subsidy returns, 1524- 25[79]

Corfton, by contrast, contained none of the wealthiest group, and this impression is confirmed by the rental, where seven of the 12 names in the assessment may be found. Five of these were yearly tenants who paid between 10d. and 16s. 8d. in rent. Only two were leaseholders, John Lutley of Lawton who leased the Farm of Corfton on an 80-year lease, and Richard Normecott who had a lease for 40 years. This is slightly surprising, as Corfton was a valley township, whose inhabitants would be expected to be rather more prosperous than the hill settlements of Middlehope and Westhope. Curiously, Westhope, normally the poorest of all the townships, contained the highest assessment for goods, Richard Lewis at £12. Although Lewis was only assessed on goods, his will mentions that he possessed land at Dudley, Ludlow, Wulstene, and Sutton.[80]

Most of those who appeared in the 1524-5 assessment would have been engaged in farming, styling themselves as yeomen or husbandmen. While this division theoretically indicated a distinction between large and small farmers, in practice this became rather meaningless, as may be seen from an examination of probate records. Most testators before 1660 omitted to note their occupation or status, though curiously inhabitants of Middlehope showed more of an inclination to do so than their fellow-parishioners in other townships. All but one of these considered themselves to be yeomen rather than husbandmen. For the period in which probate inventories are available, that is from 1660 to 1764, the terms may be seen to have covered a very wide spectrum. In the period 1660-1700, only two testators described themselves as husbandmen, one accurately with an estate of £20, and one with possessions worth £76 5s. 3d., who would more accurately be described as a yeoman. Those described as yeoman had possessions valued between £10 5s. at the lowest end, and £557 11s. at the top. In the later group of wills are two where the testators are described as 'labourers'. These often represent the rank below the husbandmen, rather than people who were dependent upon wages for their living. This is clearly shown by the values of the inventories in question, £6 13s. 6d for Richard Amies (1710), who may have been a 'genuine' labourer, and £66 5s. for Joseph Rowton (1706) (see Appendix 1).

While the lists of those who had wills proved at Hereford in the period 1660-1765 is in many ways a roll-call of the 'middling sort' in the parish, they do contain many omissions and a number of curious features. They only list those cases where probate was actually obtained, and while it is fair to assume that the majority of inhabitants were below the £5 limit above which an inventory was compulsory, it is clear that many of the leading parishioners either died intestate, or were buried elsewhere. These would appear to include a number of the husbands of the 21 widows whose names appear on the lists. An examination of Appendix 1 underlines the general rule that the wealth of the parish, apart from the significant exception of the Diddlebury Hall estate, was concentrated on the eastern side of the River Corve. This is not unexpected, due to the quality of the agricultural land in the river valley. What is unusual is the number of high-value inventories from Earnstrey Park, high in the foothills of the Brown Clee, where the situation might reasonably have been expected to resemble that of Middlehope or Westhope. The same is true of the single inventory to come from Poston, that of Daniel Stedman (1736). The distribution of wealth shown in Table 13 would suggest that there was quite a high proportion of more prosperous residents in the parish. It is significant that with 34 inventories valued at more than £100, Diddlebury appears significantly more prosperous than any of the four South Telford parishes studied by Trinder and Cox, where Broseley, with an estimated population of 1,190 in 1676 could boast only 24 such valuations.[81] It was, however, significantly behind three of the four North Telford parishes examined earlier by the same group, where the parishes of Lilleshall and Wrockwardine, with smaller populations than Diddlebury, boasted respectively 49 and 50 inventories valued at £100 or more.[82]

< £5	£5-9	£10-19	£20-49	£50-99	£100-199	£200-499	£500-999	> £1000
3	5	28	20	16	20	10	2	2

Table 13 Analysis of value of Diddlebury probates, 1660 – 1764

Two groups are inadequately represented by the surviving inventories. The absence of the professional classes, with the exception of the clergy, whose social background has been discussed elsewhere (see pp.47-55) is a reflection on their absence from their community. Those who were lawyers were categorized as gentlemen, while Diddlebury rarely had a resident medical practitioner. There is a lengthy will of John Viner 'chirurgeon' (surgeon) of Diddlebury (1617),[83] who appears to have resided at Poston, but no other medical man appears to have lived in the parish until Dr. T.R.C. Downes came to Milford Lodge after the death of his aunt in 1877. His son, Sir Arthur Henry Downes, followed a distinguished career in medicine for which he was knighted in 1910.[84]

The other group which is under-represented is the tradesmen, with only five inventories representing a miller, a tiler, a butcher, a carpenter and a glazier. This list may be augmented from the marriage licences issued at Hereford during the period 1660-1700. These mention three carpenters, two weavers, four shoemakers, a slaughterman, a felt maker, a turner, a tailor, a blacksmith, a petty chapman, a gardener and a charcoal burner.[85] This indicates a much greater variety of trades operating in the parish than suggested initially by the probate records. Of particular interest are the indications that there was something of a domestic textile industry operating in the parish in the late 17th and early 18th centuries. In addition to the weavers and felt maker noted above, the will of Joan Beddoes of Lower Parks (1720) mentions her son, Samuel Beddoes, a dyer, and her inventory includes three furnaces and two pairs of shears which would have been used in the trade.[86]

The pattern of society which had become established by 1700 continued with comparatively minor changes until the beginning of the 20th century. With the exception of the Beddoes of Sparchford and the Marstons of Moorwood, the farmers were all tenants until 1910, with the larger and more prosperous holdings being located as previously in the fertile valley of the Corve. Some tenants were remarkably long-established on their farms. The Yapp family, who had been in the parish since at least the 16th century, acquired the tenancy of Lower House Farm in Middlehope in 1831, and remained there as tenants until they purchased the freehold in 1995. The Bowen family were similarly established at Corfton, where three generations of the family farmed Hill House for a century after 1780, and a brother tenanted Lower House from 1831 to 1885.[87] By contrast, many tenancies were short, reflecting the movement of population which has already been noted above (see pp.90-92). This is graphically illustrated by the census returns for Sutton and Lawton between 1851 and 1901, where the names of 22 farmers are listed. Of these, 14 appear in only one return, and none appear in more than three successive censuses. The situation is basically similar in Peaton and Broncroft, while that in Corfton is distorted by the long occupation of the Bowen family. Generally speaking, upland tenants moved less frequently than those in the valley. It is not surprising to find that tenant farmers were largely drawn from Diddlebury and adjacent parishes, although some came from much farther afield, presumably in answer to newspaper advertisements for farms to let. These included Morgan Jones, who moved to Delbury Farm from Llantwit Major in Glamorgan in 1878, and a contingent from Westmorland who arrived at much the same time. These consisted of John Wilson from Hutton (Broncroft Parks), George Atkinson from Kendal (Great Sutton), Robert Hayhurst from Kirkby Lonsdale (Lawton), and, a few years later, James Batty from Barbon (North Sutton). Wilson and Atkinson were only in the parish a few years, but Batty and

Fig. 32 Robert Hayhurst, a prosperous tenant farmer, moved to Lawton from Kirkby Lonsdale in Westmorland c.*1880 and became a leading figure in Diddlebury affairs*

Hayhurst became well established, with the latter playing a leading role in public life as churchwarden, school manager and parish councillor.

It is possible that the increased turnover in tenant farmers in the 19th century may explain the abandonment of the practice, which had existed since the 17th century, of rotating parish office on an annual basis between the farmers, and occasionally the more substantial tradesmen, From the appointment of Samuel Handcox, the Bache Mill blacksmith, and one of the few surviving freeholders, in 1850, churchwardens began to hold office for lengthy and continuous periods.[88] Handcox was warden from 1850 to 1868, and his successor Walter Watkins of the Glebe served from 1868 to his death in 1889. Robert Hayhurst held the office continuously from 1883 to 1911. The attempted coups against this oligarchical tendency are discussed elsewhere (see p.142).

A major change which had overtaken the parish by the second half of the 19th century was a reduction in the number of trades which were not connected with agriculture. This contradicts the traditional picture of the self-sufficient Victorian rural community. In Middlehope and Westhope, apart from domestic servants, there was no-one in the 1881 census who was not connected with agriculture. In the rest of the parish, some of the trades, such as masons, carpenters and wheelwrights would have been greatly dependent upon agriculture for employment. By 1881 Diddlebury still had two grocers, one with a post office, though it had lost its butcher some time after 1851. Corfton still had its inn, which had served the parish continuously since 1616.[89] Apart, however, from one part-time shoemaker at Sutton, and a tailor and a dress-maker at Corfton, the community was not substan-

Fig. 33 Smallholders like Mr. and Mrs. Woodhouse of the Hollybush (c.1910) worked a precarious living on the poor uplands of Sutton Hill

tially better served by facilities than it is at the beginning of the 21st century, when transport is available to most of the population.

Rural communities such as Diddlebury have witnessed great social changes in the 20th century, many of which resulted from the rapid decline in agricultural employment after 1950, and from the growth in private car ownership in the same period. The latter factor has increasingly enabled people who work in towns at an increasing distance from Diddlebury to live in the country, and a significant number commute on a daily basis to the towns of the West Midlands, and in one case as far as Hinckley in Leicestershire. They have bought up the farmhouses and farmworkers' cottages which had become vacant as a result of changes in agriculture, and also moved into the redundant agricultural buildings which were converted to residential use in large numbers at the end of the 20th century. It may be remarked that this trend began before the Second World War, when P.G. Holder began to farm his lands directly, and rented out the farmhouses formerly occupied by tenant farmers to middle class people who would pay higher rents.[90] In consequence Diddlebury, for the first time in its long history, has acquired a significant middle class population which has no connection with agriculture, a growing number of whom have retired into the parish. While this development is bemoaned by some, it must be remembered that it has brought benefits, not least among which is the care with which historic properties in the parish are now maintained.

The Poorer Classes:

Labourers

It is ironic that for much of the period which is covered by this history there is hardly any documentation relating to the lives of the most numerous section of society. This is because, being generally illiterate, they left behind no written records of their own, and it is only when they became objects of interest or concern to public authorities that documentary evidence becomes available. This means that there is, for example, virtually no information on agricultural labourers before the end of the 18th century. In 1800 Archdeacon Plymley noted that 62 of the 147 households in the parish were headed by labourers, with the largest numbers being concentrated in the valley settlements of Lawton and Little Sutton (22), Corfton (17) and Peaton and Broncroft (14).[91] This figure did not include those who lived in as members of their employer's household, nor those who for any other reason were not householders, and it may reasonably be concluded that the number of labourers at the start of the 19th century was in excess of 100. The records of the census show an increase in the number of labourers until 1851, with a gradual decline which accelerates towards the end of the century, reflecting the contraction of agriculture during that period. Table 14 shows a decline in the number of live-in labourers, but the fact that the practice survived on a significant scale as late as 1901 is a reflection of the 'backwardness' of the area. Live-in labourers were usually unmarried men and boys, who would move into cottages when they married. As mentioned earlier, many labourers moved almost annually between jobs, and a clear division can be seen between those who were essentially mobile, and those who remained resident, often in the same cottage, over a long period. The more prosperous of these 'permanent' labourers often rented a few acres upon which they grazed a few livestock. A very small number even owned the freehold of their property, like Richard Fewtrell of Sparchford Cottage, who described himself as 'landowner and agricultural labourer' on the 1881 census return. A few, like William Carter of Middlehope, managed to move from the position of labourer to that of tenant farmer. After a lifetime of labouring, and no doubt of saving, by 1871 at the age of 60 Carter had become tenant of the 60-acre Wetmoor Farm. Unfortunately his subsequent career is not known, as he was not resident at the farm in 1881, and does not appear in the Diddlebury burial registers.

	1841	1851	1861	1871	1881	1891	1901
Householders	98	92	96	69	69	53	53
Live-in	69	70	58	62	51	39	35
Others*	15	39	30	34	20	25	10
Total	182	191	184	165	140	117	98

* mostly children of householding labourers, or lodgers

Table 14 numbers of farm workers from census returns 1841 – 1901

Even the more prosperous farm workers were extremely vulnerable, as illustrated by the example of the Wigley family of Sutton Hill. The Wigleys had lived in the parish since at least the 16th century, when they had been quite prosperous. Thomas Wigley would appear to have taken over the family home and 11-acre smallholding after the death of his father in 1882, but 12 years later tragedy struck. On the way home from attending the annual rent dinner at the Sun at Corfton, he collapsed in a ditch and died. A subscription was raised by the vicar to try to assist the widow to remain in her home, but she fell into arrears of £22 with her rent, and a court order was obtained for the distraint and sale by auction of her few miserable possessions on 8 August 1895 (Fig. 34).[92] Following the sale, Mrs. Wigley and her children would most likely have been forced to enter the Ludlow Union Workhouse, but unfortunately the admissions records for this period have been lost.

The records of the Ludlow Union provide a great deal of information on the lot of Diddlebury labourers, and illustrate how closely even the most industrious families lived to the poverty line. In the mid-19th century a labourer earned between 7 and 9s. a week (£18 4s. to £23 8s. per year), and generally paid about £3

Fig. 34 Handbill advertising the distraint sale of the Wigley family of Sutton Hill in 1895, following the tragic death of Thomas Wigley earlier that year

or £4 per year in rent. Somehow most managed to raise their families on these meagre wages, until illness or other misfortune struck. In that case there was no alternative to seeking relief from the Union. Two examples taken at random from the Application and Report books of the relieving officer for the Diddlebury district demonstrate the plight of those who fell on hard times. Thomas Simcox of Peaton had been ill for two months, and normally earned 9s. a week. He had a wife aged 50, and had fallen into arrears with his rent of 3 guineas a year. Under threat of distraint, he applied to the Guardians for assistance, and was granted a loan of £1. Similarly William Howard, also of Peaton, had fallen ill and had a wife, a lame son of 18 and four other children to support. When well, he had earned 9s. a week, and his rent was only £1. He applied for money to buy seed potatoes, which he could not afford, and was granted a half crown (2s. 6d.) as temporary relief.[93] Childbirth was another time of unforeseen expense, when many labourers were forced to seek the customary 5s. allowed for the services of a midwife. All too often this was followed by an application for the payment of funeral expenses of the child, and sometimes the mother. Old age and infirmity brought the threat of the workhouse to those who did not have families willing or able to assist them, though it must in fairness be stated that, at least in the middle of the 19th century, the parish of Diddlebury had a far greater number of recipients of out-relief* than any other in the district.[94] While much more work needs to be done on the poor law records, it is clear that the condition of the agricultural labourers in the parish had not improved greatly by the end of the 19th century.

The 20th century saw the continued decline in the number of farmworkers, which accelerated towards the end of the century to the point where they have become almost extinct. Mechanisation of agriculture has meant that fewer men were needed to work the land, and there is a certain tragic irony that by the time that farm labourers gained something approaching a decent wage, their numbers had dwindled. It is gratifying to note that one man who worked on farms in Diddlebury and adjacent parishes achieved the distinction of obituaries in the *Times*, the *Independent* and the *Guardian* when he died in 2001. Fred Jordan achieved national fame as a singer of traditional folk songs in the 1950s when he was discovered by the BBC, and began a secondary career which won him the Gold Badge of the English Folk Dance and Song Society in 1998.[95]

Servants are a group in society about whom there is slightly more evidence than there is for labourers. The earliest definitive record of servants to have survived is Nicholas Proude's tithe book, in which numbers of servants are listed. Unfortunately, servants are not named, and are generally merely referred to by the amount payable, although in some cases they are noted as manservant or maidservant. From the amounts levied, namely 4d. for a maid and 6d. for a manservant, it is possible to calculate the number of servants in the parish in 1657 as 27 maids and 20 men. Once again, the geographical distribution of wealth in the parish is visible, with a concentration of servant-employing households along the Sutton/Peaton/Broncroft axis, and fewer in the western uplands. It should be noted, however, that the household with the largest number of servants (five), that of Mr. Edward Caldwell, was at Westhope, normally regarded as the poorest township. Three households possessed three servants, 12 employed two, while the remaining eight managed with one, generally a maid.

The situation in 1657 compares interestingly with the position two centuries later. Although the number of servants listed in the 1851 census is greater than that of 1657, the character of the employment had changed significantly, with only five of the 60 servants being male. Of these, three were grooms, and one was employed in the Sun Inn.[96] The females were predominantly teenage girls, the youngest of whom was aged only ten. Only five were aged over 40, all of whom were classed as housekeepers. The size of households is remarkable similar to that in 1657, with the largest number of servants being four, employed by Charles Powell at Sutton Court. This is to a certain extent misleading, as Delbury Hall was untenanted at this time, and, as the largest establishment in the parish, normally contained an average of eight domestics. The social and geographical distribution of servants is interesting. As in the 17th century the largest households were in Sutton, Peaton and Broncroft, with fewest at Westhope, where two farmers each had a single servant. Not surprisingly, most farmers kept at least one servant girl, while the wealthiest, such as Richard Bowen of Hill House, Thomas Bradley of Earnstrey Park and Thomas Pitt of Lawton employed three. What is interesting is that no less than four agricultural labourers employed female servants who were not members of their own family.[97]

The vast majority of girls entering domestic service were the daughters of labourers or small tradesmen, for whom the experience was a prelude to, and no doubt preparation for, their subsequent lives as the wives of labourers. This point is graphically illustrated by analysis of the marriages performed at Diddlebury between 1851 and 1860. A total of 58 weddings took place, out of which servants accounted for 39 of the brides. Of these 32 married labourers, while six of the remaining seven married tradesmen. The vast majority of the grooms were themselves the sons of labourers, and the destiny of most couples would have been producing the next generation of domestics and labourers.

By the close of the 19th century a significant change had taken place in the pattern of domestic service, with fewer farmers keeping a servant, while the size of gentry households had increased considerably. Thus 22 of the 42 female servants listed in the 1901 census were employed in four households, the largest of which was Corfton Hall, where William Champion kept nine female and three male servants. While those employed by the farmers continued to be mostly local girls, the servants in the gentry households were drawn from a wide area. The Corfton Hall establishment consisted of a cook from Norfolk, a nurse from Northumberland, a parlourmaid from Lancashire, housemaids from Herefordshire and Worcester, a kitchenmaid from Herefordshire, together with two relatively local girls from Cleobury North. The coachman came from Warwickshire, the groom from Scotland, and the gardener from Wroxeter, near Shrewsbury. The establishment of the Swinnerton-Dyers at Westhope, and that of H.E. Whitaker at Broncroft contained servants of similarly varied origins. The employment of non-local servants was a deliberate policy in the larger households, as it reduced the amount of gossiping and the pilfering of food.[98]

While domestic service was low-paid, with long hours of work and little personal privacy, employers could be generous. Thomas Lloyd Roberts of Corfton made bequests to all his servants and estate staff, ranging from £5 to no less than £500 and a £40 annuity to his butler, William Raiswell.[99] This enabled Raiswell to pursue a second career as licensee of the Elephant and Castle in Ludlow's Bull Ring until his death in 1898. The unavailability of census records after 1901 makes it difficult accurately to chronicle the decline of domestic service during the 20th century. Certainly the gentry households such as Westhope maintained a staff of servants between the two World Wars, with the addition of new posts such as chauffeur (Fig. 35). The outbreak of the Second World War brought a sudden dramatic change, with both male and female conscription. The post-war situation was not conducive to the re-establishment of costly households, and improved transport made work in towns such as Ludlow and Bridgnorth more accessible to girls from country parishes like Diddlebury. By the end of the 20th century the resident domestic servant had become extinct, although hourly cleaners have become an important feature of the local domestic economy.

Fig. 35 Fred Wallis, chauffeur to the Swinnerton-Dyers of Westhope, with their Studebaker in 1922. In later life he served the parish church as churchwarden and lay reader

The poor

The vulnerability of the labouring classes, the most industrious and thrifty of whom could be reduced by misfortune to a state of dependence upon charity, has already been noted. The problem of poverty had existed for centuries, and in the 16th and 17th centuries it was normal for wills to make some provision, however small, for the poor of the parish. As more became demanded of the middling classes in the form of rates to support the poor, the habit of private philanthropy declined, though there were always significant exceptions, such as Mrs. Valentine of Ludlow, who in 1822 left £1,000 of government stock, the interest of which was to be used to provide a weekly bread dole for poor widows in Diddlebury.[100] Similarly, in 1885 Thomas Lloyd Roberts left £200 to the vicar and churchwardens to be invested to provide for 'poor, sick aged and infirm persons residing on the Corfton estate.'[101] Generally it was left to the authorities, firstly the parish, and after 1834, the Poor Law Union, to provide for the indigent. This is fortunate for the historian, as the growing tendency towards record-keeping by officialdom has meant that what was hitherto the most anonymous section of society begins to be identified. It is clear from the earliest surviving overseers' accounts in the 1720s that widows formed a permanent nucleus of recipients of poor relief. Illegitimate children (though not normally their mothers at this time) and sick males accounted for most of the other cases. Levels of dependency varied, from the payment of rent and the provision of coal to payment of a monthly allowance, which in 1725 varied from 2s. 6d. to 9s. Paupers were often discontented with their level of benefits, and frequently appealed to the Justices, at considerable inconvenience to the overseers.[102] Thirteen individuals received poor relief in 1725, of whom four were members of the Allen family. Three died during the year and were buried by the parish, and most of these would appear to have been at least middle-aged, with the exception of Ann Hawford, who did not die until 1757.

Sixty years later the number of recipients had increased considerably, with samples taken for the month of April between 1781 and 1790 varying between 23 and 36 beneficiaries, at least a quarter of whom were widows.[103] The increase in illegitimate births noted earlier in this section swelled the ranks of those who received poor relief, with each child receiving 6s. a month from the parish by the 1830s. Women who bore more than one illegitimate child were often doomed to a lifetime as paupers. Martha Baldwyn, who produced five such offspring between 1788 and 1800, was still receiving poor relief in 1830, as was Sarah Preece, whose single child had been born in 1809. While it was often the women from the poorest section of society who were caught in this way, the possession of a base child meant that they had few hopes of rising out of poverty. It is clear from the baptismal registers, however, that it was not merely the aged and unmarried mothers who were in receipt of parish relief.[104] The Revd. John Powell was assiduous in noting paupers in the register, and records a number of births to married couples in that state, including in the 1790s Thomas and Ann Yeats; John and Elizabeth Beddoes; John and Catherine Morgan.

It is clear that for whatever cause, the number of poor families in Diddlebury had increased rapidly during the late 18th century, and continued to do so during the following 50 years. It has been noted (endnote 93) that 98 individuals received outdoor relief in the period 1850-51. Some of these, however, would have been temporary cases, who needed relief for only a week or two, and analysis of the outdoor relief lists for the Diddlebury district of the Ludlow Union between Christmas 1850 and Michaelmas 1851 reveals a hard core of 36 individuals who were in receipt of relief throughout the period under examination.[105] It would therefore be reasonable to assume that in the region of 100 people, or some 12% of the population of the parish, lived on or below the poverty line at this time. It is likely that this level of poverty continued at least until the end of the century, but it is difficult to obtain accurate figures, as following a crisis within the Guardians over the extraordinarily high level of out-relief payments in the Ludlow Union in 1865, the provision of out-relief was drastically curtailed, with many of the most needy, such as single mothers, being denied assistance.[106] In 1867, 13 men, 28 women and 35 children from the parish received out relief, but a decade later the figure had fallen to five males, seven females and two female lunatics.[107] By 1891 the number had fallen to two males and three females, none of whom were able-bodied.[108]

This raises the interesting question of the fate of those who were suddenly denied their-out relief. It might have been thought that they would have entered the Union Workhouse, but it is clear from the surviving records that this did not happen. Between 1865 and 1916 there were usually no more than four inmates from Diddlebury, the greatest number, seven, in 1880 being the result of a three week stay by a family of four.[109] The only recipient of relief in 1867 who entered the workhouse in the aftermath of the clampdown was Ann Thomas, described as 'lunatic' or 'idiot', who was admitted in 1877, and remained until her death some time after 1886.[110] There were only three other long-term residents from Diddlebury in the period 1865-1886. Anne Banks had been a servant who, at the age of 33, had borne an illegitimate son in 1870. They both entered the workhouse in the autumn of 1871, and stayed for 14 years. The other was William Dyer, who was admitted in 1873 aged 68, and was still present at the end of 1886.

It would appear that the hard-line Guardians had been correct in their view that, faced with the workhouse as the only source of relief in most cases, the majority of paupers would prefer to manage without relief. The subsequent careers of 13 of those who had been receiving out-relief in 1867 have been traced from the burial registers. Nine of these, all but two of whom were elderly, appear to have died within five years. A further three, who had been relatively young in 1867, appear to have been fortunate enough to have ended their days in Powell's Almshouses in Ludlow in the early years of the 20th century. Private charity, exemplified by Louisa Powell's much needed provision of housing for the elderly, was the only recourse for those abandoned by the Poor Law authorities. Eight of the out-relief recipients of 1867 were among the beneficiaries of the annual payments of an average of 5s. from Mrs. Radnor's bequest, but this would have been the sum which some of them would have received weekly in out-relief.[111] The weekly dole of loaves from Mrs. Valentine's charity would also have been vital.

While the workhouse remained the last resort for those few who could not be cared for by their families or look after themselves, the advent of Lloyd George's old age pensions removed the stigma of pauperism for many elderly residents in Diddlebury and the country as a whole. The advances made by the welfare state in the 20th century have ensured that even the least wealthy today enjoy a standard of living which their counterparts a century ago could never have contemplated.

4 Education, Local Government & Housing

Education

From Grammar School to National School, 1560 – 1839

There is no documentary evidence concerning the provision of education in Diddlebury prior to the Reformation, but it is known that a grammar school was in existence by 1565. In that year William Baldwyn of Sparchford left an annual sum of 25s. 4d. in perpetuity to the parish, for repair of the church and 'the maintenance of the Grammaire Schoole there.'[1] During the succeeding 50 years a number of parishioners made similar bequests, ranging from 6s. 8d. to 50s.[2] It was during this period that the school's most distinguished alumnus, the 10-year-old Lord Herbert of Chirbury, spent two years from 1592 to 1594 under the tutelage of Mr. Newton, becoming proficient in Logic and Greek.[3]

Little more is known of the school until 1674 when Christopher Wace of St. Edmund's Hall, Oxford conducted his inquiry into the state of grammar schools in England. Wace noted that the school had two endowments of £50 and £10 in the hands of the churchwardens and a library of 40 books, most of which were 'impertinent' (i.e. irrelevant).[4] The schoolmaster was Robert Rowe, about whom nothing else is known, and the school house was situated in the churchyard. It would appear that by 1700 any pretensions to grammar school status were being abandoned, and the school was becoming a vehicle for the elementary instruction of village children. The maintenance of the building was a constant drain on the income of the parish. It is clear from the churchwardens' accounts that the building was timber-framed with infilling of wattle and daub, and was roofed with thatch. Both the walls and the roof appear to have needed fairly major repairs at intervals of about ten years, while the windows, like those of the church, were in regular need of the glazier.[5] In 1789 the school was partly rebuilt in stone at a cost of £38 12s. 1d., but soon became a drain on the parish once again.

Relatively little is known of the finances and staffing of the school at this period, as unlike the maintenance of the buildings, which was paid for from parish funds, the schoolmaster's salary was financed by various endowments known collectively as the school stock. A statement of this is, however, included with the churchwardens' accounts for 1718-19, from which it appears that the schoolmaster received £5 for his services.[6] There was evidently some dispute about the management of these funds, as in July 1718 a resolution was passed that no expenditure should be made from the school or poor stock without a public meeting of parishioners.[7] In the year 1720 the parish had purchased a house in Corve Street, Ludlow, the rent from which was to be used towards the provision of bread to 'poor housekeepers' and the teaching of charity scholars. A note in the churchwardens' accounts for 1724 shows that William Fosbroke, junior, the son of the vicar, was receiving £2 10s. from this fund for teaching the charity scholars, as well as £4 from the other endowments.[8] The younger Fosbroke was Rector of Cold Weston, and possibly the last graduate to teach at Diddlebury School.

Rather more is known about some of the later masters. John Green, who died in 1837, had held the post for almost 40 years, and although village schoolmasters were poorly paid, Green was able to leave his wife an annuity of £15, cash bequests of £60 to his sister and her child, and the rest of his real and personal estate to his son.[9] He was also accorded the honour of a memorial tablet within the church (Fig. 36), and was clearly no ordinary schoolmaster.

Jeremiah Lucas, appointed in 1816, was the son of a local farmer, and held the post jointly with that of parish clerk, which had not been the case with his predecessors. He was also paid an additional £5 per year from 1839 for teaching the Sunday School, and providing a fire for it.[10] Lucas was married with six children, four of whom predeceased him. He died in 1850, aged 58, and in 1851 his widow, living in Corfton Batch, was described as schoolmistress, and would seem to have continued for some time under her husband's successor.

In 1811, in response to fears that an uneducated working class could be subverted by revolutionary principles, the National Society for Promoting the Education of the Poor in the Principles of the Established Church was founded. In 1833 the society had become a vehicle for distributing grants made by the central government for educational purposes, and in 1839 it was resolved that Diddlebury should seek affiliation, which was successfully achieved. This

Fig. 36 Memorial on the west wall of the parish church to John Green, the long-serving schoolmaster, who died in 1807

effectively marks the beginning of outside influence over Diddlebury School, as it was now subject to an annual inspection, the results of which determined the annual grant.

NATIONAL SCHOOL, 1839 – 1903

The Buildings:

The main reason for affiliation to the National Society was to obtain funds to repair the old schoolroom, and this was done in 1844. A specification was obtained from E. Blakeway Smith of Ludlow for replacing the ruinous timber wall, re-roofing with stone tiles, and other repairs, which were duly carried out at a cost of £28 6s. 3d., to which the Society contributed £15 (Fig. 37).[11] The building, was, however, totally inadequate for the accommodation of 89 day pupils and 96 Sunday scholars, though it was not until 1873 that a replacement was provided.

The movement to replace the old school room, and also the master's house in the churchyard, had been spearheaded by the energetic Revd. Philip Pratt, who succeeded in raising over £670 in subscriptions. A piece of land near the church was donated by the Dean and chapter of Hereford, and a new school and master's house were erected to the designs of Edward Haycock the younger, a Shrewsbury architect of some standing (Fig. 38).[112] The cost of these works was £474 10s. for

Fig. 37 The old schoolroom, as rebuilt by E. Blakeway Smith of Ludlow in 1844

Fig. 38 Edward Haycock's plans for the new school, opened in 1873 (SA/ED 1564/93)

the school, and £232 for the master's house, and the new buildings, in the Gothic style, were opened with great festivities on 21 August 1873.[13] As with many public works projects, the new building was not really adequate for its purpose, nor was it particularly well constructed. In 1885 the infants were moved back into the old school to ease congestion, and two years later the school was closed for an extra week to allow essential repairs to be carried out.[14] New classrooms were built in 1887, but the school was still overcrowded, particularly in the infant department, where in 1894 H.M. Inspectors noted that 55 children were taught in a room which measured 20 by 17 feet and which had desk accommodation for only 14 children. Because so many children started school late, only 23 were true infants, the rest being aged over 7.

The schoolmaster's house as originally built was too small for a moderately sized family, and in 1894 had to be extended to accommodate the family of John Rowland Jones. Somewhat typically, the window frames had been made to the wrong pattern, and had to be replaced.[15]

The Teaching Staff

After 1850, a distinct change can be seen in the nature of the headship of Diddlebury School, with an increasing professionalism developing. After Jeremiah Lucas no local men were appointed, and apart from Frederick North (1850-55) none served as parish clerk. The training of a teacher at this time usually consisted of a period as a monitor or paid classroom assistant, followed by a form of apprenticeship as a pupil teacher for five years. Successful completion of this gave qualified status to the teacher, who could then proceed to a training college for higher qualifications. The new breed of teacher tended to move between posts more frequently than had formerly been the case. This was in sharp contrast to the previous 80 years, when there had been only three headmasters, and unlike some other schools in the area, such as Clunbury, there were ten headmasters at Diddlebury during its period as a National School. As two of these had fairly lengthy headships — Charles Cook 1855-1874 and J. Rowland Jones (1892-1909) — it is clear that there was a fairly rapid turnover in the last quarter of the century.

There were various reasons for this. As will be explained, teaching at Diddlebury was beset by many frustrations, and this took its toll on the health of the teachers. The log books show that all levels of staff suffered from what would now be described as stress-related illnesses, and three successive headmasters — George Wood (1877-1881; G.W. Winchester (1881-82); and William Summers (1882-1888) — resigned due to ill-health. Assistant teachers and monitors also suffered from frequent absences, which were often ascribed to overwork. The career of Summers' successor, F.W. Dovell, was blighted by a personality clash with Morgan Jones, a manager and one of the largest farmers in the parish. Both were strong-minded, Dovell being rather liberal in outlook, while Jones was something of a bully.[16] The main causes of disagreement were Dovell's refusal to punish boys who had committed acts of vandalism against Jones out of school hours, and the latter's persistent use of boys from the school for farm work on schooldays.

Fig. 39 John Rowland Jones, headmaster, 1892-1909, was a conscientious teacher whose logbooks provide a fascinating insight into the problems of a rural schoolmaster at the turn of the 19th century

While Andrew Pope was vicar, Dovell was safe, but as soon as he left the parish, Jones began an ultimately successful campaign for his removal. Dovell was, however, given a post at Upton Bishop, where Pope had become the incumbent. Dovell was succeeded in 1892 by John Rowland Jones (Fig. 39) and his talented family, who remained until forcibly retired at the age of 65 in 1909. As a fellow-Welshman, he enjoyed cordial relations with Morgan Jones, with whom he socialised, though he was critical of the way in which the latter flouted attendance regulations.[17]

Fig. 40 Sampler worked at the school by Martha Banks in 1847

All headmasters were assisted by their wives, with the exception of George Wood (1877-1882), whose aunt filled the role. The headmaster's wife normally took charge of the infants, and taught needlework to the older girls (Fig. 40). In addition, according to pupil numbers, there were monitors, pupil teachers, and qualified assistant teachers. Some, like Hannah Duce, appointed monitress in 1885, did not proceed to pupil teacher status, and instead entered domestic service. Edwin Cox, who was a pupil teacher in 1865, completed his course and became employed at Munslow. He subsequently worked for the Ludlow Union as an attendance officer, before taking over from his father as licensee of the Sun at Corfton in 1891. When the public house was sold over his head in 1909 he took over the tenancy of the Glebe Farm, and ended his days a manager of the school where he had begun his career.

The case of another pupil teacher, W.H. Turner, is of interest. Appointed in July 1884, he was soon the subject of complaints about violence towards his pupils. After an official complaint in February 1885, he went absent without leave, and left with the consent of the managers in June. It is interesting to note that excessive violence was not tolerated, and that in fact there was remarkably little corporal punishment. Successful teachers often left for posts in larger schools, or to be married. The scale of the celebrations for the marriage of Elizabeth Hall, who had been assistant teacher for nearly four years, in 1890 shows that an assistant could become a highly valued member of the community. It is interesting to compare this with the treatment of Henrietta Rowland Jones, the widow of the headmaster, who continued teaching until she reached the age of 60 in 1924. There is no mention of her retirement in either the log book or the managers' minutes, although she was the longest serving assistant for over a century.

The Pupils

In 1881, a formula for the calculation of fees listed three categories of parents for whose children the school was intended. These were labourers, artisans and farmers, and these categories fairly accurately covered the parental spectrum of the parish. There were few if any middle class families, who would have educated their children privately, as did the gentry. Two of the wealthiest farmers in the parish, Robert Hayhurst of Lawton and Morgan Jones of Delbury both sent their children to the school, and both became active managers.[18] In practice, the great majority of pupils were the children of labourers, the poorest social group, for whom the payment of fees (2d. per week for the first child; 1d. each for the second and third; fourth and subsequent children free) would have been a considerable burden when school attendance became compulsory after 1870. In theory, after this time, children entered school at the age of 5, and left at 14, or when they had attained the required 'Standard' (officially Standard V, but in practice Standard IV). Few children in fact commenced school at 5, some not starting until as late as 9 or 10, and few stayed long enough to attain the official qualifications for leaving. For example, of 58 pupils admitted in 1876, 15 had left by the end of that year, and most had gone by the end of 1879. Only 10 of the 1876 intake completed their education at the school, one of whom obtained Standard VI and one gained Standard V.[19]

Many children were poor, badly clothed and undernourished. Shoes and clothing were usually unsuited to walking to school (it was calculated that the average pupil walked 4 miles per day), which made pupils susceptible to illness. Many were verminous, but it was not until the very end of the 19th century that the authorities began to intervene in matters of health. Some attempts were made to improve the dietary conditions of the pupils in the 1880s, when the Popes set up a weekly soup kitchen in the vicarage, but this stopped with the vicar's departure, and it was not until 1947 that school meals were provided. Impressions of the pupils varied. George Cattle, whose brief headship lasted from January 1876 to November 1877, noted that 'the children seem very much given to lying and underhand dealing' and criticised 'their rough and unkind manner one to another.' The inspectors provide a more impartial assessment, in 1871 describing

Fig. 41 J. Rowland Jones, his wife Henrietta (to left of door), and pupils of Diddlebury School c.*1900*

the children as 'clean, cheerful, well-mannered and orderly,' though in 1873 they wondered whether 'spirit and intelligence have not, to some extent, been sacrificed to strictness of discipline.' There was general agreement over the period that the pupils were weak in arithmetic, read haltingly, and were slow to answer the questions of the inspectors. Towards the end of the period, headmasters began to record their responses to such criticisms in the log book. In July 1890 Dovell commented that neither he nor the pupils could understand the 'peculiar twang' of the inspector, a Londoner, while Rowland Jones was particularly scathing on several occasions.[20]

Problems

The school was beset by problems of attendance which doubtless lay behind the poor standards criticised by the inspectors. These were the result of migration, the weather, illness and truancy. The question of the migration of labourers each Lady Day has been mentioned in connection with population, and had a drastic effect on the school. Pupils who had been prepared for the examination by the inspectors left a few weeks before it took place, to be replaced by those from other schools who had followed different syllabuses. This was of particular importance when grants were awarded on the basis of performance in the examination, and Rowland Jones, who confided his views to the log book, frequently deplored the migration of pupils.

The weather caused considerable problems when all children walked to school, generally without suitable clothing and footwear. Many parents kept their children at home in wet weather to avoid them spending the day in wet clothing, and perhaps contracting rheumatic fever. In times of heavy or prolonged rain, the Corve rose and effectively cut off the eastern parts of the parish for days at a time. Snow, which occurred more frequently in the 19th century, often blocked the roads for days. The comment in the log book for 16 January 1891 is typical: 'Roads still impassable. Children suffering from chilblains and colds. Despite good fires, the stoves are inadequate to keep warm. Severity unsurpassed for 50 years. 32° of frost.' For the next four days the temperature did not rise above 5°F.

Under such conditions, it is not surprising that many children were prey to disease, particularly as they were often undernourished, lived in unsanitary cottages, and spent their days in an overcrowded school. In the earlier part of the period serious disease was noted in the log books in a matter of fact way, as between 22 and 26 May 1865: 'Smallpox at Middlehope, six or seven absent,' but gradually infection became a cause of concern, even panic. In June 1885, the Hince children from Fernalls Mill were ordered to stay away from school as there was smallpox in the house,[21] and during an outbreak of scarlet fever in February 1889, Mr. Groome of Peaton Hall ordered his cottagers to keep their children at home. During the following 12 months, the school was subjected to further epidemics of whooping cough and influenza. Disease was so prevalent that the Medical Officer of Health intervened, and from January 1896 the school was regularly subjected to long periods of closure on his orders.[22]

Truancy

While the foregoing factors caused major disruption to teaching, they were matters over which no human control could be exercised. This was not the case with truancy, which caused considerable problems well into the 20th century, and to which, before schooling became compulsory, the school seems to have had a relaxed attitude. Charles Cook gave permission for children to miss school for a variety of reasons, including Ludlow Fair, rook-scaring, and a meet of hounds at Delbury Hall. He commented that some farmers' sons only attended in the winter when they were not needed to work at home. When school attendance was made compulsory in 1880, it was widely resented by both parents and employers. Parents resented having to send their children to school, and having to pay to do so. Children's earnings could supplement a meagre family income, and children performed many useful jobs such as rook-scaring, beating, leading plough horses, and assisting with harvesting, cider-making and other tasks. Girls were often absent helping hard-pressed mothers, often by looking after younger siblings. As employers valued child labour, it was difficult to enforce school attendance.

Diddlebury was typical of most rural parishes in the wholesale ignoring of compulsory schooling. By the later 1880s it was causing great concern, and Summers began the process by which headmasters attempted to crack down on truancy. In October 1888 Darvell obtained summonses against a number of parents whose children were persistently absent, and attendances improved dramatically. However, when the courts refused to punish the offenders, absenteeism began to escalate, and attempts to punish children for truancy sometimes met with abuse and violence from parents. In April 1890, Darvell was abused and threatened by a Mr. Williams for punishing his son, and the following November a Mrs. Davies from Titrail, Westhope gave the master 'her mind' for reporting her son to the Attendance Officer. This would have been a fairly empty gesture, judging by the frequent comments of Rowland Jones on the supine nature of the Attendance Committee Just over a year after his appointment, he wrote, on 7 April 1893, that the 'School A[ttendance] Committee for this District is a nonentity. It is really disheartening for an anxious Teacher.'[23] By 1901 Jones had become so disheartened that he handed in his resignation, but later withdrew it. The situation had not improved by the time of his retirement in 1909.

Teaching and learning

The basis of the Victorian curriculum was the so-called 'three Rs', which formed the basis of the annual examination upon which the 'payment by results' was calculated. In addition, as a Church school, there was a heavy emphasis on instruction 'in the Holy Scriptures, and in the Liturgy and Catechism of the united Church of England and Ireland.'[24] This was the subject of a second annual examination, conducted by a representative of the diocese, which continued until the reorganisation of the school in 1964. In 1882 the examiner had found the children backwards in Religious Knowledge, but three years later, partly under the influence of the Revd. Andrew Pope, the school was receiving letters from the bishop congratulating the pupils on their performance in this area. Pope continued and expanded his predecessor's practice of teaching in the school, and increased the number of occasions when the children attended church. This had to be done in designated Religious Knowledge periods to comply with the law, which necessitated juggling with the timetable. It is significant that in 1900 Jones, an ardent churchman, complained that the work of the school was disrupted by frequent diocesan examinations, and noted that the school had attended church 27 times in the previous year.

Attempts to broaden the secular curriculum were frowned upon by government inspectors, and met with little success. In 1882 the new headmaster, G.W. Winchester, had begun to teach English Literature to children who had 'little or no knowledge, I may say, none at all.' Scott's *Lady of the Lake* may not have been a wise choice with which to start, and in October he was sternly admonished by the

Inspector to confine himself to the three elementary subjects. As the government became more interested in education, so the syllabus became more prescriptive, and the content for each year had to be approved by the Inspectorate. The infants were largely taught by object lessons, which in 1891 included topics as diverse as Tea; The Forge; Leather; Sunlight; and the Shark. All Standards of the main school were taught geography and history, with Standard IV and upwards being given a chronological grounding in English history from 1603 onwards. By 1900 English literature, drawing, music, elementary science and drill had been added to the compulsory subjects, the last occasioned by the lack of fitness among recruits for the Boer War. Jones wrote despairingly on 25 May 1900 of the difficulty of teaching music by note to children, 'several of whom were unable to sing an octave in C with the harmonium.'

VOLUNTARY SCHOOL, 1903 – 1980

The Education Act of 1902 brought the voluntary schools under the control of the Salop County Council. This brought little major change, though in 1904 Jones ruefully remarked that the supply of materials had been much better under the old system. The opening of a short-lived rival establishment at Westhope had a temporary effect upon numbers at Diddlebury. After the First World War, a gradual decline in numbers began to take place, which was temporarily offset by an influx of evacuees during the next war, but was accelerated by the very belated reorganisation of the school in 1964. In 1980 the school finally closed, to be reopened in 1982 as the Corvedale School.

The Westhope Experiment

One probable consequence of the transfer of the educational responsibilities of the National Society to the County Council was to make policy decisions more vulnerable to pressure from influential individuals, and soon after the new arrangements were in place, the formidable Mrs. Martin, whose historical researches have been frequently quoted in this work, began to lobby for a school at Westhope. As Westhope was the most remote and inaccessible township in the parish, there was some logic in the suggestion. Mrs. Martin provided the site, and erected the school building, which was duly opened in April 1908.[25] The new school provided accommodation for 60 children, and began with 35 on the roll. This number gradually declined, until by the autumn of 1918, when closure was being sought, there were only 16 pupils.[26]

This decline is difficult to understand initially, as by many criteria the school could have been counted as a success. Visits by school inspectors had revealed the children to be very capably taught, although the standard of cleaning of the premises was condemned. Furthermore, two children had obtained free places for the Grammar and High schools in Ludlow.[27] Though, like all schools, Westhope suffered long periods of closure by order of the Medical Officer, it was not plagued by the absenteeism which drove the Diddlebury heads to distraction. The log book noted on 20 June 1919, a month before the school closed, that it had been the 29th week with full attendance since the school had opened, which was a truly remarkable achievement.

Unfortunately the cause of some of these strengths was also that of its downfall, namely the personality of Mrs. Martin. The official attendance officer was never needed, as absences had to be reported to and sanctioned by Mrs. Martin. As all the parents were employees or tenants of the Westhope Estate, there was no possibility of the sort of truancy which occurred in Diddlebury. But it was not just the pupils and their parents who were subject to the rule of Mrs. Martin. It extended to the schoolmistress, of whom there were no fewer than six during the school's short life. As a manager and the Correspondent for the school, Mrs. Martin was in constant attendance, having made 55 official visits during the first six months of the life of the school. As Mrs. Martin regularly inspected the school log books, there was no opportunity for the head teacher to engage in the confessional entries which characterised Rowland Jones at Diddlebury. By the summer of 1918, Mrs. Martin had decided that the school was too small to survive with 16 children, and the managers duly requested the Local Education Authority to close the school and provide transport for the pupils to Culmington. The authority was inclined to accede to the request, but the Board of Education in London was not so amenable. An extraordinarily frank internal memorandum from G.R. Theobald, HMI, gave a perceptive interpretation of the situation:

> This proposal is, I think, the result of a 'mood' of Mrs. Martin, the owner, who apparently got her knife into the retiring headmistress. Mrs. Martin is, from what I hear, a lady of moods, anxious to be good so long as she can boss a show. She is spoken of as 'ruling Westhope' and an awkward widow. She spent a good deal of trouble and money in starting the school, and now she wants to close it.[28]

In the ensuing battle of wills between the Board and Mrs. Martin, the latter took the initiative by closing the school when Mrs. Cook, the headmistress, left in the summer of 1918. According to Theobald, the case had 'been thoroughly muddled by Mr. Wale [the County Education Secretary] in accordance with his usual practice'. Eventually an agreement was reached that the school should be reopened as soon as a head teacher could be appointed, with the promise of a review in April 1919 if the war had ended.[29] Reluctantly in March 1919 Theobald agreed that the school could close, provided that suitable arrangements could be made to transport the children to Culmington. The school duly closed on 31 August 1919, Mrs. Martin noting in the log book that she had made 226 visits to it during its short life.[30] The building was subsequently converted into a dwelling, which survives today.

Delbury School 1903 – 1980

It has already been noted above that John Rowland Jones spanned the period in which overall control of the school passed from the National Society to the County Council until his enforced retirement in March 1909.[31] He was succeeded by Mr. J.H. Gornall, although Mrs. Jones continued to work as assistant teacher until 1924. Tragically, Jones died after a fall from his tricycle after only six months of retirement. Though Gornall initially received a promising report from H.M. Inspectors, by 1912 he was being criticised for being insufficiently exacting, while in May 1914 he was called to account for failing to develop the children's powers of expression, and 'accepting indiscriminate or chorus answers or slovenly speech'.[32] This led to a prolonged dispute with the managers, who desired a change of headmaster.[33] This was achieved in March of the following year when Gornall was replaced by Joseph Benson, from Pantglas School, Oswestry, who remained for three years before removing to a post in Birmingham.

The departure of Benson led to a conflict between the managers and the Local Education Authority, who wished to appoint a woman as head. The authority was victorious in this instance, and Miss Nellie Walker was engaged as the school's first and only headmistress. Miss Walker was fortunate to have inherited Mrs. Rowland Jones as her assistant, and to have secured the appointment of her daughter Olga a few months after taking up her headship. Miss Walker was highly regarded by the educational establishment. In June 1924 the inspector commented glowingly that 'harmony and goodwill characterise the relation of teacher and taught as the work is carried on with an efficient industry that leaves the children keen and fresh at the end of a session'.[34] Miss Walker had, however, suffered from

Fig. 42 Staff and pupils assembled outside the school. The pricture is undated, but must have been taken prior to 1918, when the school gained its first headmisterss. The headmaster (in trilby) is probably Joseph Benson (1915-18)

illness in 1924, and resigned at the end of November. The Education Authority wished to appoint another female head, but none of the short-listed candidates was acceptable to the managers, who successfully lobbied the county council for a headmaster. Whether this was purely chauvinism or something deeper is not clear. However, the supply teacher put in charge pending a permanent appointment wrote a scathing critique of his predecessor, and references to 'modern methods' may well hold the key to the managers' dislike of Miss Walker.

The short headship of Griffith Thomas, who succeeded Miss Walker in February 1925, was marked by a rapid turnover in assistant staff, and what the school required was a period of stability. This was acquired in March 1927 when Sidney Leach began his long headship which lasted until 1948. It is interesting to note that in 1932, the government inspector commented very favourably on the school, which had a 'pleasant and healthy tone' with the children conducting themselves in 'an orderly and natural manner'. He also noted that the majority of the infants were able to read. This contrasted with the opinion of the Diocesan Religious Knowledge Inspector who deplored the time lost to religious education for cookery classes.

The most serious occurrence during Leach's headship was the Second World War which, although no lives were lost from the parish, in many ways affected Diddlebury far more than the Great War had done. For the school, the most obvious effect was the presence of evacuees, 50 of whom had arrived from Gwladys Street School in Liverpool on 1 September 1939. Many of these had returned to Liverpool the following spring, but small contingents continued to arrive from a number of Roman Catholic schools in Liverpool during 1940 and 1941. In September 1941 there were 61 local children on the roll, together with 35 'official' evacuees and four 'private'. School holidays were arranged to fit in with harvesting, and in August 1941 the school was used for billeting a number of secondary school boys and their masters from Wolverhampton who were helping on local farms. This camp was abandoned after three weeks when one of the boys was killed, an event noted in the school logbook but not in the local press.

The presence of evacuees had temporarily masked the problems which a declining birth rate was causing for small rural schools. The school opened in September 1945 with 40 on the roll, the lowest number ever recorded. This was significant, as Diddlebury still catered for all ages up to statutory leaving age at 14. In 1948, shortly before the departure of Mr. and Mrs. Leach, Holdgate school was closed, and its pupils transferred to Diddlebury, raising the roll to 72, and heralding a future pattern of closure and amalgamation of small schools. Considerable advances had been made during Leach's headship. In April 1947 the newly opened school kitchen served its first meals to the children. The previous year children from the outlying areas of Peaton and Bouldon, shortly followed by Middlehope, were provided with bus transport to school, a luxury which Westhope children had enjoyed since 1919. Another feature of the post-war years was a dramatic increase in the number of children who won places for a grammar school education. In 1946 no fewer than five children were successful, two of whom were 13 year olds who had 'developed late'.[35] This trend to both educational and social improvement continued under the next headmaster, Mr. James, and in September 1951 the number of pupils on the roll briefly reached 100. The transport revolution which was occurring enabled educational visits to be made, with cultural excursions to places such as Cardiff (1954), Bath (1955) and Aberystwyth (1956) by motor coach. Trips to the cinema at Craven Arms to see educational films such as the *Coronation*, the *Conquest of Everest* and Shakespeare's *Julius Caesar* provided additional experiences which had been unavailable to pre-war pupils.

When James moved to Broseley at the end of 1957 he was replaced by the school's last headmaster, Frank Mitchell. Mitchell greatly increased the scope of the school excursions to include such varied destinations as the British Empire and Commonwealth Games in Cardiff (1958) and Wolverhampton Football Club and the Goodyear tyre factory (1962). A keen bee-keeper, musician and local historian, Mitchell involved the children in his interests, with the school regularly competing at national and local levels in honey shows, and entering music festivals. It is ironic that at a time when the quality of educational experience of the pupils was improving out of all recognition, the shadow of closure began to fall on the school. For some time pupils who had not passed for a grammar school had transferred to Stokesay at 13 to complete their education in a larger school, leaving only a small number of senior pupils at Diddlebury. In 1964, 20 years after the Butler Education Act, Diddlebury was reorganised as a primary school, with pupils leaving at 11 to go to Ludlow Grammar or Secondary Modern schools. By 1970 the number of pupils had fallen to 36, and by the end of the decade proposals were afoot for the amalgamation of small schools in the area. In December 1980 Diddlebury school finally closed, with the children transferring temporarily to Munslow. Frank Mitchell, whose health had been failing for several years, died shortly afterwards, having lived to see the publication of his booklet on Molly Morgan, Diddlebury's notorious convict transport.

Postscript: Corvedale School

In February 1982, following extensions and refurbishment, the school reopened as the Corvedale School, taking children from the parishes of Diddlebury, Munslow, Culmington and Stanton Lacy. Initially 83 children were on the roll, but grew in size, making new building necessary. In 1992 the appointment of Mrs. Templeman as head teacher ended the run of male heads which had only once before been broken. The school continues to flourish with 107 children on the books in 2006, and a staff of five full-time teachers. The link with the church is still maintained, with the Vicar regularly taking classes.

LOCAL GOVERNMENT

Given that local government is such an established feature of the political organisation of the United Kingdom at the start of the 21st century, it is remarkably difficult to establish terms of reference whereby the subject is to be dealt with in a parish history. This is because the concept of local government involves two separate, but often interlinked elements. These are the operation of the central or national government of the country in the localities, and also that of a distinctive and locally based system of administration. Historically the former may in a sense be regarded as the longer-established of the two, which for much of its early history was concerned with two vital areas of operation: the raising of money for the crown, and the maintenance of the king's peace in the localities. The evolution of a separate system of local administration, which in rural areas developed around the parish, was largely the result of a need to provide services, particularly the care of the poor. This distinction is in many ways unsatisfactory, as there was often a considerable overlap. The justices of the peace, for example, whose office was originally conceived as one of social control, steadily accumulated a variety of administrative tasks. These included oversight of highways and bridges, licensing, and fixing wages and prices, as well as supervising semi-parochial officers such as the constable, the waywarden (surveyor of the highways) or the overseers of the poor. Most of these functions, with the exception of licensing, were taken away from the justices when county councils were established in 1888. While recognising these areas of overlap, the present section will consider local government in Diddlebury largely from the standpoint of the provision of services at a parish level.

When churchwardens are sworn in at the annual archdeacon's visitation, they are formally admitted to the 'ancient office', which does indeed boast a far greater antiquity than any other lay post in the parish. The origins are obscure, but date from at least the 14th century when their duties were primarily ecclesiastical and concerned with the upkeep of the church (except the chancel), and the provision of the goods and ornaments required for the performance of the services. In Diddlebury, as in the majority of parishes, there were two wardens who were elected by the parishioners and served in rotation.

At the end of the medieval period the other significant official in the parish was the constable, of whom virtually nothing is known in a Diddlebury context. The constable was an official of the manor, who was responsible for enforcing the orders of the manor court, particularly in matters such as the regulation of alehouses and the treatment of beggars. The workings of the manor court may be seen from the surviving court rolls of Diddlebury and Corfton. In addition to the registration of changes of tenant, and the never-ending efforts to prevent the illegal grazing of the common fields, which has already been discussed (see p.27), may be found the prosecution of petty crimes and the control of various nuisances. Thus in October 1562, four Diddlebury residents were fined for selling ale without the necessary licences, and a further two were presented for selling meat.[36] In 1610 the court baron of Corfton imposed a heavy 10s. penalty upon householders who 'shall maintain inmates or strangers in their houses in the harvest time or any other time'.[37] In a similar manner the laws against cottagers were enforced, with four being presented at Corfton in 1610, including Thomas Madox, 'a cottar under Thos. Stedman freeholder, who useth him for a thatcher.'[38] Another example occurred in 1658, when permission given by Thomas Lewis of Sutton for Thomas Hopton to live in a cottage on his land was upheld by Quarter Sessions, and the constable was ordered to cease proceedings against the cottage. These measures were intended to prevent an increase in the number of poor inhabitants who might have become eligible for relief out of the rates.[39]

The care of the poor

These measures were the product of an increasing concern about the rising number of poor. Throughout the 16th century the real or perceived threat to the public order from the growing number of poor people, and particularly the more unruly elements, the 'rogues and vagabonds', exercised the minds of those in authority. The problem had been noted by Sir Thomas More and others early in the century, and the countrywide disorder of 1549, which included two major rebellions, had brought the full extent of the problem to the forefront. While the rebuilding of farmhouses in Diddlebury which has been noted in the second half of the 16th century is an indication of the growing prosperity of the yeomen, this was not shared by their poorer neighbours. Although past writers have dwelt on the dissolution of religious houses, and the consequent loss of monastic charity, as a cause of the problem of poverty after 1540, this can have had little effect in Diddlebury. The nearest religious houses, in Ludlow and Bromfield, would have been too far away to provide regular assistance, and were no doubt fully occupied relieving their own poor.

Before 1597 private philanthropy was the main instrument of relieving the poor, and was irregular and unpredictable. The small surviving sample of wills dating from before 1558 contain bequests to the church (see above p.62), but, of those examined, only that of William Mynton of Peaton (1546) contains provision for the poor.[40] Between 1560 and 1660 the number of bequests to the poor increases but still represents a minority of testators, most of whom were drawn from the wealthier section of the community.[41] Bequests to the poor were generally small, ranging from 5 to 40s., and it was not until the 19th century that there was any almshouse provision for the parish, and these were situated in Ludlow. Lifetime gifts to the poor were in many ways more significant, and enabled the parish to purchase stock, the interest of which could be employed in relief. A list of donations drawn up in 1624 produced a total of £54, which included a substantial contribution of £30 from Thomas English of Middlehope.[42] After

1660 a number of bread doles were established. John Baldwyn of Middlehope gave £2, the interest on which was to be laid out on 2d. white loaves to be distributed on the first Sunday in November. Dr. Goode, the vicar of Wistanstow was more generous, in that the initial stock of 40s. given in 1662 for a similar purpose was augmented annually by a further 20s. until 1671.[43] However, provision for the poor in wills comes effectively to an end after 1660, except for occasional isolated cases such as Joyce Harwell who left 10s. in 1682. This trend is paralleled in Highley, where the last such bequest was made in 1678, and may be explained by the fact that having contributed in their lifetime through the rates, testators no longer felt obliged to make provision for the poor in their wills.[44] Diddlebury must be typical of most rural parishes in the lack of sufficient private charity, a situation which had led to the central government passing the first Poor Law in 1597. This required the appointment of overseers (theoretically by the justices) to work alongside the churchwardens to provide relief for the poor financed by a rate or lewn which was to be levied on the inhabitants of the parish.

The Elizabethan statutes of 1597 and 1601 effectively mark the beginning of the concept of local government as we know it today, a system of services provided at local level, and financed and administered by the local community. The Highways Act of 1555 had established a precedent with the provision of surveyors of the highways or waywardens appointed on a parish basis, and the poor laws developed the idea further, retaining the supervisory role of the justices alongside a system which was operated by the parishioners. Each spring the leading inhabitants of the parish would meet in the annual parish vestry to receive the accounts of the churchwardens and elect the officers for the ensuing year, although this latter aspect of the vestry did not start to be recorded until 1686.[45]

In the 17th century the parochial officers consisted of the two churchwardens, who were elected annually by the vicar and parishioners. The vestry then went on to nominate four overseers of the poor rather than the more usual two, in recognition of the size of the parish; and ten supervisors of the highways, one for each hamlet. These were theoretically subject to approval by the justices, and the entry for 1686 added the rider 'if please his Maties. Justices of the Peace.' Subsequent entries omitted this deferential appendix.[46] In the earlier years of the 17th century a rather shadowy body known as the 'twelve men', who may have been the sidesmen, seem to have exercised some authority in the parish. In 1609 permission was granted to Thomas Baldwyn to build a chapel on the north side of the church in the names of 'the churchwardens ..., the twelve men ... and the minister' of Diddlebury.[47] By the middle of the century the twelve men seem to have disappeared from the records of the parish.

The churchwardens, as formerly noted (see p.108) were chosen almost exclusively from the higher ranks of the farming community, some of whom were 'perceived gentry'. This is hardly surprising, for the post required a degree of literacy and numeracy which would have been absent further down the social scale, and too much should not be read into the existence of a 'rural oligarchy'. In the first half of the 17th century a small group of farmers held the office, sometimes serving for up to four consecutive years. This had the advantage of continuity, but in 1650 the system was replaced by the more usual pattern of rotating the office annually among the different townships of the parish, a practice which remained in place until the office became less onerous in the mid-19th century. The overseers were appointed in the same manner, but represented grouped townships, namely Middlehope and Westhope; Diddlebury and Corfton; Lawton and the Suttons; and Peaton and the Parks (Earnstrey and Broncroft). The overseers were responsible for the day to day administration of poor relief, and, after the first years of the system, collecting the lewn, and the allocation of specific parts of the parish to an individual overseer made for a more efficient discharge of their functions.

The churchwardens, who had many other responsibilities both religious and secular apart from the relief of the poor, exercised a more supervisory role. At first they tended to conduct relations with the magistrates, which could be complex and time-consuming. The aggrieved poor would often appeal to the justices, who could then order the churchwardens to carry out certain obligations. On 16 July 1657 the churchwardens were ordered to pay 2s. 6d. weekly to Richard Baker until they should find him a home, while in 1687 they were ordered to pay 20s. a year to Ralph Habberley 'an old soldier of Charles I'.[48] In 1662 parliament had introduced legislation governing settlement and removal, which gave entitlement to relief in only one parish, which proved a great barrier to mobility of labour, and saw many disputes between parishes as to which had responsibility for individual paupers. These occurred frequently throughout the period of the old poor law,[49] and often led to unseemly actions. The maintaining of the extra-parochial enclave at the Skirmadge as a dwelling for unmarried mothers, so that their children had no settlement was a particularly unpleasant practice.[50] Paupers without a settlement had to be returned to their own parish, as in 1728 when the wardens, after obtaining an order from Mr. Baugh at Onibury, transported 'a child from the Wetmore' to Pontesbury, at a charge of 5s. to the parish.[51] By the 1720s, however, it was becoming more usual for the overseers to undertake routine visits to the justices concerning complaints by paupers. The 18th-century benefit claimant was generally as well-versed in his entitlements as his latter-day counterpart, and the surviving overseers' accounts of the 1720s contain references to complaints from Bridget Owen, Mary Brown, and John Smart, all of which required several meetings with individual magistrates.[52] By the end of the 18th century the overseers appear to have organised their office on a regular basis. Each overseer dealt with casual payments to applicants for relief from his or her division, (female overseers were uncommon but not unknown, see below) but took turns to pay the regular recipients who received a monthly allowance from the parish. After 1785 one overseer became responsible for the workhouse accounts, and was left out of the regular payments rota. The office of overseer was filled by most of the farmers in the parish, including many of the wealthier members of the farming community. Substitution appears to have been resorted to very rarely, most noticeably between 1827 and 1834 when Thomas Keysall and Richard Dyer acted as paid assistant overseers in place of the elected nominees.

The parish would appear to have occasionally built cottages for the poor, as the Register of Papists' Deeds note in 1717 that William Yates held a cottage in Middlehope built by the parish of Diddlebury, for which he paid no rent.[53] In 1720 the churchwardens took the unusual step of buying a house in Corve Street, Ludlow, in order to use the proceeds of the rent to pay for the school and provide relief for the poor (see p.118). This was initially formalised as a distribution of 6d. loaves to poor householders on four occasions in the year, but by 1727 these had become cash payments. It is noticeable that of the 38 recipients of this charity in 1727, only Widow Hall had been in receipt of poor relief from the overseers in 1725.[54] The accommodation of the poor remained a problem throughout the 18th century, and in 1781 Diddlebury began sending paupers to workhouses in Ludlow and at Hatton, in Eaton parish.[55] This was obviously unsatisfactory, and in 1784 the parish opened its own workhouse at Corfton, in a building rented from the Corfton estate, to accommodate those who, for whatever reason, could no longer manage in their own homes.

Corfton workhouse appears to have been unusually generous in its provision for the inmates. Vegetables were grown in the garden, pigs were fattened, and beer brewed for the paupers in the workhouse brewhouse. In addition, astonishing quantities of meat and cheese were purchased. In 1787 the workhouse had bought no less than 1,498lbs. of beef for an average of 24 inmates. In 1800 this had risen to 3,127½lbs., and the following years to 5,362lbs., at a cost of £48 8s. 4½d.[56] Unfortunately, a record of average numbers of inmates was not kept at this time, so that it is impossible to tell whether there was an unusually high occupancy. The years 1800 and 1801 do, however, coincide with the periods of office of Robert Dawes of Elsich, and his widow who succeeded him. Mr. and Mrs. Dawes appear to have followed a 'tax and spend' policy, for not only did workhouse expenditure reach unprecedented heights, so also did the overall expenditure, and the amount of lewn which was required. It may be noted that while overall spending on poor relief had increased dramatically after 1800 independently of the Dawes, workhouse expenditure remained reasonably constant on either side of their period of office (Table 1). Even in 1810-11, the worst year of the period apart from 1801-2 for expenditure, the cost of the workhouse was not disproportionately higher.

Year	Income	Expenditure	Workhouse costs
1780-1	£376	£340	Not applicable.
1785-6	£349	£338	Not applicable
1790-1	£362	£365	£133
1795-6	£509	£488	£160
1796-7	£754	£697	£208
1797-8	£483	£439	£162
1798-9	£547	£533	£172
1799-00	£680	£572	£197
1800-1	£1079	£1005	£472 [Dawes]
1801-2	£1121	£1262	£453 [Dawes]
1802-3	£1151	£875	£196
1803-4	£1020	£937	£183
1804-5	£580	£647	£139
1805-6	3657	£726	£189
1810-11	£1177	£1136	£282
1815-6	£919	£855	£136
1820-1	£987	£876	£107
1825-6	£720	£682	£93
1830-1	£444	£392	£121

Table 1 Expenditure and Lewn Income for selected years, 1781 – 1835. Sums have been rounded up or down to the nearest pound

There was some attempt to bring the cost of maintaining paupers in the workhouse under control following a steady increase in cost after 1809. From 1811 the overseer in charge included the average number of paupers by month and year in his accounts from that year onwards, and calculated the unit cost of keeping a pauper for a week. This was 4s. 6½d. in 1811, and gradually fell until the lowest amount of 2s. 5d. was reached in 1821 and 1822. For the last decade of the life of the workhouse the average cost of maintaining an inmate was between 2s. 6d. and 3s. This was partly attained by a reduction in the amount of beef consumed. In 1818/19, 510¾lbs. of beef were bought, when on average the number of inmates was nine. In addition a further 210lbs. of mutton was purchased while, in an economy drive in 1822/23, 264lbs. of mutton and 711 of cheese were bought for the workhouse, rather than beef. It is likely that even under this more economical regime many workhouse inmates enjoyed a far higher standard of nourishment than they had in their own homes. Diddlebury does appear to have managed its workhouse with a degree of humanity which was to disappear rapidly after the system was reformed and centralised in 1834. When an inmate died, a proper shroud and coffin were provided, and 5s.-worth of beer was allowed to the mourners. On occasions the parish even paid for the ringers to mark the occasion. A human touch not usually associated with workhouses was the purchase of milk and eggs for pancakes to celebrate Shrove Tuesday in 1811.

It is obvious that the Diddlebury parish authorities were guilty of most of the charges laid against the old poor law system by the reformers of the 1830s. The workhouse provided a reasonable standard of living for the inmates, and it is unlikely that it posed to great a deterrent to future applicants for relief. In addition, the increase in the number of poor who were given relief outside the workhouse towards the end of the 18th century led to a dramatic increase in expenditure, and in consequence to rises in the lewn. The notorious Speenhamland system, which linked the amount of relief to the price of bread, depressed wages and created greater demands for assistance, thus forcing up the rates. The enormous burden of the poor rates nationally, which had more than doubled to over £4 million between 1785 and 1837, led to demands that the system should be reformed.[57] The result was the Poor Law Amendment Act of 1834, which established unions of parishes which were to provide a central union workhouse. The unions were under the strict centralised control of the commissioners established under the act, who were known popularly as the 'Three Bashaws [Pashas] of Somerset House' by virtue of their almost unlimited power. The new system embodied the principle of 'less eligibility' dear to the Utilitarians* who had framed the Act. This meant that fewer people were to be eligible for assistance by restricting out-relief* to those who were not able-bodied. For the able, relief could only be obtained within the union workhouse, where conditions were intended to be a deterrent to all but the most desperate. To inmates used to the comparative luxury of the Diddlebury workhouse, the dietary regime in the Ludlow workhouse must

Fig. 43 Memorial window placed in the church in memory of Walter Watkins (d.1889), who had served for many years as churchwarden and poor law guardian

have been something as a shock, with a weekly allowance of only 9 ounces of meat for each adult pauper.[58]

The parochial system was completely swept away by the 1834 Act, with such local control as existed being exercised by the Board of Guardians of each union, who were elected annually by the ratepayers. Diddlebury guardians were drawn largely from a small coterie of the principal farmers who held the office in rotation. The exceptions were Samuel Handcox, the Bache Mill blacksmith, who served in 1845 and 1858, and Walter Watkins of the Glebe, who farmed only 80 acres. Watkins' father had been the first guardian in 1836, and had served again in 1840. The younger Watkins was Guardian from 1862 to 1889, apart from a small gap in his service in 1878. An attempt to unseat him in 1888 was unsuccessful, the vicar remarking that 'never had he heard a greater injustice proposed than this opposition to Mr. Watkins after 25 years' service'.[59] The task of administering out-relief was carried out by the relieving officer, a paid official who served a district comprised of several parishes.[60] Applicants for relief applied to the relieving officer, who presented their case to the fortnightly meeting of the Board of Guardians to decide whether relief was appropriate, and if so whether it should be available inside or outside the workhouse.[61] Overseers of the poor continued to be elected at the annual vestry meeting as late as 1895, but their work would seem to have consisted merely of administering the private charities which operated in the parish and apprenticing parish paupers to local employers.[62]

Other local government functions of the union

While there are undoubtedly many features of the post-1834 system which were as shocking to contemporary eyes as they are today, it recognised one incontrovertible fact, that the parish was not an efficient unit for administering costly services which required a degree of uniformity of provision. In setting up the unions, the government had created a useful framework for developing other functions. The guardians were made responsible for the civil registration of births, marriages and deaths, which was made compulsory in 1837, and four years later were given responsibility for the administration of the census. In 1854, with less success, as part of the Victorian obsession with the gathering of data, the union became responsible for the gathering of agricultural statistics.[63] In 1872 the Ludlow Union became the Rural Sanitary Authority for the area, and occasionally took a desultory interest in Diddlebury, as in 1870 when an attempt was made to prevent the contamination of the Bache Brook by privies at Delbury Hall and another property, which were polluting water used for domestic purposes by residents downstream.[64] The Union also became responsible for providing an elementary health service for the poor, which was administered by its medical officer. The role of the medical officer could prove crucial in assessing out-relief as well as providing treatment in the paupers' own homes or in the infirmary ward of the workhouse. The curious affair of Hannah Painter of Bache Mill in 1887 shows that the concept of patients' rights was not unknown even at this period. Hannah was a consumptive who brought a complaint of neglect against the medical officer, Dr. Malley and his deputy, who, it was claimed, was drunk on two occasions when he visited the patient. The incident led to the holding of an official Local Government Board inquiry at the Crown Inn, Munslow, following which Dr. Malley and Sambrook, the relieving officer who had falsified the records of attendance, were forced to resign. Unfortunately Hannah died a few weeks after gaining her victory.[65]

The coming of elected local government

As Dr. Williams points out, the poor law authorities possessed a bureaucratic machinery which might well have evolved into a new form of local government, but for their traditional unpopularity in the community and oligarchic nature.[66] In consequence, new local authorities developed from different origins.

The parish had carried out in conjunction with the justices a number of functions connected with the maintenance of law and order and the repair of the highways. While the petty constable was traditionally the butt of ridicule, epitomised by Shakespeare's Dogberry, he provided the only mechanism for maintaining law and order in the villages until the county police force, established by the justices of the county in 1839, spread to the Corvedale. The supervisors of the highways or waywardens had been established under the Highways Act of 1555 to supervise the maintenance of the highways by 'statute labour', that is the compulsory obligation upon parishioners to work on the roads for four days a year, or to provide substitutes. Until 1691 the waywardens were elected by the parish, and in Diddlebury they would appear to have been drawn from the same group who served as overseers and churchwardens.[67] In 1691 appointments were made by the justices at their 'Highway Sessions', but following the general Highway Act of 1835, Diddlebury returned to the practice of electing its waywardens at the Easter vestry meeting.[68] Perhaps as a consequence of the reduced responsibilities of the office, after 1835 waywardens appear to have held the post on a semi-permanent basis.[69]

The 19th century witnessed a great extension of government activity in the localities, and for much of the time the favoured method was the creation of statutory authorities such as highway boards, urban and rural sanitary authorities and school boards. Towards the end of the century the inefficiency of a mass of often overlapping authorities became increasingly recognised, and a system of unified authorities based on three tiers came into being. The Local Government Act of 1888 created county councils, which took over most of the administrative functions previously carried out by the county magistrates, to which in 1902 was added responsibility for education. In 1894 the sanitary and highway authorities were incorporated into new urban and rural district councils, and a third tier was added in the form of parish councils. A three tier system of elected local government was created which has lasted, with modifications until the start of the 21st century, though at the time of writing its future looks increasingly uncertain.[70]

The county council was initially dominated by members of the county magistracy, who possessed considerable experience in administering the county, while the initial election to the Ludlow Rural District Council suggested that the farmers would continue to control the new system, with the election of Morgan Jones of Delbury and Richard Evans from Bouldon.[71] That this was not entirely the case is seen when the first years of the parish council are examined. The first elections were conducted by show of hands at a parish meeting held on 4 December 1894, at which 16 candidates stood for nine seats. The vicar and six other candidates represented the group which had controlled parish affairs for the preceding decades, while the remainder, with the exception of Evans, were smaller farmers, a number of whom were members of the Peaton Strand Methodist chapel.[72] Evans, and Smith of Sutton Hill, succeeded in gaining eighth and ninth places, while all the 'establishment' candidates were elected. By the time of the next election, which was held on 31 March 1896 and went to a poll, Evans appears to have been incorporated in to the 'establishment' list, whose candidates swept the board. Party feeling appears to have undergone a brief revival in 1919, when Robert Chester, the Liberal Party agent who lived in Bache Mill, was elected to the parish council and organised a contest for the rural district council. Five candidates stood for two seats, and it is noticeable that the vicar, Harold Mason, and the Primitive Methodist minister were both adherents of the Chester group. Chester and Mason, with 31 and 26 votes respectively were roundly defeated by G.W. Hide of Lawton Farm (84) and H.E. Whitaker of Broncroft Castle (78).[73] After this brief outburst, party feeling subsided, with most elections to both district and parish councils being uncontested until the last decades of the 20th century.

It is probably fair to say that for most of its 80-year existence the attitude of the Ludlow Rural District Council to Diddlebury was reactive rather than proactive. The problems associated with concentrations of population, often in poor housing, in Craven Arms and Clee Hill were always of a more pressing urgency than those of more remote rural communities like Diddlebury, and questions of water supply and drainage in Craven Arms dominated the council's proceedings for much of the period. Initially most of the district's activity in the parish was concerned with maintenance of the network of minor roads, a responsibility which it had inherited from the Rural Highways Board. In October 1898 the Ludlow Borough steam roller was hired to resurface the road at North Sutton aided by the 'new water cart', and these technological wonders were soon in demand on a stretch further north at Peaton.[74] The problems of road maintenance were to increase as motor traffic slowly made its appearance in the parish in the early 20th century.

Unlike the district council, the parish council had few executive powers, although its responsibility for footpaths was diligently performed. This provoked a clash in 1911 between the parish council and Captain Wingfield-Stratford, the new owner of Delbury Hall, over the latter's attempts to close a bridleway and footpath through the park. The parish council, chaired by Captain Smythe of Milford Lodge, took the dispute to the county court at Leominster, where a compromise verdict was obtained.[75] Chiefly, however, the role of the parish council was that of a pressure group acting on behalf of the local community, and attempting to draw the attention of the higher tiers of local government to local problems and needs, a role which it still fulfils. In the 1920s the main problems were the lack of low cost housing and public transport, both of which still occupy much of the council's time. In 1919 the council was lobbying the county to encourage the provision of a motor bus service from Bridgnorth to Ludlow through the parish, and the rural district council to provide housing.[76]

The rural district council's attitude to housing was cautious. In 1930 it had been given responsibility for dealing with unfit and overcrowded housing, and in 1936 pronounced eight houses in the parish to be overcrowded and one unfit. The building of 44 houses in the district, of which two were to be in Diddlebury, was recommended, but nothing was done before the outbreak of war in 1939.[77] After the war Diddlebury finally gained its council houses in Mill Lane (Fig. 44) and the

Fig. 44 Diddlebury's first council houses in Mill Lane were completed in 1948

Moors, though the delays in commencing the work through 1947 were a constant cause of frustration for the parish council, which had enthusiastically supported a suggestion that the village should be expanded as a central settlement for the Corvedale.[78] The rural district council had been greatly aided by the considerable provision of housing which had been made by the Church Commissioners in the eastern part of the parish, which they had assisted by grant aid, at a considerable saving to the ratepayers and benefit to the lower paid section of the community.

The Ludlow Rural District Council ceased to exist in 1974, having been incorporated into the much larger South Shropshire District Council. Diddlebury shared a member with Culmington, and this situation exists at the time of writing, although it is likely that the existing two-tier arrangement of county and district authorities will shortly be replaced by some form of single authority, as in Herefordshire. Behind such proposals lurks the spectre of regional government, which would inevitably be dominated by the urban areas of the West Midlands. Whatever form these changes take, the role of the parish council, if it is allowed to survive, will become increasingly important as the only effective voice of rural communities such as Diddlebury. The wheel may well turn full circle, with the parish becoming the only organ of really local government, as it was four cenuries ago.

DIDDLEBURY HOUSES

Any attempt to provide an architectural and historical summary of houses in Diddlebury is beset by the evidential problems which have been noted in other contexts in this work. In the case of houses, this includes the problem of physical survival. There is very little surviving medieval work, despite the fact that neighbouring parishes contain some of the earliest domestic buildings in the county.[79] Indeed, Diddlebury would appear to confirm the truth of W.G. Hoskins' now largely discredited theory of a great rebuilding between 1570 and 1640,[80] with a large number of buildings surviving from this period. In the matter of documentary evidence, the usual problems exist. While there is a relative abundance of material on the larger dwellings, including those which have long since been destroyed, there is disappointingly little evidence about the cottages in which the majority of the parish lived until well into the 19th century. With these reservations, it is still possible to make some generalisations about houses in Diddlebury and how they were used.

ARCHITECTURAL AND HISTORICAL SURVEY

The larger houses

The dearth of larger medieval buildings in the parish is explained by the nature of medieval landholding. Not only was Diddlebury divided into a number of estates, but these were also in the main small and formed subsidiary members of much

Fig. 45 Aerial view of the remains of Corfham Castle. The foundations of the curtain walls and four circular towers are visible, as indicated on the inset (courtesy of Clwyd-Powys Archaeological Trust 88-MB-45)

more important holdings based elsewhere. This was true even of the largest and most important manor of Corfham, which despite its local status was a relatively minor part of the larger holdings of the Clifford, Le Strange and Talbot families. The premier building of the period was without question Corfham Castle, of which not a stone remains above ground, although it was originally a substantial stone building. An early 17th-century description mentions that it had declined rapidly since the reign of Henry VIII, and mentions a strong curtain wall with corner towers, of which one, Rosamund's Tower, was still standing.[81] The associated earthworks and former water features (Fig. 45) are strongly suggestive of a medieval garden, and it is known that the LeStrange family were particularly interested in landscape creation.[82]

Other gentry houses in the parish were constructed as newer estates were carved out of existing holdings, as described in Section 1. Broncroft in the 14th century was followed by Diddlebury, probably in the early years of the 16th century, with Elsich and Earnstrey later in the same century. Broncroft Castle was almost certainly built by the Tyrell family, who held the estate from at least 1243 to 1361 as undertenants of Corfham. It was famously described by Leland in 1540 as 'a very goodly place like a Castle,' but has since suffered from extensive demolition during the Civil War, and large scale rebuilding in the 19th century which has transformed the remains into what is largely a Victorian gentleman's house.[83] The plan would appear to have been similar to that of Stokesay, with a great hall set between two defensive towers. One of these is largely medieval, but the other, the Library Tower (Fig. 46), has generally been regarded as Victorian, though the lower parts at least appear to contain medieval work. The great hall would appear to be completely Victorian. Broncroft is nevertheless of interest as one of only a handful of domestic buildings in the county constructed of stone between the mid 14th and early 16th centuries.[84] This decline in stone building, which is noted in ecclesiastical as well as secular building in 15th-century Shropshire, has been explained in terms of the siphoning away of much of the county's wealth by absentee landlords like the Talbots and FitzAlans, both of whom were major landholders in Diddlebury.[85]

The earliest of the gentry houses to have been erected unfortunately no longer remains, the old hall at Diddlebury having been demolished in 1752 when

Fig. 46 Broncroft Castle. Despite considerable Victorian rebuilding, medieval work survives in the towers

the present Delbury Hall was constructed. A very comprehensive inventory dating from 1639 provides much information about the house and its rooms,[86] from which a number of inferences may be made. It is clear that the principal and most lavishly furnished room of the house was the great chamber. The inventory mentions six other living rooms, including a gallery chamber and a painted chamber.[87] It may be significant that the hall and the old parlour are included at the end of the inventory after the domestic offices. By 1639 neither room played a major role in the house, the hall having been relegated to a form of gun room. It is possible that these two rooms remained from a former house on the site containing an open hall with a gallery, which had become eclipsed by the great chamber after a rebuilding. It is likely that the demolished building was of timber-framed construction, and in 1985 a quantity of large structural timbers was unearthed when the pool in front of the house was excavated. The old house may have stood immediately adjacent to the present building, and may have been demolished after the completion of the latter, as happened at nearby Millichope in 1843.[88]

Another estate carved out of the old manor of Corfham when the Talbots began to dispose of parts of their estates at a distance from their power base in Sheffield was Earnstrey, which was purchased by Oliver Briggs of Shifnal in 1558. Briggs was clearly creating a new estate on the flanks of the Brown Clee, and in 1565 he bought Clee forest from the earl of Shrewsbury. His son bought the manor of Abdon from Richard Cressett of Upton in 1598.[89] The house at Earnstrey, now known as Upper Earnstrey Park, was probably the lodge of the

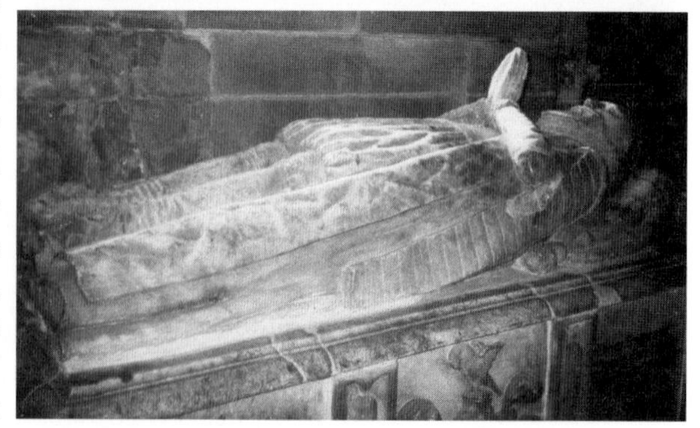

Fig. 47 (a) Upper Earnstrey Park, originally the residence of forester of Earnstrey Park, was rebuilt in the later 16th century, most probably by Oliver Briggs of Shifnal, and is likely to have been the first building in the parish to be constructed in brickwork
(b) The tomb of Oliver Briggs in Shifnal church

Fig. 48 Elsich, a typical Elizabethan gentry house built by the Baldwyn family has undergone alterations since this 19th-century photograph was taken. The wing on the right of the picture is currently being restored after nearly three decades of ruin following a major fire in 1976

medieval forester, and was extensively rebuilt in the later 16th century (Fig. 46). It is notable for the use of brick as well as stone, particularly in the elaborate chimney stacks. Characteristic diaper patterns* of dark bricks are used in some of the external walls.

The building of Elsich has traditionally been ascribed to Richard Baldwyn II of Diddlebury as a residence for his younger son, William, at some time in the second half of the 16th century. The building followed a conventional **U**-shaped plan which was becoming the norm for smaller gentry houses of the period, with a central two-storied hall range and two shallow wings. Extensive alterations took place in the 17th century, for which the accounts survive. These refer to work carried out on the parlour, study and cellar during the spring and summer of 1627, which were probably accommodated in the enlarged eastern wing.[90] Items recording payments to John Smallman for 'making the roofs' of the two dormers may indicate that the unusual stepped windows in the gables date from this time (Fig. 48). Similar windows may be found at Crowleasowes, Bitterley and Ludstone Hall, Claverley, both of which date from the early 17th century. Further works were carried out between 1634 and 1637, which included the building of an ox house and hen house in the yard.

The other substantial house which dates from this period, Sutton Court, has been so thoroughly rebuilt in the 19th century that it is difficult to make any

Fig. 49 Delbury Hall (completed 1756; wings added 1836) was the first house in the parish to be designed by architects rather than local builders. It is typical of the work of the Hiorn brothers of Warwick

deductions about its original plan or extent. It does contain, apparently *in situ*, a pair of grotesque human heads which bear a striking resemblance to those on the roof of Diddlebury church, and may be by the same hand.

The rebuilding of the hall at Diddlebury (hereafter referred to by its post-1793 name of Delbury) between 1752 and 1756 gave the parish its first taste of so-called 'polite'* (as distinct from vernacular*) architecture. Captain Cornewall employed the brothers David and William Hiorn of Warwick, who had taken over the practice of the renowned William Smith there in 1747. Delbury is one of a group of fairly plain country houses in the Midlands by the Hiorns, and is unusually well documented.[91] The house was built of brick, seven bays in width and three storeys in height. The exterior was plain, with such display of ornament as there was being confined to the interior (Fig. 49). The main feature of the house is the entrance hall, with its staircase, modelled on a Chippendale design, which was created by William Earl, the Clerk of Works and principal joiner.[92] A recent writer has commented that the planning of the house, although in many ways rather old-fashioned for its date, is unusual in that the entrance hall does not command the best view from the house. This is obtained from the north front, in which reception rooms were placed.[93] Delbury was a fairly modest house, and cost £1,756 10s., which included the architects' 5% commission. In 1836 it was extended by Frederick Hamilton Cornewall by the addition of two wings flanking the original building. Later additions included a large kitchen block (now demolished), a single storey billiard room, and an elaborate palm house (also demolished).

The greatest period for the building of gentry houses was the century between the end of the Napoleonic Wars in 1815 and the outbreak of the First World War. This era began with the erection of Milford Lodge by the Downes family on 35 acres of freehold land which they owned adjacent to their rented estate in Aston Munslow. This was a small country house in the Regency style, no doubt intended as a more modern residence than the 17th-century Aston Hall.[94]

About 1840 Sutton Court underwent a large scale rebuilding, which transformed it into a three storied U-shaped house, with characteristic sash windows and low-pitched slate roofs.[95] No architect has yet been identified, although a local architect such as one of the Steads or Edward Blakeway Smith of Ludlow may be responsible.[96] Like Milford, the style is still basically Regency.

The architect who transformed Broncroft Castle from a farmhouse set within a ruin into a comfortable gentleman's residence in the gothic style was J.P. Seddon, the designer of the Old College at Aberystwyth.[97] This work must date from between 1867, when it was described by Mrs. Stackhouse Acton as having the appearance of a farmhouse, and 1888 when the last of the Johnstones died. The 1860s also saw the building of Corfton Hall for Thomas Lloyd Roberts, who had inherited the estate in 1854. There had been no mansion house on the estate for some time, the previous Roberts owners having lived in Bewdley.[98] Roberts engaged the Munslow-born architect Samuel Pountney Smith to design him a brick house in the Jacobean style, similar to that which he was to use at Ferney a decade later with somewhat unhappy results.[99] Corfton was an imposing structure which attempted to increase its authenticity by adopting the motif of stepped windows in the gables, which has been noted at Elsich (Fig. 50).

Fig. 50 Corfton Hall, designed by Samuel Pountney Smith for Thomas Lloyd Roberts, was demolished in 1953

The final gentleman's house to be built in Diddlebury was at Westhope at the very end of the 19th century. Like Corfton, Westhope had been without a principal residence for several generations. The Dannetts and the Flemings must have possessed a suitable house, but by 1900 no-one knew where it had

Fig. 51 The large Arts and Crafts house designed at Westhope for Leonard Swinnerton-Dyer by Guy Dawber, seen shortly after completion

been situated.[100] Between 1898 and 1902 Mrs. Swinnerton-Dyer commissioned Guy Dawber, later the president of the Royal Society of British Architects, to design a house at Westhope as a wedding present for her son, Leonard. Westhope Manor was a large and rambling Arts and Crafts mansion, heavily influence by the Cotswold vernacular style which Dawber particularly favoured (Fig. 51). Sir Leonard and his wife lived at the Manor for their lifetimes, but their son and his wife preferred the Cottage (now Westhope College), and in 1948 the Manor was converted into three dwellings.

The last piece of significant country house building took place in 1921, when Sir Basil Stallybrass added a music room to Sutton Court, then the home of Lionel Powell, a noted London impresario. The following half century was a bad time for country houses generally, and it is fortunate that in Diddlebury only Corfton fell victim to the demolition contractors. At the time of writing (2006) Broncroft, Delbury, Sutton, Milford and Elsich all flourish as family homes, while Westhope continues to be well maintained as three separate dwellings.

Farmhouses and other middle-sized dwellings

While there is a relative abundance of documentary evidence concerning the medieval peasantry of Diddlebury and their properties, it can be safely asserted that next to nothing remains of any of these buildings before the 16th century. There are two great periods of building evident in the parish, one of which approximates to the period of Hoskins' 'great rebuilding', the other being the early 19th century. It is significant that the earlier of these two periods shows a widespread building or rebuilding of farmhouses in all parts of the parish, whereas in the later period its was largely confined to the larger and more prosperous farms of the valley of the Corve. The relative poverty of the upland parts of the parish at this time doubtless accounts for the survival of Middlehope as a settlement of timber-framed houses to the present day.

Timber-framed farmhouses

Farmhouses of the 16th and 17th centuries were constructed of timber-framing or stone, and sometimes a combination of the two. As both materials were to be found in abundance in the locality, there is no significant difference in distribution between the upland and valley parts of the parish.

The plan and design of timber-framed farmhouses was generally conservative, being based upon a hall and one or two cross-wings. Little evidence of medieval open halls has survived in the historic parish, although Bouldon Farm, formerly in Holdgate, and built of stone and timber frame, does contain an early 16th-century hall with smoke-blackened timbers in the roof.[101] The larger farmhouses, like Bouldon, tended to retain elements of the medieval plan well into the 17th century. This consisted of a hall, to which one or two cross wings were added to provide further accommodation. This arrangement can be clearly seen at Sutton Court Farm, which may originally have been the site of the manor house of the de Suttons. The present building, which probably dates from two phases in the 16th century, has a hall and a square-framed service wing, to which a close-studded* parlour wing was added subsequently to create an H-plan (Fig. 52). This parlour wing contains the remains of 16th-century wall paintings, which have faded since their discovery in 1986. The hall at Sutton, despite being eclipsed in importance by the parlour, retains elements of its former cross passage,[102] and this arrangement may also be seen at Lower House, Middlehope. This is another 'sub-medieval'* house which comprises a hall block, which would appear

Fig. 52 Sutton Court Farm. The addition of two cross-wings and external chimney stacks to the original hall transformed the building into a conventional 16th-century H-plan house

to have been two-storied from the start, with a cross passage between it and the close-studded two-storey service wing (Fig. 53). One medieval feature which has survived, at North Sutton, is a detached kitchen, which has subsequently been converted to a separate cottage. Detached kitchens were employed to limit any damage which might have been caused by outbreaks of fire.[103]

One of the most important developments of the 16th and 17th centuries was the spread of chimneys into a far wider range of properties than hitherto. Massive chimney stacks added to lateral or end walls of existing buildings are a characteristic feature of the transition from medieval to modern house types. At Sutton Court Farm they have been inserted rather clumsily, with the consequent reversing of the frontage of the house. At Glebe Farm and at Hall Farm, Middlehope, both examples of hall and cross-wing houses, the stacks have been inserted on lateral walls. While most of the larger farmhouses preserved a sub-medieval layout until at least the middle years of the 17th century, there are a number of more innovatory designs.

Fig. 53 Lower House Farm, Middlehope. (a) The exterior shows the hall and cross-wing, with a later extension to the right of the picture. Despite the relatively low height of the building, it would appear always to have been two-storied
(b) The ceiling beams of the ground floor reveal the division which marked the original through passage

Fig. 54 Upper House Farm, Middlehope.
(a) The house from the east, showing the projecting upper floor and diagonal patterned timber framing
(b) The exposed ceiling timbers in the main ground-floor room, with the dragon beam which originally supported the jetty

One of these may be seen at Upper House Farm at Middlehope, which has undergone many alterations and additions since the 16th century. The core of the building survives as a rectangular structure which may possibly have originally been free-standing and jettied* on all four sides.[104] The upper storeys are composed of square-framing with diagonal bracing, presumably of a 17th-century date. The main ground floor room contains deeply chamfered spine beams,* and a well preserved dragon beam* (Fig. 54). The original appearance of the building has been much altered by the addition of a cross-wing, and on the eastern side by the construction of a timber-framed outshut.* This house is of interest as the only example so far located in the parish of a surviving building which can be

Fig. 55 Broncroft Parks (formerly known as Lower Parks). This 1922 photograph shows the elaborately decorative timber framing which was covered with render during the 1950s

confidently linked to a probate inventory. That of John Baldwyn (1671) lists seven living rooms, together with cellar and buttery.[105] The cellar survives today, and it is likely that the main downstairs room containing the dragon beam was the great parlour, but it is virtually impossible to make any other conjectural identification of rooms.

Another larger yeoman farmhouse which moved completely away from the medieval plan was Lower Parks, a large T-plan building with high quality decorative timber framing of a mid- to late 17th-century date (Fig. 55). Most of this was covered by render in the 1950s by the Church Commissioners who then owned the property. It is possible, but not completely certain, that this was the house of Arthur Stedman, whose 1669 inventory was valued at £337 9s. 8d.[106] The final phase of large-scale timber building is represented by Great Sutton Farm, a large and plain rectangular building with thin framing forming square panels which were almost certainly not intended to be exposed, unlike the decorative motifs of Lower Parks (Fig. 56). This may date from the very last years of the 17th century, or even the early years of the following century.

The houses which have been discussed so far were all the homes of the wealthier yeoman farmers, some of whom may well have perceived themselves as gentry.[107] All the foregoing examples were also of box-frame construction,* with crucks* being uncommon in the parish, which probably implies nothing more

Fig. 56 Great Sutton Farm represents the end of the timber-framed tradition in the parish, and dates from the very end of the 17th century

than the accident of survival. This is corroborated by documentary evidence for the use of crucks at the medieval vicarage, which would seem to have been a high status building.[108] The one verified domestic example of cruck construction was in a smaller building, Fernalls Mill in Middlehope, which was photographed in 1967 prior to its collapse (Fig. 57).[109] The majority of smaller timber-framed farm-

Fig. 57 Fernalls Mill at Middlehope, now collapsed, was the only known example of cruck construction in the parish

houses date from the 17th century, and follow a simple rectilinear plan with the chimney placed inside the building either centrally as at No.9, Lower Corfton (Fig. 58), or at the end of the building as at Lydehole or Green Farm, Middlehope. Both internal and end wall chimneys are to be found at the somewhat larger New House in Peaton. Where the stack was placed centrally, it was often customary for the door to the house to be placed opposite to it with access to the rooms on either side, creating a baffle-entry.* Such houses usually contained two rooms on the ground floor, with the fireplaces placed back to back in the central stack. The examples quoted were all houses of smaller farmers, and were probably very similar to the larger cottages of the parish.

Fig. 58 No.9, Lower Corfton with its centrally placed chimney stack is typical of smaller 17th-century timber-framed houses in the parish

Stone houses to 1700

As noted above, many of the farmhouses in the parish were originally built in stone. Some houses which started their lives as timber-framed structures were subsequently clad in stone, either almost wholly as at North Sutton and Bouldon Farm, or partially as at Glebe Farm, Diddlebury, where one wing has been encased in stone, while the framing of the other remains exposed. It is sometimes almost impossible to tell from the exterior of a building like Middle Westhope Farm, which follows the traditional plan of hall and cross-wing, whether it was originally built in stone or has been subsequently cladded. While some houses which were stone-built from the start followed a conventional plan, others like Peaton Hall, a double pile* pile building, were far more experimental. This impressive sandstone building was erected in 1663 by Edward Pulley, according to a date stone which has been re-set into the front of the house (Fig. 59a). Peaton Hall for most of its history has been the largest and most prosperous holding in the parish, and Pulley was perceived by himself and his neighbours to be 'gentry'. The building was much altered in the early 20th century by its then owner, W.H. Atherden,

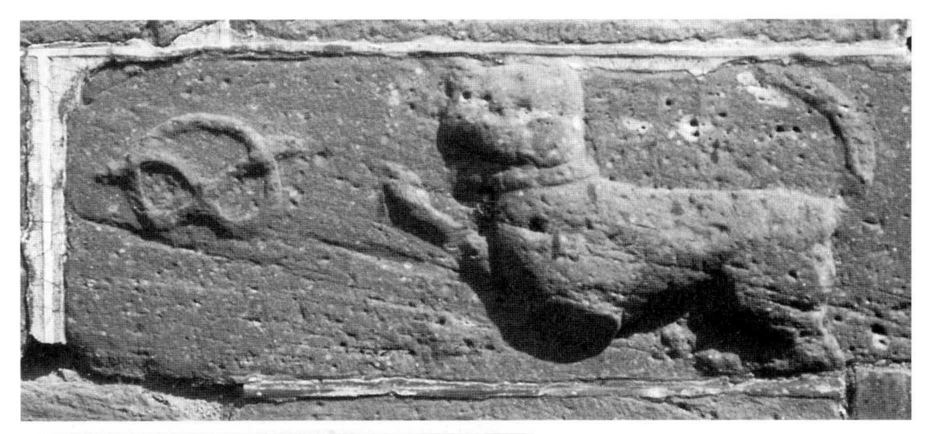

Fig. 59 Peaton Hall.
(a) Date stone of 1663,
with the initials of Edward Pulley
and his wife
(b) Talbot and Staffordshire knot on
a stone in an outbuilding

a Ludlow banker, but preserves some of its 17th-century arrangements. A carved stone in the wall of an outbuilding features the Staffordshire Knot, and the Talbot of the earls of Shrewsbury, commemorating the two noble families which had owned the estate in the 17th century (Fig. 59b).

Another stone double pile building, also much altered over the centuries is the Sun Inn at Corfton, which has been in continuous use as an inn since at least 1616.[110] Other stone farmhouses of 17th-century origins which have been much altered over the years include Delbury Farm, which is the only house in the parish to preserve a two-storeyed porch, and Westhope Hall, which is dated 1617 on the chimney.

Farmhouses and other middle sized dwellings after 1700

The second quarter of the 18th century saw the first houses in the parish to be constructed entirely of brick. This material was beginning to become fashionable and less expensive, and the rebuilding of much of Ludlow in brick had begun about 1720. Both the Diddlebury examples were rebuildings of existing high status houses, the Rectory at Corfton and Lodge Farm at Broncroft. Unfortunately there are no documentary records for either, though the Rectory would appear to be the slightly older of the two. It is an elegant two storeyed building of seven bays, with a characteristic doorcase positioned centrally and sash windows (Fig. 60a). Lodge Farm was formerly a large, probably timber-framed house, for which a detailed inventory of 1654 exists, listing no less than 18 rooms, including a porch with a room over.[111] This was rebuilt about 1750 by Edward Turner, who in addition to the tenancy of the Lodge owned freehold lands at Clee St. Margaret,

Fig. 60(a) The former rectory at Corfton is probably the first house in the parish to have been rebuilt in brick in the 18th century
(b) Lodge Farm, Broncroft, is a nid-18th-century rebuilding of a much larger house which formerly occupied the site

Wigmore and Aymestrey. Turner's house was much smaller than its predecessor, being rebuilt as a three bay brick house of two storeys with attics (Fig. 60b). At the same time the farm was provided with a set of brick outbuildings of a very high quality, which still survive unconverted. Brick was also used to build the great barn complexes erected for Elsich, Upper House and Lower House, Corfton on the lands enclosed from Corfton Wood in 1779. Of these only the last, known as Hale Barns retain anything resembling their original appearance.

The late 18th and early 19th centuries saw a considerable rebuilding of farmhouses in the valley area. This generally took the form of a symmetrical front of three bays and two or three storeys, with chimneys placed on each end wall. Hill House, Corfton; Peaton Lodge; Sparchford; and Lawton Farms are all typical samples of this period of rebuilding. Peaton Lodge (Fig. 61) is a fine example of a type of house with distinctive elliptical-headed windows which is found the length of the Corvedale. The origin of the design has yet to be located. In view of the agricultural depression which hit the country after 1870, it is not surprising that there is little evidence of later Victorian building of farmhouses. A couple of Edwardian examples, Milford Farmhouse and Milford Hut, the latter now altered out of all recognition, demonstrate how, by the early years of the 20th century, the designs of contemporary suburban villas were being adapted to agricultural dwellings.

The imposition of increasingly rigid planning controls in the latter part of the 20th century has wisely restricted new building to within so-called 'village

Fig. 61 Peaton Lodge is typical of Corvedale farmhouses built or rebuilt in the late Georgian period. The elliptical window heads are characteristic of these houses

Fig. 62 Barn conversions, such as this at Middlehope, were undertaken throughout the parish at the end of the 20th century. In this instance a great deal of the historic character of the building was retained

envelopes', which has prevented sporadic development in the countryside, and in the case of Diddlebury has largely restricted the building of owner-occupied housing to Mill Lane. This now links the village centre to Bache Mill, reversing the migration process which had taken place over preceding centuries. A largely unforeseen consequence of the tight controls over development in the countryside has been the conversion of redundant agricultural buildings into houses, a process which has affected the country as a whole. Diddlebury has been no exception, with the result that there are relatively few old farm buildings in the parish which are still used for agricultural purposes. On the whole the process has been beneficial, giving new life to buildings many of which would otherwise have been demolished. Some particularly good conversions have been made (Fig. 62), though there have been others which are less successful. The scale of the process did, however, conflict with the planners' aims to relate new development to the availability of services and similar factors, with the result that South Shropshire District Council now follows a policy of only permitting the conversion of farm buildings for holiday letting.

Workers' housing

Little is known or survives relating to the cottages in which the majority of the inhabitants of the parish lived until the early 19th century. It may be assumed that the majority were poorly built, often comprising two or three rooms, and roofed with thatch. Undoubtedly many were overcrowded and insanitary, and when abandoned they quickly disintegrated. This may be seen when comparing 19th-century Ordnance Survey maps of Sutton Hill, then a populous part of the parish, with those of today, upon which few dwellings are marked. Some idea of the appearance of local cottages before improvement may be gained from a photograph of Bache Mill taken about 1900 (Fig. 63).

A letter from Thomas Lloyd (later Thomas Lloyd Roberts) to his father Wilson Aylesbury Roberts dated February 1824 throws an interesting light on the problems of maintenance.[112] Roberts sought to persuade his father to re-roof a cottage on the estate, and to raise the walls by two feet to create additional headroom upstairs. This would 'make it a comfortable cottage' whereas 'if it is thatched up it will always want repairing.'

Thomas Lloyd Roberts was the first landowner in the parish to attempt the systematic improvement of his labourers' homes. On inheriting the estate in 1854, he wrote that 'there are about 30 cottages on the estate and such is their condition that I intend taking down and rebuilding 2 annually till all are put in tenantable order'.[113] While he did not completely achieve his aim, he did rebuild many of the cottages on the estate in an attractive and instantly recognisable neo-Tudor style. Many have been altered, particularly by the replacement of their original diamond-paned casement windows, and at least one has been extended out of all recognition (Fig. 64).

Other landowners began similar improvements towards the end of the 19th century. J.H. Atherden, who purchased the Peaton estate in 1897, engaged

Fig. 63 These cottages at Bache Mill, c.*1900 were typical of working-class housing at the start of the 20th century*

the Powis Castle estate office to design semi-detached stone cottages, four of which were built (Fig. 65).[114] At much the same time the Swinnerton-Dyers at Westhope began a cottage building programme. The first were the Crossways Cottages, a semi-detached pair of brick with lattice panes. Others which followed included a curious pair of cottages built under long tiled sloping roofs to give a wedge-shaped effect, which were designed by the multi-talented Mrs. Martin. A curious feature of housing on the Westhope estate was the construction of a barracks to house workers who were engaged in building Ward Farm about 1910. These consisted of a prefabricated dormitory and a small house for the foreman.[115]

Fig. 64 An estate cottage at Lower Corfton rebuilt by Thomas Lloyd Roberts after 1854. All these cottages featured 'Tudor' details such as lattice casements and hood moulds, but many have been extensively altered in recent times

Fig. 64 Cottages on the Peaton Estate were desgned by the Powis estate offices for J.H. Atherden of Peaton Hall. (Shropshire Archives, 552/9/430)

When the work was completed, the barracks were converted into three cottages for estate workers, and fully modernised in the late 1980s. Although Ward Cottage had been built by Mrs. Martin in 1906 as a headmistress's house, in 1919 the unfortunate Mrs. Cook and her children were living at the Barracks.[116]

The last major building of estate cottages took place after the Second World War when the Church Commissioners, who had purchased the Holder estates in 1943, began a programme of constructing cedarwood houses at Sutton, Peaton, Peaton Strand and Bouldon. These represented a major improvement in the housing stock of the parish. Although the parish council had first lobbied the Ludlow Rural District Council to build council houses in Diddlebury as early as June 1919, it was not until 1946 that a scheme was finally adopted to build houses in Mill Lane.[117] These were followed in 1947 by further development on the Moors field. Changes in government housing policy in the 1980s meant that many of these houses were bought by their tenants, and those which remained were transferred from the council to the South Shropshire Housing Association, who completed a small scheme of social housing for renting to local people in 1997.

Appendix 1

Diddlebury Probates at Hereford : Names 1660 – 1700

Date	Name	Residence	Occupation	Value
1675	Charles Baldwyn	Elsich	Esquire	No inventory
1671	John Baldwyn	Middlehope	Gentleman	152: 05: 08
1689	Deborah Baxter	Earnstrey Pk.	Widow	147: 00: 00
1683	Richard Baxter	Earnstrey Pk.	Yeoman	557: 11: 00
1661	Cornelius Bennion	Peaton	Yeoman	No inventory
1699	John Blucke	Peaaton	Yeoman	15: 15: 06
1683	Thomas Bluck	Sparchford	[Yeoman]	127: !9: 00
1700	Richard Brecknock	Peaton	[Yeoman]	36: 02: 09
1677	Francis Collins	Corfton		66: 17: 02
1688	Griffith Davies	Middlehope	Yeoman	37: 14: 08
1670	Richard Downes	Diddlebury		11: 00: 00
1681	William Ensom	Corfton	[Agriculture]	14: 12: 03
1669	Edward Evans	Moorswood	[Yeoman]	68: 06: 00
1676	Edward Fewtrell	Diddlebury	[Yeoman]	30: 12: 04
1670	John Hall	Middlehope	Yeoman	20: 15: 00
1685	William Handson	Peaton.	[Yeoman]	148:12: 00
1685	Adam Hanson	Broncroft Pk.	Yeoman	193: 18: 04
1671	Anna Hanson	Broncroft Pk.	Widow [Ag.]	206: 06: 08
1678	Richard Hanson	Diddlebury	Yeoman	113: 17: 06
1677	John Harris	Lt. Sutton	Yeoman	107: 05: 00
1686	Richard Harris	Lt. Sutton		52: 04: 00
1682	Joyce Harwell	Diddlebury		22: 16: 06
1666	Anne Hashould	Bache Mill	Widow	11: 11: 10
1669	Thomas Haynes	Diddlebury	Yeoman	37: 13: 03
1699	Francis Head	Diddlebury	Butcher	89: 00: 00
1680	Thomas Hosier	Diddlebury	Yeoman	34: 18: 00
1661	Roger James	Diddlebury	Yeoman	No inventory
1685	Francis Johnson	Earnstrey Park	[Yeoman]	75: 18: 06
1683	Charles Jones	Gt. Sutton	Husbandman	76: 05: 03
1679	Edward Jones	Gt. Sutton	[Husbandman]	10: 11: 06
1673	Mary Jordan	Diddlebury		No inventory
1661	Edward Lewis	Wetmoor		No inventory
1674	Thomas Lewis	Middlehope	[Agriculture]	06: 19: 08
1674	Peter Mathew	Diddlebury		10: 00: 00
1697	Richard Millichap	Earnstrey Pk.	Yeoman	194: 19: 00
1679	Anne Minton	Diddlebury	Widow [Ag.]	88: 13: 04
1665	Thomas Minton	Diddlebury	Yeoman	26: 04: 04
1682	William Minton	Diddlebury		No inventory
1681	Thomas Nornecott	Lt. Sutton	[Yeoman]	22: 12: 04
1675	Thomas Penny	Westhope	Yeoman	20: 09: 08
1666	Stephen Powell	Diddlebury		04: 00: 06
1675	Elinor Powles	Diddlebury	Widow [Ag.]	33: 08: 00
1667	Miles Powles	Diddlebury	[Yeoman]	14: 14: 00
1689	Oliver ap Hugh	Westhope	Yeoman	10: 05: 00
1666	Thomas Radnor	Diddlebury	[Yeoman]	15: 12: 00
1676	Richard Shepheard	Diddlebury	Vicar of Diddlebury	24: 08: 08
1675	William Simmons	Peaton	Tiler	13: 02: 04
1674	Thomas Smart	Broncroft		51: 10: 00
1666	George Smith	Corfton	Husbandman	20: 11: 00
1669	Arthur Stedman	[Broncroft Pk.]	[Yeoman]	337: 19: 08
1663	Henry Stedman	Diddlebury	Yeoman	32: 16: 06
1680	Katherine Stedman	Corfton	Widow	09: 19: 06
1664	Margery Stedman	Diddlebury	Widow	No inventory
1687	Margery Taylor	[Burwood]	Widow	85: 10: 00
1687	Richard Taylor	Gt. Sutton	Yeoman	154: 09: 10
1696	Edward Thomas	Diddlebury	Yeoman	81: 14: 10
1683	Thomas Wall	Earnstrey Pk.	Yeoman	371: 11: 05
1672	Richard Ward	Lt. Sutton		03: 05: 00
1665	Edward Wellens	Gt. Sutton	[Yeoman]	70: 02: 02
1675	William Wigley	Diddlebury	[Yeoman]	33: 13: 10
1684	Richard Wigley	Corfham	Miller	113: 05: 02
1675	William Wigley	Peaton		No inventory

Diddlebury Probates at Hereford: Names 1701 –1762

Date	Name	Residence	Occupation	Value
1708	Edward Adams	Diddlebury		No inventory
1709	Joan Ambler	Corfton	Widow	No inventory
1710	Richard Amies	Westhope	Labourer	36: 13: 06
1729	Thomas Amies	Westhope	Yeoman	No inventory
1734	Thomas Baker	Lower Parks	Yeoman	192: 15: 00
1713	Alice Beamond	Peaton	Widow	18: 03: 00
1729	John Beamond	Peaton	Yeoman	16: 01: 00
1720	Joan Beddoes	Lower Parks	Widow	1 9: 12: 06
1715	Timothy Benion	Peaton	[Yeoman]	121: 18: 00
1713	William Bottfield	Lawton	Yeoman	19: 18: 06
1723	Benjamin Boundford	Peaton	Yeoman	90: 06: 06
1721	Richard Bradley	Diddlebury		11: 17: 01
1743	William Caldwell	Gt. Sutton	Yeoman	No inventory
1730	Mary Child	Corfton	Widow	09: 12: 06
1716	Richard Childe	Gt. Sutton		No inventory
1706	Richard Clee	Diddlebury		15: 02: 06
1740	Richard Crudgington	Diddlebury	[Yeoman]	169: 07: 06
1709	Elizabeth Crump	Peaton	Widow	14: 10: 00
1712	Elizabeth Dale	Diddlebury	[Widow]	13: 00: 00
1710	John Dale	Elsich	Gentleman	1573: 10: 00
1719	Thomas Dupper	Peaton	Labourer	15: 14: 02
1763	Edward Deuxall	Sutton		493: 00: 00
1738	Thomas Evans	Diddlebury	Yeoman	No inventory
1740	Joan Farmer	Diddlebury	Widow	03: 16: 06
1715	George Fernalls	Middlehope	Carpenter	11: 03: 00
1729	Elizabeth Fleming	Westhope	Widow	No inventory
1705	Edward Floyd	Sparchford	[Yeoman]	199: 06: 00
1726	William Fosbrooke	Diddlebury	Vicar of Diddlebury	No inventory
1707	Anthony Gettens	Gt. Sutton	Yeoman	No inventory
1731	Richard Gough	Diddlebury	[Yeoman]	220: 05: 00
1706	Thomas Gough	Diddlebury		No inventory
1729	Mary Handson	Peaton	Widow	189: 18: 00
1724	Henry Haynes	Sparchford	[Yeoman]	309: 17: 00
1716	Nicholas Jarrett	Diddlebury		36: 17: 00
1738	Elizabeth Keysall	Peaton	Widow	No inventory
1739	Mary Keysall	Peaton	Maid [i.e. unmarried]	18: 18: 06
1728	Thomas Keysall	Peaton	Yeoman	169: 10: 00
1736	John Knowles	Diddlebury		No inventory
1712	John Lelloe	Middlehope		15: 14: 00
1716	William Lelloe	Middlehope	[Yeoman]	No inventory
1717	Bartholomew Lutley	Lawton	Gentleman	2501: 00: 00
1707	John Meredith	Peaton	Yeoman	114: 05: 00
1705	Richard Millichap	[Earnstrey Pk.]	[Yeoman]	489: 17: 00
1732	Elizabeth Morris	Moorswood		No inventory
1742	Elizabeth Morris	Diddlebury	Widow [Ag.]	14: 05: 06
1730	Richard Morris	Moorswood		No inventory
1715	William Morris	Peaton	Yeoman	37: 15: 00
1722	Edward Mytton	Corfton	Gentleman	No inventory
1706	Edward Niff	Sparchford	Yeoman	107: 04: 06
1719	Thomas Nornecott	Corfton	[Yeoman]	68: 16: 00
1736	Thomas Pearkes	Diddlebury		06: 05: 00
1721	Samuel Powell	Diddlebury		No inventory
1709	Thomas Powles	Corfton	Yeoman	51: 17: 02
1746	Thomas Radnor	Diddlebury	Husbandman	No inventory
1706	Joseph Rowton	Lawton	Labourer	66: 05: 00
1721	John Smyth	Westhope	[Yeoman]	109: 00: 00
1709	Catherine Squire	Corfton	Widow	254: 10: 02
1712	Edward Squire			07: 04: 00
1711	Thomas Squire	Westhope		10: 10: 00
1714	Ann Stedman	Corfton	Widow	259: 11: 04
1736	Daniel Stedman	Poston	[Yeoman]	552: 06: 00
1708	John Stretton	Lawton	Weaver	16: 00: 00
1728	Edward Taylor	Middlehope	Yeoman	182: 16: 00
1741	John Taylor	Burwood	Yeoman	19: 15: 00
1730	John Thomas	Corfton	Labourer	No inventory
1706	Elizabeth Tipton	Diddlebury	[Widow]	42: 08: 00
1731	Francis Tipton	Diddlebury	[Yeoman]	466: 17: 00
1741	Edward Tipton	Diddlebury		No inventory
1741	Francis Tipton	Diddlebury	[Yeoman]	32: 17: 00
1704	Jeremy Tipton	Diddlebury	Yeoman	50: 02: 00
1741	Thomas Tomson	Corfton	Glazier	17: 14: 00
1762	Samuel Wilks	Peaton	Yeoman	17: 05: 00

Glossary of terms

a) General historical terms

Advowson: The right of presenting a clergyman to a benefice or living.
Agistement: The right to graze stock on the lands of another, generally the lord of the manor, on payment of a fee.
Alienation: The granting of land from a tenant to an under-tenant.
Appropriators: Persons who leased the right to collect the tithes in a parish or township.
Caput: The administrative centre of a manor or hundred.
Churching of women: A service of thanksgiving for childbirth in the Book of Common Prayer.
Coppicing: A process of timber culture whereby the trees were cut down to the stool to allow the growth of poles, which could be harvested. Practised extensively with willow, hazel, and birch.
Dower: A portion of an estate (generally a third) granted to a widow out of her husband's lands to maintain her until her death.
Knight's fee: An area of land held of the king or another overlord in exchange for the service of one knight for a fixed period (generally 40 days).
Hide: A unit of land approximating to 120 acres.
Hundred: An administrative unit originally based upon a hundred townships.
Hundred year rule: A measure prohibiting public access to certain documents such as census returns for a century.
Inquisition post mortem: An inquest taken to establish the extent of the lands of a tenant of the Crown after his or her death.
Justices in Eyre: Itinerant judges who travelled the country on circuits hearing cases. The origin of Assizes.
Mort d'ancestor: A legal process whereby the rightful owner of an estate could claim against one who had wrongfully claimed it on the death of an ancestor.
Novel disseizin: A legal process which enabled freeholders to take action against those who were alleged to have unjustly deprived them of their lands.
Nucleated settlement: One in which the settlement is concentrated round a central feature such as a green or cross-roads, rather than consisting of dwellings dispersed over a wider area.
Out-relief. Payments made to paupers who remained in their own homes rather than entering a workhouse.
Oyer and Terminer: A commission to a justice or justices to gather evidence and determine the outcome of an alleged infringement of the law.
Pannage: The right to graze pigs (and in Westhope, goats) on the land of another.
Seneschal: A manorial administrator of considerable responsibility.
Serjeantry: A form of military service performed in exchange for land, such as providing an armed escort for royal officials or revenue.
Surplice fees: Charges levied by the clergy for performing marriages, churchings etc.
Thrave: A measure of corn in the sheaf, usually 12 or 24 in number.

Utilitarians: A group of political thinkers in the early 19th century who believed that usefulness should be the sole criterion for judging institutions and practises. A great influence (often with disastrous results) on the Liberal government of 1832-35.

Vestry meeting: An annual meeting of parishioners to elect churchwardens and other parochial officers, to set church rates etc. Vestries often sat other times in the year, as business demanded.

b) Architectural Terms

Arts and Crafts: A movement of William Morris and others at the end of the 19th century which favoured craftsmanship over mass-production, and often employed vernacular styles.

Baffle entry: An arrangement where the entrance door of a house is placed opposite to the chimney stack, with living rooms opening off each side.

Box frame: A common form of timber frame construction in which the walls form a 'box' upon which the roof is supported.

Close studding: A style of timer framing in which a wall is composed of closely-spaced vertical timbers, generally as an indication of wealth.

Cruck construction: A form of timber framed building when the bay divisions of a house are formed by arches formed from split oak trunks.

Double pile: An arrangement of two parallel ranges of rooms in one building, each having their own roof.

Dragon beam: A diagonally placed timber which enables a jetty to be carried round the corner of a building.

Imposts: Horizontal blocks placed at the base of an arch, especially in pre-Conquest buildings.

Jetty: The projecting upper storey of a timber framed building

Lavatorium: A washing place.

Outshut: An addition of a building formed by extending the eaves to a lower level to form a lean-to.

'Polite' architecture: The product of architects, often employed by wealthy clients and generally following national and international fashions, rather than using local or vernacular styles.

Sheila-na-gig: An obscene representation of a female figure, perhaps with undertones of pagan survivals.

Spine beam: The main ceiling beam running the length of a whole room.

Sub-medieval house: A house which retains the medieval 'three unit' ground plan, but with upper rooms in all parts. A transition from medieval to 'modern' building types.

Three unit plan: The common form of medieval house plan, comprised of a hall, cross-passage and service area.

Vernacular architecture: The architectural style of smaller buildings before *c.*1750, built by local craftsmen with local materials, and exhibiting many local characteristics.

References

Abbreviations used

Cal. I.P.M.	Calendars of Inquisitions Post Mortem
CPR	Calendars of Patent Rolls
HCR	Hereford Cathedral Records
HRO	Herefordshire Records Office
PRO	Public Records Office (now the National Archives)
SA	Shropshire Archives
SPR	Shropshire Parish Registers series
TSAS	Transactions of the Shropshire Archaeological and Historical Society
TWNFC	Transactions of the Woolhope Naturalists Field Club

Section 1

1. The author wishes to acknowledge his debt to M.A. Scard, *The Building Stones of Shropshire*, (1990), for much of the information upon which the foregoing paragraph is based.
2. Bache Brook is the older name for this stream, which is now popularly (but erroneously) known as the Diddle. The origins of the name 'Diddlebury' will be discussed later in this section.
3. The origin of the term is the Old English 'baece' meaning a stream or valley. The usage is largely confined to Shropshire, Herefordshire and Cheshire. M. Gelling, *Place Names in the Landscape*, (2000), 12. In Munslow parish the term 'deans' is preferred, and originates with another Old English word for a valley, 'denu.' *Ibid.*, 97.
4. *VCH Shropshire*, Vol. X, (1998), 2
5. Salop SMR, 8609. It is believed to have originated from the Penzance area
6. S.C. Stanford, *The Archaeology of the Welsh Marches*, (1980), 67-71.
7. 250 m. S of Corfton Farm, Salop SMR 7367.
8. Stanford, *op.cit.*, 155.
9. A.W. Houghton, The Roman Road from Greensford through the Central Welsh March, *TSAS*, 56, (1960), 233-43.
10. M. Gelling, *op.cit.*, 88.
11. *ibid.*, 41-49 discusses the usage of 'hamm' in great detail with reference to recent scholarship.
12. H.P.R. Finberg, *Early Charters of the West Midlands*, (1972), 203.
13. T. Rowley, *The Making of the Shropshire Landscape*, (1972), 50-52.
14. It may be significant that the name Merewalh means 'famous Welshman'.
15. M. Gelling and H.D.G Foxall, *The Place Names of Shropshire, Part I*, (1990), 54; 98-9; 288-9.
16. Dr. Gelling suggests that the 'bolle' element may refer to an unrecorded plant name, and that the 'dun' may imply a change of site from the hill to the valley of the Clee Brook. *Ibid.*,
17. SA, 6001/6862.
18. W. Byford Jones, *Earl Baldwin's Country*, (1938), 63-4. Jones claimed to have been told 'it's an unfortunate name – sounds like part of a music hall joke. You'll find places much quicker if, when asking for directions, you use the name Delbury.'
19. For a discussion on nucleated settlements and their dating see C. Taylor, *Village and Farmstead*, (1983), Chapter 8.
20. For an examination of this organisation with reference to one of the greatest marcher families and their estates, see C. Hopkinson and M. Speight, *The Mortimers: Lords of the March*, (2002), Chapter IX.
21. J. Morris (ed.), *Domesday Book: 25, Shropshire*, (1986)
22. It was most unusual for a magnate to hold so much land in the area from which he took his title, the earldom of Chester being the other great exception. *VCH Shropshire*, Vol. I, (1908 rep. 1968), 288.
23. R.W. Eyton, *History of Shropshire*, Vol. V, (1847).

24. There is thus no truth in the tradition which names Corfham as Rosamund's birthplace, nor is there any link between Rosamund and the nearby well which bears her name.
25. *Cal IPM*, Edward I, Vol . III, 544.
26. Not knowing that they were related. A papal dispensation allowing the marriage to be regularised was obtained in 1307. H. LeStrange, *Le Strange Records, A.D.1100-1310*, (1916) 293.
27. A most spectacular example was Roger Mortimer V. When he succeeded in 1331, his mother, grandmother and great grandmother all held parts of the estate as dower. He finally inherited the last portions shortly before his death in 1360, when the process began again for his son Edmund, who was outlived by his own mother. Hopkinson and Speight, *op.cit*, 108-112.
28. A.J. Pollard, 'The Family of Talbot, Lords Talbot and Earls of Shrewsbury in the Fifteenth Century', unpublished University of Bristol Ph.D. thesis (1968), 64. The first earl had intended Corfham to be the centre of a separate patrimony in south Shropshire. The deaths of both Lewis (1460) and Humphrey (1496) without issue saw the purchased properties return to the main Talbot line.
29. B Ross (ed.), *Accounts of the Stewards of the Talbot Household at Blakemere, 1392-1425*, (2003), 62.
30. *ibid.*, 52.
31. Pollard, *op.cit*, 296 ff.
32. *Cal. IPM,* Edward III, Vol. VIII, 451. Hugh Tyrell, 1340.
33. *Cal. IPM,* Henry VII, Second Series Vol. III, 203.
34. Eyton, *op.cit.*, Vol. V, 90ff.
35. *ibid.*
36. Eyton, *op.cit.*, Vol. V, 90 ff.; *Rotuli Hundredorum*, (1815), 72.
37. Eyton, *op.cit,*, Vol. V., 96.
38. *ibid*, 92.
39. A.W.B. Simpson, *A History of the Land Law*, (1986), 21-2.
40. *Cal. Close Rolls*, Henry VI, Vol. 3, 203.
41. For convenience I shall use the term land *owner* for the period after 1500, although there is in fact little difference in tenure before or after this date. Even today, no-one actually *owns* land in the United Kingdom other than the monarch. It is technically held of the crown free of feudal obligations by *freeholders* who, as will be seen, emerged during the medieval period.
42. Inquisition p*ost mortem*, quoted in E.H. Martin, 'History of Several Families connected with Diddlebury: I. The Baldwyns', *TSAS*, 4th ser., Vol. II, (1912), 143-4.
43. Stafford WSL, 350/40, Hardwick Ms, 19.
44. *ibid*, 22.
45. Baldwyn papers, Cardiff Library (Glamorgan RO), 66; M.E. Speight, *Some Diddlebury Houses*, (2000), 56.
46. H.T. Weyman, 'Some Account of the Early History of the Foxe Family', *TSAS*, 2nd. ser., Vol. XII, (1900), 141.
47. The date when this purchase was made is not clear. It is mentioned in Foxe's will, dated 12 October 1590 (summarised in Weyman, *op.cit.*), but a roll of the Court Baron of Sir John Savage at Corfton for September 1593 survives (Staffs. RO, D1788, F1.) It is not impossible that this was a clerical error.
48. Details of these transactions are to be found in SA 1093/40D, a 19th century copy of a long deposition made by Thomas Baldwyn in the reign of James I in connection with a dispute over rights of common in Diddlebury wood.
49. Staffs.RO, D1788, P33, B10 1600 is a typical example. Later in the century there are a number of similar exchanges between members of the Baldwyn family.
50. The author has as yet been unable to locate a record of this transaction among the vast collection of Baldwyn deeds at Stafford. Lady Long died in July 1665. On 19 October 1665 the Court Baron of Samuel Baldwyn was held for the manor of Corfton. Staffs. RO, D1788, F1.
51. Staffs. RO, D1788, undated early 18th century survey; D1788/F1/1/13 rental (made between 1710 and 1714).
52. A detailed account of the dispute may be found in Weyman, *op.cit*, 161-169.
53. Cardiff Library (Glamorgan RO), 75. Lease of possession.

54. *ibid*, 101.
55. Glamorgan RO, 6176.
56. This accounts for the happy survival of Baldwyn papers among the Aqualate deposit at Stafford (D1788). The Baldwyns would appear never to have willingly disposed of any document relating to title to property, which has created a comprehensive, if somewhat disorganised, archive.
57. Worcs. RO, 705/658BA5467/67, Bundle 3.
58. Stafford WSL 350/40, Hardwick Ms.,24.
59. C.G.S Foljambe and C. Reade, *The House of Cornewall*, (1908), 141.
60. Held by them as early as 1524. M.A. Faraday, *op.cit*.
61. SA, Morgan Coll. 783, Box 79.
62. E.H. Martin, 'Bromcroft', *TSAS,* 4th ser., Vol. VI, (1917), 225-276.
63. E.H. Martin, 'History of the Manor of Westhope', *TSAS*, 3rd ser., Vol. IX, (1909), 196.
64. *Country Life*, 8 June 1967.
65. *TSAS*, 4th ser., Vol. VIII, 25
66. *Ludlow Advertiser*, 22 July 1911.
67. *VCH Shropshire*, Vol. X, 156.
68. The dispute between Capt. Wingfield-Stratford and the parish council is recounted in Section IV, iii.
69. Powell had been agent for many of the leading theatrical and musical figures of the 1920s, whom he often entertained at Sutton. He died after contracting a chill, which turned to pneumonia.
70. SA, 4440/2. The surveyor handling the negotiations described Holder as' an extremely nice old fellow… perfectly hopeless when it comes to talking about the essential data necessary to make a valuation'.
71. A.W.B. Simpson, *A History of the Land Law*, (1986) Ch. 1; S. Reynolds, *Fiefs and Vassals*, (1994), 38-45; 374-379.
72. 'Two FitzAlan Surveys', *Sussex Record Society*, Vol. 67, (1968), 62-64.
73. *Roll of the Justices in Eyre for Gloucestershire, Warwickshire and Staffordshire, 1221-22,* Selden Society, Vol. 59, (1940), 292. Despite the title, this volume includes cases heard at Shrewsbury.
74. A. Harding (ed.), *Roll of the Shropshire Eyre, 1256*, Selden Society, Vol. 96, (1981), 137.
75. PRO E315/410/5.
76. These are to be found in Staffs. RO, D1788.
77. SA 1093/40D.
78. Staffs. RO, D1788, P40,B4.
79. SA, QE 3/3/1, Register of Papists' Deeds.
80. PRO, C/103/164.
81. SA QE3/3/1, 249.
82. SA, 4011/45.
83. PRO, MAF 32/622/104.
84. Lower House is currently (2006) an equestrian centre and Wetmore operates as an organic pig and vegetable business on a very reduced acreage.
85. These raids continued into the 14th century. The *Chronica Landavensis* [BL Cotton Nero, A, iv] notes 'a slaughter of Welshmen at Culmington in Corvedale' in 1228. I am grateful to Michael Faraday for this reference. As late as 1306, Peaton was one of a number of townships petitioning for relief from taxation as they had been 'burnt, plundered and destroyed by the Welsh'. (C.J. Train, *The Walls and Gates of Ludlow*, (1999), 19.)
86. J. Morris, *op.cit.*, 4. 21, 15, 17.
87. *ibid.*, 4, 1, 6.
88. Probably 600 acres. Historians in the past have expended much discussion on a putative 'five hide unit. If such existed, Corfham is a good example.
89. E.H. Martin, *TSAS*, 3rd series, Vol. IX, (1909), 155-6; D.C. Skemer, 'The Perambulation of Shropshire, 1298', *TSAS*, Vol. LXXI, (1996), 22-32.
90. Staffs. RO, D1788, P39, B8.
91. Staffs. RO, D1788, P44, B6.
92. SA, 6001/6868 (19th century transcript of deed of 1336); Staffs. RO, D1788, P38, B2.
93. Staffs. RO, D1788, P36, B10.
94. Survey of 1720, SA, 6001/2600.
95. A. Harding (ed.), *Roll of the Shropshire Eyre, 1256*, Selden Society, Vol. 96, (1981), 220; Eyton, *op.cit.*, IV, 14-15.
96. *VCH Shropshire*, Vol. IV, (1989), 60.
97. 'Two FitzAlan Surveys', *Sussex Record Society*, Vol. 67, (1968), 63.

98. *VCH Shropshire*, Vol. IV, (1989), 90.
99. Staffs RO, D1788, F1/1/5-10 for Foxe period as lords of the manor of Corfton.
100. P. Turner (trans.), Thomas More, *Utopia*, (1965), 46-8.
101. H.M. Auden, 'Medieval Enclosures in Shropshire', *TSAS*, 4th Series, Vol. XI, 211. In 1524 William Barker was assessed at 46s. 8d. on his goods for the subsidy, for which he was the collector. This was the largest assessment in Middlehope. M.A. Faraday, *The Lay Subsidy for Shropshire 1524-7*, (1999), 235.
102. Staffs. RO, D1788, P45, B11. Elsich lies on the western side of the parish towards Seifton. Although the name may originate with Aelsi, the Saxon lord of Corfton, the author has been unable to find any reference to the name prior to the building of the Baldwyn house in the 16th century.
103. *VCH Shropshire,* Vol. IV, (1989), 124.
104. Staffs. RO, D1788, F1/1/7 (1610); F1/1/10 (1637).
105. PRO, C/103/164.
106. Staffs. RO, D1788, p35, B11.
107. T. Rowley, 'History of the South Shropshire Landscape, 1086-1800', unpublished Oxford B.Litt. thesis, (196), 127. Rowley quotes two copies of this survey, Gloucester RO, Sudeley Ms. 518 and Bodleian Library, Oxford, Gough Salop Ms. 10. It is probable that these are copies of the survey in SA, 6001/2600.
108. SA, QE3/3/3.
109. SA, 6001/2600.
110. *ibid.*
111. HRO, Microfilm Box 64.
112. B. Trinder and J. Cox, *Yeomen and Colliers in Telford*, (1980), 80-1. The average flock in Lilleshall, Wellington and Wrockwardine was 30, but just over 20 in Dawley.
113. The author wishes to thank Mr. and Mrs. Woodhouse for kindly supplying this information.
114. PRO, Prob.11/119, 48 Fenner. I am very grateful to Michael Faraday for his verbatim transcript of this valuable document.
115. J. Bathurst and E.J.L. Cole, 'Leominster Fair, 1556'. *TWNFC*, Vol. XLII, (1976), 78.
116. Wigmore Fair toll books, BL, Add. Mss 70063; Notts. RO, DD4P 74. I am most grateful to Brian Smith of Vowchurch for these Diddlebury references.
117. SA, LB7/1059. This class contains a series of 17th and 18th century toll books, but most are too fragile to be handled. The example used illustrates clearly the regular use made of Ludlow by Diddlebury farmers.
118. SA, BB/C/6/1/2. This box contains over 70 toll books for Bridgnorth from 1656 to 1679 . A sample taken of six books across the period revealed only two transactions involving Diddlebury residents.
119. SA 4340/Pl/1.
120. SA, D641/3/E/4/12, Survey of Shifnal etc. 1769; 438/2, lease 1789 Rouse-Boughton and Woodhouse to Rowlands.
121. This definition is based upon J.P. Dodd, 'High Farming in Shropshire, 1845-1870'. *Midland History,* Vol. 8, (1983),148-168.
122. *ibid.*, 154, quoting *Journal of the Royal Agricultural Society*, XIX, (1858).
123. SA, 6000/15001.
124. Johnstone and his neighbours were in touch with the latest techniques. It was in 1842 that the firm of Anthony Gibbs & Co. had begun to import guano from the islands off the Peruvian coast, making themselves the vast fortune, which led to the clerihew 'Mr. Gibbs made his dibs/ Selling the turds of foreign birds'. *Tyntesfield*, National Trust Guide, (2005), 6.
125. SA, Pl9/35/1/10.
126. It is likely that the departure of John Groome from Peaton Hall in 1897 was due to overstretching, as he had tried to create one large 900 acre holding at Peaton. It is interesting that all three attempts to do this failed.
127. J. Cherrington, *On the Smell of an Oily Rag: my Fifty Years in Farming*, (1979),6-9; 51-52.
128. As late as 1954, Smiths Gore, agents for the estate, wrote to the Church Commissioners condemning this legacy from Holder. SA, 4440/2.
129. Cherrington, *op.cit.*, 52.
130. PRO, MAF32/622/104/57.

131. *ibid.*, 104/58
132. Sir Leslie Fielding, personal communication. I am, however, informed by Peter Bolton that such a company did actually exist.
133. The poor living conditions prompted a protest in 1944, which is discussed in M.E. Speight, 'The Land Girls' Lament', *Salopian Recorder*, Summer 2003, 10.
134. SA, 4440/02.
135. *Picture Post*, 15 September 1951, contains a fairly low-key account of some of Edwards' exploits. His own writings are more colourful.
136. *Cal. Pat.Rolls*, Vol.2, p.306; Edward I,1272-1281, 363-4.
137. SA, QE1/2/21. This is a copy and translation of the original documents [now lost] made in 1809.
138. *ibid.*
139. Rowley, B.Litt. thesis as above, 80.
140. SA 1093/40D. This is a 19th century copy of a lengthy account made by Thomas Baldwyn early in the 17th century as part of a legal dispute with the Smiths of Aston. While undoubtedly one-sided, it gives a valuable insight into this major clearance.
141. *ibid.* An intriguing passing reference. The Long Forest is described as being 'much diminished and decayed by such enclosures and defalcations of woods as one Leonard Dannatt Esq. in making of glass hath committed in his manor of Westhope'. It is not known whether Dannatt was exporting timber to glassworks elsewhere, or if he had established one at Westhope.
142. *VCH Shropshire*, Vol. X, (1998), 150.
143. Eyton, Vol. IV, 341-2.
144. *Cal. IPM*, Edward III, Vol. IX, 490.
145. M.E. Speight, *op.cit.*, 40.
146. Staffs. RO, D1788, 45, 11. There are a bewildering variety of spellings for this name. In this reference it has been rendered as in the document.
147. Delbury Hall archives. I am grateful to Mr. Patrick Wrigley for allowing me access to these documents. The windmill is mentioned specifically in a sale deed of 1870 (Cooke to Yorke), but is described as disused on the first edition Ordnance Survey 25 inch to the mile map of 1884. The platform upon which it stood may still be seen.
148. Bouldon Mill was not in the parish until 1884. An account of the mill will be found in the *VCH Shropshire*, Vol. X, 149-50.
149. *Cal. IPM*, Edward III, Vol. VIII, (1913), 451.
150. Kelly, *Directory of Shropshire*, 1922.
151. *VCH Shropshire*, Vol. II, 86.
152. HCA, 2144
153. Inquisition *post mortem* of William Baldwyn, summarised in Martin, *TSAS*, Series IV, Vol. II, (1912), 143.
154. A.Hardin (ed.), *The Roll of the Shropshire Eyre, 1256*, Selden Society (1961), 633.
155. PRO, CP40/48/65a. I am grateful to Michael Faraday for this reference.
156. Cal. IPM, Vol. III, Edward I, 194 (Hugh Burnell); Staffs. RO, D1788, P45 B11.
157. Staffs. RO, D1788, 45, 11.
158. Sussex Record Society, *op.cit.*

Section 2

1. E. Duffy, *The Voices of Morebath: Reformation and Rebellion in an English Village*, (2001).
2. A.T. Bannister, *The Cathedral Church of Hereford*, (1924), 47 *et. seq.*; HCA 1853 [326].
3. HCA 1849 and 1408 (22 February 1252/3); 1392 (12 January 1256/7.)
4. W.W. Capes, *Charters and Records of Hereford Cathedral*, (1908), xiii.
5. J. Barrow (ed.), *English Episcopal Acta, VII, Hereford 1079-1234*, (1993), 53.
6. Capes, *op. cit.* xii-xiv; HCA 2128-2130; 2132; 1060.
7. HCA 1836.
8. HCA 2146
9. SA 6001/4411, E.H. Martin, manuscript History of the Parish of Diddlebury, 155, quoting Williams Mss. 4/448.
10. A.T. Bannister, 'Visitation Returns in the Diocese of Hereford', *English Historical Review*, Vols.44 & 45 (1929, 1930).
11. HCA2136; 2137; 2140-3; 2156-7.
12. E.H. Martin, *op.cit.*, 39-40. Mrs. Martin's reference to Mershton chapel in 1689 is incorrect. The Marshton referred to there is in fact in Sussex.

13. Deed dated 7 January 1655 Walcot to Baldwyn, Ludlow Library, Southern Collection.
14. J. Morris (ed.), *Domesday Book – Shropshire*, (1986), 4, 1, 6.
15. HCA 2133, 24 March 1285/6.
16. HCA 2145, 6 April 1309; 1879, 11 June 1333.
17. HCA 2149, 29 June 1422.
18. HCA 2148 2 July 1533.
19. *Valor Ecclesiasticus*, Vol. III, 202.
20. Transcribed by E.H. Martin, *Trans. Shropshire Archaeological Society*, 3rd Ser. vii (1907), 139-49.
21. I am grateful to Christopher Potter for drawing my attention to this as yet unnumbered document in the Diocesan Registrar's papers in the HRO.
22. HRO, HD4/27.
23. A. Tindal Hart, *The Eighteenth Century Country Parson*, (1955), 99.
24. *Crockford's Clerical Directory*.
25. HCL 4836, Dean and Chapter endowments.
26. I am most grateful to Mrs. Audrey Youngman and Mrs. Jo Bristow of the Ludlow Historical Research group for supplying me with transcripts of these two grants, which were found in the Southern papers in Ludlow library.
27. J. Barrow (ed.), *English Episcopal Acta, VII, Hereford*, (1993) lxii.
28. Staffs. RO D1788 P36 B10.
29. *Reg. John Gilbert*, 124.
30. *Reg. Mascall*, 187.
31. *Reg. Edmund Lacy*, 120.
32. *Reg. E. Lacy*, 116; *Reg. Mayew*, 212; *Calendar of Papal Letters, Vol. XVI, Alexander VI, 1492-98*, (1986), 92.
33. Reg. Mayew, 88; *SPR Onibury*,
34. Two Fitzalan Surveys, *Sussex Record Society, Vol. 67*, (1968), 63.
35. HCA, 2136; 2141-43; 2146-48; 2151; 2156-57.
36. *Reg. John Trefnant*, 180; *Reg. Stanbury*, 191.
37. *Reg. Myllyng*, 52-3.
38. A.J. Pollard, 'The Lords Talbot and Earls of Shrewsbury in the 15th century', unpublished University of Bristol Ph.D. thesis, (1968), 296.
39. SA 567/2A/6. Quitclaim to Richard of all accounts arising out of his service to Sprenchose.
40. VCH Shropshire, Vol. VIII, 108; SA 567/2A/5 (n.d., 1291-98)
41. Eyton, Vol.V., 95-6.
42. *Roll of the Shropshire Eyre 1256*, Selden Society Vol. 96, (1980), 651.
43. PRO, CP40/369. I am indebted to Michael Faraday for this reference.
44. Unless otherwise stated, information on the educational background and careers of clergy is taken from Foster (Oxford) or Venn (Cambridge) with additional material from *Crockford's Clerical Directory* for those living in or after 1865.
45. He signs the 1637 Glebe Terrier.
46. J.E. Auden, 'Ecclesiastical History of Shropshire', *TSAS*, 3rd Series, Vol. VII, (1907), 269.
47. Ludlow Library, Southern Collection, deed 7 January 1655, Walcot to Baldwin.
48. Venn, Vol. I, 403.
49. Tithe Book of Nicholas Proude 1657-1662, HRO uncat.
50. HRO, AA20 Box 30.
51. M.E. Speight, *Some Diddlebury Houses and their History*, (2000), 35; will of W. Fosbroke, HRE Mic. Box 60.
52. All but three baptisms in the period 1787-1799 were performed by Powell, and all but nine weddings between 1764 and 1797 were conducted by him. SPR, *Diddlebury*.
53. SA, 6001/6862, Archdeacon Plymley's Visitation, Ludlow Deanery, 51.
54. D.J. Lloyd, *Country Grammar School*, (1977), 87.
55. SA 6001/6862, p.65.
56. PRO, ED49/6324, Diddlebury School and Poor Charity, contains a vast correspondence on the topic. The capital sum [about £150] is still [2006] in the hands of the Commissioners.
57. SA, P91/C/2/1. Minute Book, Church Restoration.
58. *Shrewsbury Chronicle*, 29 August 1873.
59. SA, ED 4322/2/1, Diddlebury School Log Book 1863-1896, 214.
60. I am grateful to Mrs. Anne Watkins, daughter of Mr. Purcell, for this information, and for permission to use the pho-

tograph of the vicar in his pony cart. He spent his last years at Church Stretton, and was buried at Diddlebury.

61. Diddlebury PCC Minutes, 6 November 1974.
62. *TSAS*, 3rd Series, Vol. I, part iii, (1901), 413.
63. W.J. Smith (ed.), *Herbert Correspondence*, (1968), no. 345.
64. HRO, HD7/24/55.
65. Speight, *op. cit.*, 50.
66. Photocopies of originals in HRO, formerly in possession of Mr. F. Mitchell of Diddlebury
67. Downe: HRO 42/1/7; Mynton, PRO, Prob.11/138.
68. PRO, Prob. 111/146.
69. SA 3544/3/1, Primitive Methodist Circuit Book.
70. *VCH Shropshire*, Vol. II, (1973), 14-15.
71. PRO, HO/129/352.
72. Photocopy *ex* Frank Mitchell in possession of the author.
73. M.E. Speight and K. Woodhouse, *Portrait of Diddlebury*, (2002), 7.
74. SA, 2612/16-17, Baptismal Register, Peaton Strand Chapel.
75. *Shrewsbury Chronicle*, 20 March 1880.
76. *ibid.*, 4 August 1877.
77. PRO 34 Hogen, quoted in E.H. Martin, History of the Manor of Westhope, *TSAS* Vol. IX, (1909), 247-8.
78. *Reg. John Trefnant*, 12-13.
79. *Reg. Myllyng*, 206.
80. PRO, Just.1/726 fo. 47f. I am grateful to Michael Faraday for this and the following reference.
81. PRO, Just. 1/741
82. A.T. Bannister (ed.),Visitation Returns of the Diocese of Hereford in 1397, *E.H.R,* 1927, 455.
83. *Calendar of Inquisitions Post Mortem, Edward III*, Vol.3, 59; 159.
84. *ibid.*, 59.
85. *ibid.*, Vol. 2, 547.
86. The fate of the Diddlebury screen is problematical. It was probably destroyed at the Reformation, although only the removal of the lofts above screens was required by law. Over the entrance to the chancel there is a beam placed in the position where the rood beam, which supported the crucifix and the attendant figures of the Blessed Virgin and St. John, would normally have been positioned. At each end of this is a grotesque mask of 17th century date similar to those on the corbels of the nave roof. Does this indicate an intention, never completed, to erect a screen in the Laudian period, as at Abbey Dore in Herefordshire? It is interesting that the one planned feature of the 1881-1883 restoration never to be executed was the chancel screen.
87. HRO 21/3/6, will of William Heyns of Sutton, 1544.
88. e.g. Richard Bawdewyn 1547 HRO AA20/X/001; Elizabeth Barker 1548 Thomas Barker, 1548 HRO, AA20/X/02; Elizabeth Mason, 1548 HRO, AA20/X/06. Bawdewyn and Thomas Barker both use the traditional preamble to their wills, while both women use the 'reformed' version.
89. HRO, AA20/X/06.
90. HRO, 46/2/22.
91. Inventories of Church Goods, Temp. Edward VI, *TSAS*, 2nd Series, Vol. XII, (1900), 301.
92. John Bowdeler, HRO, AA20/X/02; Richard Normecote (1556), HRO, AA20/X.06; Philip Spencer (1556), HRO, AA20/X/08; Margaret Scharlett (1554), HRO, AA20/X/07.
93. E. Duffy, *The Stripping of the Altars*, (1992), especially Chapters 16 and 17.
94. Duffy, *op. cit.*, p. 590.
95. HRO, 34/3/33
96. J.E. Auden, *op. cit.*, 251-2.
97. HRO, HD4/2/16, deposition no. 87 states that Edward Parton was about 1659 'married to ... Margaret Parton in the house of one Mr. Churchman clerk in the parish of Munslow.' The marriage ended in divorce in 1671. In 1646, Churchman had baptised the son of 'Dr' Richard Baldwin. P. Klein, 'The Churchman Monument', *TSAS*, Vol. LXXIV, (1999), 86. This article contains fascinating information on the esoteric interests of this unusual clerical family.
98. HRO, HD7/11 1669/157.

99. HRO, HD4/31, 10 a-d.
100. P.E.H. Hair, *Before the Bawdy Court*, (1972), 23.
101. HRO, HD4/2/16 (87); HD7/10 (294), Parton v. Parton, 1668-1671.
102. HRO, HD4/36-37, Fleming v. Fleming. I am most grateful to Christopher Potter for bringing this extraordinary case to my notice.
103. E.H. Martin, *op.cit.*, 206-8.
104. A. Rowan, Sibdon Castle, *Country Life*, 1 June 1967, 1452. Further detals of the bizarre matrimonial affairs of the Fleming family may be fond in J. Verasanso, 'A 'Mushroom' Family: the Flemings of Westhope, Sibdon and Shadwell', *TSAS*, Vol. LXXIX, (2004), 128-133.
105. SA P91/B/2/1 (1685-1761) and P91/B/2/2-5 (1761-1870). My task in dealing with these documents has been considerable eased by the use of the index compiled by the late Frank Mitchell, and kindly passed to me with others of his papers by Mr and Mrs. R. Edwards of Diddlebury, who had rescued them at the closure of Diddlebury School. Examples taken from the accounts for this period will not be separately referenced.
106. HRO, HD5/15/102, visitation return 1719.
107. SA 6001/6882, 67.
108. *ibid.*, 125.
109. PRO, HO 40/129/352, 1851 Religious Census. For Diddlebury parishioners at Culmington see 'Population' below.
110. Communion register, SA, P91/B/2/7.
111. *ibid.*
112. *ibid.*
113. SA, P91/A/7/1- 3; Service registers, 1921-1965.
114. *ibid.*
115. *ibid.*
116. The calculation of the financial quota paid by parishes has on occasions been determined, at least in part, by the number on the Church electoral roll. This presented a temptation to keep numbers on the roll as low as possible.
117. HCA 1836 (1315); 2146 (1355); *Visitation of the Diocese of Hereford, 1397*, 55.
118. E. Mercer, *English Architecture to 1900: The Shropshire Experience,* (2003), 2-6. G. Baldwin Brown, *The Arts in Early England,* (1925), 245-6, had claimed that the herring-bone was a veneer added by Norman masons to an Anglo-Saxon wall. This was thoroughly refuted by H.M. and J. Taylor, *Anglo-Saxon Architecture,* (1965), Vol. I, 211-4.
119. I am grateful to the Revd. Ian Gibbs for drawing may attention to the marked similarities between the west front at Diddlebury and the (destroyed) chapel of Bishop Robert of Lorraine (1079-95) at Hereford. Peter Bolton has also pointed out a very similar arrangement to that of Diddlebury, but dating from the 13th century, at Bottisham, Cambridgeshire.
120. Mercer, (2003), 6.
121. H.M. Taylor, *Deerhurst Studies1, The Anglo-Saxon Fabric,* (1977), 15.
122. Mercer, *op.cit., 47-8.*
123. Tugford and Holdgate. For a discussion of the significance of these curiously obscene figures, see W.J.Hemp, Some Unrecorded 'Sheela-na-gigs' in Wales and the Border, *Arch. Camb.* XCIII, Part 1, (June 1938), 136-9. Hemp discusses the Holdgate and Church Stretton examples, but was obviously unaware of Diddlebury and Tugford.
124. These two aisle windows were accurately replicated in the conservative restoration of 1859-60. The other aisle windows do not resemble the much smaller ones which they replaced.
125. Staffs.R.O, D1788, P38, B12.
126. Stafford, William Salt Library, Hardwick Mss., Vol. V, 35.
127. SA, P91/B/1/1.
128. HRO, HD7/22/18. There is no evidence to suggest that the church ever possessed a west gallery for singers.
129. *ibid.*
130. SA, P91/B/2/1.
131. SA, P91/B/2/2-5.
132. When the ropes were last renewed in 2001, a set of four cost nearly £400. The quality of 18th-century rope must have been much poorer than those of today.

133. SA, 6001/6882, 64.
134. SA4454/16, Bill of Edward Powell for work done for bishop of Hereford.
135. SA1704/32.
136. SA, P91/2/2/1, Minute Book, Church Restoration. Overton took the old windows back to his house in Corfton as rockery stones. The present owner is still unearthing pieces of tracery.
137. SA,6001/6862, p.67; Stafford, William Salt Library, *op.cit.*
138. According to the date inscription which survives. Curiously there is no mention of this in the churchwardens' accounts.
139. Fortunately these had been recorded earlier in the century . William Salt Library, Stafford, Hardwick Mss., Vol. V, p.40.
140. *Shrewsbury Chronicle*, 31 August 1883; SA, P91/C/2/1, Minutes of Church Restoration.
141. E.H. Martin, *TSAS*, Ser.3, Vol. IX, 231; Will at HRO, AA20, Box 62.
142. Plymley, *op.cit.*, p.125.
143. *Shropshire Star*, 17 April 1997.
144. The chapel has been recognized as a private chapel for many years, and as such is not covered by faculty jurisdiction.
145. E.H.Martin, SA6001/4411, p.94.
146. Staffs. R.O., D1788, P.46, B.8.
147. Staffs. R.O., D1788, P.46, B.8.
148. SA, 6001/6862, p.53. The exterior drawing by Williams backs up Plymley's comments on the state of repair.
149. Hardwick, *op.cit,* Vol.V, p.11.
150. Speight and Woodhouse, *op.cit.*, p.5.

Section 3

1. J. Morris (ed.), *Domesday Book, Shropshire*, (1986), 257.
2. W.G.Hoskins, *The Making of the English Landscape*, (1955), 106.
3. *TSAS*, 2nd Series IV, 320.
4. *Two FitzAlan Surveys*, Sussex Record Society, Vol. 67, (1968), 63.
5. *The Book of Fees,* (1923), 1184; *Rotuli Hundredorum*, Vol. II, (1818), 70-73. The amount of detail is probably due to the need of the government to sort out the details of the alienation of land because the manor was held in serjeantry (see p.12).
6. *TSAS*, 2nd Series, IV, 320.Thomas, son of Hugh; Richard Brid, presumably the son of the Widow Brid of the survey.
7. R.E, Glasscock (Ed.), *The Lay Subsidy Roll of 1334*, (1975) 254.
8. It is generally assumed to have been located near the Corve, somewhere between Broncroft and Corfham.
9. *Cal.I.P.M.*, Edward III, Vol.IX , 223.
10. *ibid*, 224.
11. *Inquisitions of the Ninth*, (1807), 188
12. *Cal. I.P.M.*, Edward I, Vol. III, 544.
13. *Cal. I.P.M.*, Edward III, Vol.II, 547; Vol. III 59; 139.
14. M.A. Faraday, 'Mortality in the Diocese of Hereford, 1442-1551', *TWNFC*, Vol. XLII, (1977), 163-174.
15. The individual acts are listed on fiche in M.A. Faraday and E.J.L. Cole, *Calendar of Probate and Administration Acts ... in the Court Books of the Bishops of Hereford*, (1989).
16. PRO, E179/255/35 (1662); W. Watkins-Pitchford, *The Shropshire Hearth Tax Roll of 1672*, (1949).
17. Though this is not always possible. Some entries do not differentiate between offerings and other payments. Where this leads to an odd number such as 5d., it has been assumed that offerings have been made for two persons, and that the penny represents a small payment such as for a garden. Similarly, when a parishioner has paid for three or four years, the sum has been divided by that number. The result is generally, though not completely accurate.
18. G. Nair, *Highley*, 112.
19. This is considerably higher than my estimate in the first draft of this section, before Christopher Potter had introduced me to the Hearth Tax exemption certificates. The total number of households in 1672 would appear to be inarguable. Nair's figure of 4.3 per household seems a very conservative estimate.
20. SA, 6001/6862.
21. All references to census material are taken from microfilm copies in the SA. The originals are, of course, lodged with the National Archives at Kew.

22. Details of Diddlebury residents buried at Culmington were abstracted by the late Frank Mitchell, whose notes, in the author's possession, are gratefully acknowledged. Peaton Strand Methodist registers are in SA, 2612, 17/18.
23. Shropshire County Council, Planning Division, *1991 Census for Shropshire*; Census 1831
24. www.shropshireonline.gov.uk/factsfigures.
25. SA, ED4322/2/1, Diddlebury School Log Book.
26. SA, ED 4273/1, Diddlebury School Admissions Register.
27. P.M. Bolton, 'What became of the labourers? Wellesbourne agricultural labourers after the strike of 1872', *Warwickshire History*, Vol. XII, No.5,(2004).
28. I have attempted to examine most English counties (with the exception of Lancashire, which is too daunting by virtue of numbers). I cannot claim 100% accuracy, as it is inevitable that some entries will have been missed among the many hundred thousands examined. The inaccurate recollections of people as to their birthplace, the problems faced by enumerators in other parts of the country in entering local names, and the same problems encountered by the Mormon transcribers, also mean that some entries may have been missed. The overall conclusion, is, however, quite striking.
29. The category of servants has been interpreted widely to include gamekeepers and butlers as well as the more common general domestic servants. It also includes housekeepers, a number of whom were family members.
30. This mobility was not confined to one social class. The fact that virtually all farmers were tenants tended to produce a lot of movement, while the growth of the class of 'tenant gentry' (see below) meant that country houses had frequent changes in occupier.
31. The original enumerator gave the population of Peaton and Broncroft as 119, but this contains an arithmetical error, and should be 129
32. T. McKeown, R.G. Record, and R.D. Turner, 'An interpretation of the decline of mortality in England and Wales during the twentieth century', *Population Studies*, 29, (1975), 391-422.
33. Nair, *op.cit.*, 195.
34. 263 vaccinations in 1840, compared with 85 in the rest of the Ludlow district of the Poor Law Union. I am grateful to Dr. Derek Williams for this interesting statistic. The Diddlebury School logbooks [SA ED4322/2/1] record smallpox at Middlehope (May 1865) and Corfton (February 1872)
35. Although employed, Beddoes regularly received out relief from the Poor Law Union for expenses during his wife's confinements; for medical relief for sick children; and for clothing when the children started work. (Ludlow Union, Applications and Report Books, SA, PL9/2/4/1-11.)
36. G. Nair, *Highley*, (1988), 234-9; P.Laslett, *The World we have Lost,* (1983), 159-61. Laslett quotes a study of 98 parishes to reach a national average. The Diddlebury percentages between 1800 and 1850 are at least double his figure.
37. G. Nair, *op.cit.*, 120-127.
38. SA, Morgan Collection 786, Box 43, Bundle 17.
39. M.E. Speight, *Some Diddlebury Houses*, (2000), 61.
40. SA, P91 fiche 129, Diddlebury Overseers' Accounts.
41. *ibid.*
42. SA, PL9,/19/1/2, Ludlow Union, Register of Admissions and Discharges, 1848-1857.
43. *Cal. I.P.M., Edward III*, Vol.II, 547; Vol. III., 139.
44. see above p.59.
45. Inquisition dated 8 June 1413, *Cal.I.P.M.*, Vol. XX (1-5 Henry V), 114.
46. Eyton, Vol. V., 51-55.
47. *ibid.*
48. *C.P.R., 1281-92*, 131; 141; 251; 258; 264.
49. E.H. Martin, 'History of several families connected with Diddlebury I. The Baldwyns', *T.S.A.S.*, 4th series, Vol. II, (1912), 133-185; 299-385.

50. *ibid.*, 152-3. The official charge against him was counterfeiting coin, which seems unlikely. This is the time at which Queen Mary was removed from the custody of the earl of Shrewsbury, who was deemed too sympathetic a gaoler, into that of the puritan, Sir Amyas Paulet. It is possible that Baldwin may have been suspected of involvement in one of the plots with which Mary was associated.
51. *V.C.H. Shropshire*, Vol. III, (1979), 62-3.
52. E.H. Martin, 'Bromcroft and its Owners', *TSAS*, 4th series, Vol. VI, (1917), 223-276
53. A.J. Pollard, 'The Family of Talbot, Lords Talbot and Earls of Shrewsbury', unpublished Ph.D. thesis, University of Bristol (1968), Appendix III, 417.
54. *V.C.H. Shropshire*, Vol. III, (1979), 63.
55. *Cal. I.P.M.,* (Second series), Vol. II, Henry VII, (1915), 909. She also managed to outlive her father's cousin Edward Trussell, who appears to have had a reversionary interest in the estate. *Ibid.*, 326
56. M.A. Faraday, (ed.), *The Lay Subsidy for Shropshire 1524-7*, (1999).
57. John Wellens (£9), William Heynes (£7), Roger Maunde (£6), and Richard Hiskys (£5)all from Sutton. William Mason of Diddlebury was assessed at £5 for goods in addition to his 20s. on land.
58. The upper group rarely served as churchwardens, and it is tempting to suggest that herein may lie the origin of the expression 'county' families.
59. E.H. Martin, *T.S.A.S*, 4th series, Vol. II, (1912), 133-185.
60. 'Genere oriundus antique et illustri' (from the monumental inscription of Capt. Frederick Cornewall died 1788 in Diddlebury church.
61. M.E. Speight, *op. cit.*, 60-62. The descent from Meredith Powell is based on a Hardwick pedigree of 1850, (SA6001/4646), which seems rather more plausible than some others. There is a lease of 99 years from Henry, Lord Herbert to Rowland Powell dated 10 October 1713 in Glamorgan RO, but no other record of dealings between the families has yet emerged.
62. Mary Morgan was shipped to Australia on the notorious Second Fleet after her conviction for stealing flax in Corfton. She escaped and returned to England in 1794, and was transported again, under another name, in 1803. Having served her sentence she took up farming, to become a major landowner in the Hunter valley, N.S.W., by the time of her death in 1835. F. Mitchell, *Molly Morgan: Convict to Queen*, (1980).
63. Staffs. R.O., D1788/41.15.
64. HRO, AA20, Box 27.
65. All at HRO, AA20.
66. HRO, AA20, Box 54.
67. HRO, AA20, Box 51.
68. SA, 6001/6862, 61. (Archdeacon Plymley's Visitation, 1793).
69. M.E.Speight, *op.cit*,, 14; 44.
70. *ibid.*, 8; 14.
71. *Roll of the Justices in Eyre for Gloucestershire, Warwickshire and Staffordshire, 1221-1222*, Selden Society, Vol. 59, (1940), 474. This volume includes pleas made at Shrewsbury.
72. Eyton, Vol. IV, 14-15; *Shropshire Eyre Roll, 1256*, Selden Society Vol. ,220.
73. W.G.D. Fletcher, *TSAS,* 2nd series, Vol. IV., (1892), 287-338. The present writer is sceptical of Fletcher's identification of the three de Borleye entries under Diddlebury with the Broncroft family. They more likely represent a less illustrious family originating at Burley in Culmington.
74. *ibid.*
75. *ibid.*
76. PRO, Just1/744, 72d [33 Edward I]; Just1/1381,33f, [14 Edward II]; CP40 /258 72d [19 Edward II]; 361f; CP40/276, 15f, [2 Edward III]. I am most grateful to Michael Faraday for allowing me to use his abstracts of these PRO sources.
77. It should, however, be remembered that the majority of the small number of medieval deeds which have survived are in the Baldwyn Collection in Staffordshire RO (D1788), and refer to lands in Diddlebury and Corfton which were subsequently acquired by the Baldwyns. The Child family might well be expected to loom large in such a context.
78. PRO E315/410.

79. Faraday, *op.cit.*, (1999).
80. PCC, 34 Hogen, 17 April 1536 in E.H. Martin, *T.S.AS.* 3rd Series Vol. IX, (1909), 247-8.
81. B. Trinder and N. Cox, *Miners and Mariners of the Severn Gorge*, (2000), 10.
82. B. Trinder and J. Cox, *Yeomen and Colliers in Telford*, (1980), 4-5. The Wrockwardine figure does, however, form a similar percentage of surviving inventories to that of Diddlebury.
83. PRO, Prob11/130,
84. Information kindly supplied by Mr. Frank Downes, of Mickle Trafford, Chester.
85. I am most grateful to Mr Christopher Potter for allowing me to use his findings concerning Diddlebury marriage licences.
86. HRO, AA20, Box 56.
87. Speight, *op.cit.*, (2000), 17-18; 36.
88. This may also reflect the fact that the post was becoming less onerous as secular responsibilities passed to other bodies.
89. SA, QE2/2/1 Alehouse keepers' recognizances.
90. This practice, years ahead of its time, was condemned as economically foolish by the agents who were employed to buy his estates for the Church Commissioners in 1941. SA 4440/2.
91. SA, 6001/6862.
92. *Diddlebury Parish Magazine*, February 1892; SA, 4924/1/21/18/1.
93. SA, PL9/24/3/2.
94. In 1850/51 there had been 98 recipients of outdoor relief at a total cost of £112 3s. 8d. This represents about 25% of both the recipients and the budget for the whole district of 14 parishes. SA, Pl9/25/2/1. Once again, I am indebted to Dr. Derek Williams for bringing this to my notice.
95. *Shropshire Star*, 30 December 2004.
96. Only those men who can obviously be identified as domestic servants have been included. Enumerators were sometimes careless about categories, for example, the entry for Delbury Farm includes eight males and two females as house servants, when it is clear that most, if not all, of the men were live-in farm workers. It is equally clear that Thomas Strefford, in the household of Thomas Jones of Middlehope was a house servant, as he is distinguished from his farm servant colleague.
97. Cases where daughters and other relatives are included as housekeepers etc. have been disregarded. The examples quoted are John Morris, Bache Mill; Edward Griffiths, Middlehope; Thomas Edwards, Corfton; and Richard Kerry, Poston.
98. I am grateful to Peter Bolton for this point.
99. SA, 783, Box 145/26
100. Details are given on a benefactions board in the south aisle of the church.
101. SA, 783, Box 145/26.
102. SA, P91/L/2/1. Overseers' accounts, Caleb Stedman's disbursements 1725-6. Complaints by John Smart, the highest paid pauper in the year, involved two meetings in Tugford, one in Ludlow and one in Bromfield.
103. SA, P91/L/2/2. Overseers accounts 1781-1790.
104. It is also clear from the registers that many unmarried mothers managed to avoid the additional stigma of pauperism.
105. SA, Pl9/25/5/1-2.
106. Detailed studies of this may be found in I. Hall, 'Out Relief in the 19th Century Ludlow Union', in *Victorian Ludlow*, (2004), 144-157; D. Williams, 'The Ludlow Guardians 1836-1900', *TSAS*, Vol. XXVII, (2002) 110-118.
107. SA, PL9/25/8/5, Michaelmas 1867; PL9/25/8/7, Lady Day 1877.
108. SA, PL9/25/8/18.
109. SA, PL9/19/9/6-13, Indoor relief lists 1865-1916 [but contains a large gap between 1886 and 1909].
110. She appears in the 1886 register, but is not present in 1909. She does not appear in the Diddlebury burial register.
111. Accounts of Mrs. Radnor's Charity, 1843-1879, SA, P91/B/2/6 (at end of churchwardens' accounts).

Section 4

1. Will proved at Hereford, 20 March 1565, quoted verbatim in E.H. martin, TSAS, 2nd series, Vol. II, (1912), 150.

2. John Astoke, 1581, 6s. 8d. [HRO]; William Downe, Middlehope, 1585, 10s.; Johan Stokes, Peaton 1594, 6s. 8d.; John Hanson of Broncroft Park, 1607, 6s.8d.; Richard Lewis, Middlehope, 1617, 20s. [PRO].
3. J.M. Shuttleworth (ed.), *The Life of Lord Herbert of Chirbury written by Himself*, 1976, 15.
4. Wace Mss., Bodleian Library, CCC390/ii (schools). Wace records that Ludlow Grammar School had no books in its library. The Diddlebury library is mentioned in the churchwardens' accounts for 1690-1. SA P91/B/2/1. An earlier edition edited by S. Lee (1906), p.21, suggested that Mr Newton may have been Thomas Newton who taught near Macclesfield. While confusion between Diddlebury and Didsbury, south of Manchester, is not impossible, the latter being sometimes rendered Didlesbury at the time, Herbert's statement that he was sent to Diddlebury in Shropshire should probably be taken as correct.
5. The accounts show repairs to the walls in 1686; 1697-8; 1710-11; 1714-5; 1725-6; 1734-5. Thatching was redone in 1692; 1703-4; 1710-11; 1734-5.
6. SA, P91/B/2/1, Churchwardens' Accounts, 1718-19.
7. *ibid.*
8. *ibid.*
9. Will proved at Hereford 23 June 1808.
10. SA, P91/B/2/6, Diddlebury Sunday School accounts [at back of churchwardens' accounts].
11. Information from a file of photocopied material obtained by the late F. Mitchell from the National Society in 1974, and now in possession of the writer.
12. *Shrewsbury Chronicle*, 29 August 1873.
13. *ibid.*
14. SA, ED4322/2/1-3, Diddlebury School Log Books, 1863-96; 1896-1923; 1923-56. Unless otherwise noted, subsequent references are to entries in these log books.
15. *Diddlebury Parish Magazine*, July 1894.
16. He had convictions by Ludlow magistrates for cruelty to horses and beating an employee. *Shrewsbury Chronicle*, 6 June 1879;
17. In addition to a copious log book, Rowland Jones also kept a personal diary in which social engagements with the Morgan Joneses are noted. I am most grateful to Mr Maldwyn Thomas of Haverfordwest, grandson of Rowland Jones, for allowing me access to this source.
18. During Jones's dispute with Dovell, some of the children were sent to a private school which was run for a time by Miss Groome, the sister of the owner of Peaton Hall.
19. SA, ED 4273/1. Admissions Registers, 1875-1919.
20. 'To meet the Examiner's views, it would seem advisable to equalize the attainments and capabilities of the children by cramming a subject they are weak in, and so save confusion to the Examiner and the children on Examination Day!!' Log book entry, 29 March 1893. SA, ED 4322/2/1.
21. Between January 1884 and June 1886, disease claimed the lives of Mr. Hince and five of his children.
22. This process seems to have begun much later than at Clunbury, where intervention and closure began in a diphtheria outbreak in 1878. It is interesting to note that only one of 19 epidemics which closed Clunbury school between 1886 and 1919, namely scarlet fever in January 1896, coincided with outbreaks at Diddlebury. C. Train, *A Country Education*, (1999), 47.
23. The attitude of the Attendance Committee of the Ludlow Union contrasts with that of the Clun Union, as shown in the case of Clunbury. Train, *op.cit.*, 37-40.
24. Application for affiliation to the National Society, 1839. See endnote 11 above.
25. SA 262/14, Westhope School Log Book, 1907-1919.
26. PRO, ED21/14782, correspondence re Westhope School.
27. SA 262/14. This is interesting because Evelyn Hall, who won a place at the Grammar School in 1916, was the son of the estate gamekeeper. The other, Lillian Cook, who was awarded a place at Ludlow High School in 1918, was the daughter of the headmistress. The first pupil from Diddlebury School who was not a child of the

headmaster to win a place at the Grammar School would seem to have been Cecil Stanley Yeates in 1921.

28. PRO, ED21/14782. Minute of 7 September 1918.
29. *ibid.*, November 1918.
30. SA 262/14.
31. He had written in his private diary on 15 October 1908, when he received notice of his impending retirement: 'Fancy! Compelling a man to resign after working for the State 45 years of his manhood; and all that is offered him is two fifths of his salary, which has never been what it ought to be for services rendered ... Shabby treatment!!' I am grateful to Mr. Maldwyn Thomas for allowing me to use this diary.
32. SA, ED4322/2/2, Diddlebury School Log Books, 1896-1923. Unless otherwise noted, all references are to this source.
33. SA, ED4322/2/4B. Managers' Minutes, 1903-1982.
34. SA, ED4322/2/3, Diddlebury School Log Books, 1923-1956. One of Miss Walker's more unusual achievements was organising the collection by the children of almost 12 cwt of blackberries in the autumn of 1918, for dispatch to the jam factory in Hereford as part of the war effort.
35. One of the 11 year olds to pass was the headmaster's daughter Rosemary, who subsequently achieved fame as an actress.
36. Staffs. RO, D1788 P61 B4.
37. Staffs. RO, D1788, F1/1/1.
38. Staffs. RO, D1788, F1/1/5. An act of 1589 'against the erecting and maintaining of cottages' was designed to limit the number of cottages constructed, and therefore the number of poor persons in a parish. S. Coleman, 'Houses into Cottages', *Vernacular Architecture*, Vol. 12, (1981), 54.
39. *Quarter Sessions Order Book,* Vol. I, (1899), 56.
40. At a generous level – 3s. 4d. to be distributed quarterly for ten years after his death. HRO, 31/3/2.
41. Eight out of 12 wills from this period containing benefactions to the poor of Diddlebury were proved at Canterbury rather than Hereford.
42. SA, P91/B/1/1. While listed as Churchwardens' Accounts 1624-1674, in addition to some accounts from 1601, this document contains a miscellaneous collection of notes by parish officials of the time.
43. *ibid.*
44. G. Nair, *op.cit.*, 133.
45. SA, P91/B/1/1. records the presentation of accounts (with the names of churchwardens) from 1601 to 1656, with incomplete entries for the following two decades. Elections of parochial officers from 1686 to 1750 were recorded in Volume II of the parish registers, and are printed in *Shropshire Parish Registers*, Vol. XV, (1912), 26-52. Supervisors of the Highways are only recorded until 1692.
46. *ibid.*, 27.
47. Staffs. RO, D1788 P38 B12.
48. *Quarter Sessions Order Book*, Vol. I. (1899), 49; 116.
49. The printed *Quarter Sessions Order Books* contain 48 such cases between 1689 and 1816.
50. Between 1784 and 1796 there were no fewer than 52 illegitimate births at the Skirmadge. *TSAS*, Vol. LIII, 293-5.
51. SA, P91/B/2/1.
52. *ibid.*
53. SA, QE3/3/1.
54. SA, P91,B/2/1; P91/L/2/1.
55. SA, P91/L/2/2.
56. SA, P91/L/3/1 Corfton Workhouse Accounts.
57. W.E. Tate, *The Parish Chest*, (1969), 236-7.
58. D. Williams, 'The Ludlow Union Workhouse 1839-1900', *Victorian Ludlow*, (2004), 132.
59. SA, P91/C/2/1, Diddlebury Vestry Minutes, 9 March 1888. Watkins had been opposed by John Groome of Peaton Hall. As Watkins died in 1889, Groome may have had a valid point.
60. The Diddlebury district comprised the parishes of Abdon, Clee St. Margaret, Cold Weston, Culmington, Diddlebury, The Heath, Holdgate, Munslow and Tugford.
61. For a detailed discussion of the workings of the system see I. Hall, 'Out Relief in

the 19th Century Ludlow Union', *Victorian Ludlow*, (2004) 144-158.
62. SA, P91/C/1/1. Vestry Minutes.
63. D. Williams, 'The Ludlow Guardians 1836-1900', *TSAS*, Vol. LXXVII, (2002), 115.
64. SA, PL9/2/1/12, Ludlow Guardians' Minutes, 2 and 16 August 1870. I am grateful to Dr. Williams for drawing my attention to these references, and to those concerning Hannah Painter.
65. SA, PL9/2/1/17, January-February 1888.
66. *TSAS*, Vol. LXXVII, (2002), 115.
67. W.G.D. Fletcher (ed.), *Shropshire Parish Registers, Diddlebury*, (1912), 27-29.
68. W.E. Tate, *The Parish Chest*, (1969), 245.
69. SA, P91/C/2/1, Diddlebury Vestry Minutes.
70. A good account of the changes in this period may be found in *VCH Shropshire*, Vol. III, (1979), 135-224.
71. SA, DA22/100/1, 181. Minutes of Ludlow RDC.
72. John Smith, Sutton Hill; Charles Hince, Sutton Hill; John Smith, Peaton.
73. SA, PC91/3/1.
74. SA, DA 100/2, 420; 422;430; DA 100/3, 130. Ludlow RDC minutes.
75. SA, CP 91/3/1.
76. *ibid.*
77. SA, DA/22/114/1, 150. Ludlow RDC Housing and Public Health Committee minutes.
78. SA, CP91/3/1. Minutes for 1946. Happily this scheme came to nothing.
79. For example, the Forester's Lodge at Millichope (Munslow), of the late 13th century, and Great Oxenbold (Monkhopton) dendro-dated to 1247.
80. W.G. Hoskins, 'The Rebuilding of Rural England, 1570-1640,' *Past and Present,* no. 4 (Nov. 1953), 44-59.
81. SA, 1093/40D. This appears to be a 19th century copy of an original deposition by one of the Baldwins concerning a dispute over encroachments upon the commons by neighbouring landowners.
82. Shropshire SMR-9084.
83. J. Leland, *Itinerary*, (ed. Toulmin Smith), Vol. V, 15.
84. E. Mercer, *English Architecture to 1900: the Shropshire Experience*, (2003), 115-6.
85. *ibid.*, 133.
86. Staffs. R.O., D1788/41/15, Inventory of Richard Bawdewyn.
87. Painted decoration in houses in the 16th century is discussed in M. Moran, *Vernacular Buildings of Shropshire*, (2003), 323-351.
88. *V.C.H. Shropshire*, Vol. X, (1998), Pl.20.
89. *ibid.*, 122.
90. Staffs. RO, D1788, P46B8.
91. Discussed in detail by A. Gomme, 'William and David Hiorn' in R. Brown (ed.), *The Architectural Outsiders*, (1985), 45-62.
92. Photocopies of the building accounts, the originals of which are in the ownership of Mr. Patrick Wrigley, are filed in the Shropshire Archives at 4454.
93. Mercer, *op.cit.*, 197. Since the demolition of the large Victorian extension which accommodated the kitchens etc., the most impressive of these ground floor reception rooms has been used as a kitchen/living room.
94. It may also have had another purpose. The Downes family were large tenant farmers, but were unable to vote before 1832, and a freehold would have conferred the franchise. The family were prominent in Liberal politics in Ludlow and the surrounding area at this time.
95. Piggott's *Directory* of 1850 describes it as 'newly erected'.
96. Blakeway Smith was engaged in building the commemorative tower on Callow Hill for Benjamin Flounders of Culmington in 1838, about which time Sutton was rebuilt. Charles Powell of Sutton was the agent and a close friend of Flounders.
97. J. Newman and N. Pevsner, *Shropshire*, Buildings of England series, (2006), 247.
98. The location of the early manor house is a mystery. It was possibly the 'capital messuage' known variously as Tarporley or Tarpley Hall for which a series of deeds survives at Stafford (D1788P40 B4) dating from 1546 to 1716. It had clearly come down in the world by 1546, when it was leased by a butcher, but from 1566 it was

owned by the Stedman family, who were prosperous yeomen. The name Tarporley may have some connection with the Savage family from Cheshire who were lords of the manor.

99. Slated by Pevsner as 'intolerable neo-Jacobean'. (*Buildings of England: Shropshire*, (1958), 130.) Both Corfton and Ferney were partly demolished in the early 1950s. While some of the main buildings survive in ruins at Ferney, all that remains of Corfton are the stables and the lodge.
100. Mrs. Martin (*TSAS,* 3rd series, Vol. IX, (1909), 222-3) mentions an oral tradition concerning a timber framed manor house on Callow Hill which was demolished at some time in the 18th century.
101. M. Moran, *Vernacular Buildings of Shropshire*, (2003), 429-30.
102. *ibid.*, 431.
103. *ibid*, 432.
104. There is clear evidence for jettying on three sides. The eastern side has been obscured by later work.
105. HRO, Microfilm box 27.
106. HRO, Microfilm box 25.
107. As John Baldwyn of Upper House actually was, being a younger son of the main landowning family. 'Perceived gentry' would have been wealthier than many of their neighbours, but still came of yeoman rather than gentle stock.
108. HCA 1856, 1315. This mentions six pairs of crucks originally intended for a *lavatorium.*
109. Upper crucks may be found in the former agricultural buildings at Sutton Court Farm.
110. SA, QE2/2/1, Alehouse keepers' recognisances.
111. A 19th-century transcript may be found in SA6001/6868.
112. SA 1671/19. Marcy Hemingway Collection.
113. Worcs. RO 7051658BA5467/67. The Marcy Hemingway collection in which the Corfton Hall papers are housed is inconveniently divided between the Worcester and Shrewsbury archives.
114. SA 552/9/430.
115. A. Dyer, 'Twentieth Century Westhope', [typescript], (2000), 77. Copy in SA at 9QD 64.9
116. *Electoral Register, 1919.*
117. SA CP91/3/1, Diddlebury Parish Council minutes.

Index